2/99

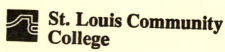

HOMOPHOBIA

Description, Development, and Dynamics of Gay Bashing

MARTIN KANTOR

PRAEGER

Westport, Connecticut
London

Library of Congress Cataloging-in-Publication Data

Kantor, Martin.
   Homophobia : description, development, and dynamics of gay bashing /
Martin Kantor.
     p.   cm.
   Includes bibliographical references and index.
   ISBN 0–275–95530–3 (alk. paper)
    1. Homophobia—Psychological aspects. 2. Heterosexism—
Psychological aspects. 3. Homosexuality—History. 4. Gay men—
Crimes against. 5. Lesbians—Crimes against. 6. Paranoia.
7. Toleration. 8. Antisemitism.   I. Title.
HQ76.25.K35   1998
306.76′6—dc21   97–22808

British Library Cataloguing in Publication Data is available.

Library of Congress Catalog Card Number: 97–22808
ISBN: 0–275–95530–3

First published in 1998

Praeger Publishers, 88 Post Road West, Westport, CT 06881
An imprint of Greenwood Publishing Group, Inc.

Printed in the United States of America

The paper used in this book complies with the
Permanent Paper Standard issued by the National
Information Standards Organization (Z39.48–1984).

10 9 8 7 6 5 4 3 2

Copyright Acknowledgments

The author and publisher gratefully acknowledge permission to reprint the following
previously published material. Selected passages: from *After the Ball* by Marshall Kirk
and Hunter Madsen. Copyright © 1989 by Marshall Kirk and Hunter Madsen. Used by
permission of Doubleday, a division of Bantam Doubleday Dell Publishing Group, Inc.;
Theodor W. Adorno, Else Frenkel-Brunswik, Daniel J. Levinson, and R. Nevitt Sanford,
The Authoritarian Personality (abridged edition), W. W. Norton & Company, Inc., 1982;
and Otto Fenichel, *The Psychoanalytic Theory of Neurosis*, W. W. Norton & Company,
Inc., 1945.

To M.E.C.

Contents

Preface   ix

Part I
General Characteristics of Homophobia

1 How All Homophobes Are Alike   3

2 Homophobia as a Manifestation of Sexophobia   13

3 Models of Homosexuality—I: The Homophobic
      Medical Model of Homosexuality   17

4 Models of Homosexuality—II: Other Models   39

5 Homophobia in Gays and Lesbians   51

6 Is It Ever Rational to Be Homophobic?   63

7 The Negative Effects of Homophobia on Gays and Lesbians   67

Part II
The Syndromes

8 Paranoid Homophobes   75

9 Mood (Affective) Disorder Homophobes   93

10 Phobic/Avoidant Homophobes   101

11 Obsessive-Compulsive Homophobes   109

12 Personality Disorder Homophobes—I   119

13 Personality Disorder Homophobes—II: Hysterical
      (Histrionic) Personality Disorder Homophobes   131

14 Personality Disorder Homophobes—III: Passive-Aggressive
      Personality Disorder Homophobes   143

Part III
Cause

15 Psychological and Biological Factors   161

16 Cognitive Errors   177

Part IV
Treatment

17 Treatment of Homophobes   191

18 How Gays and Lesbians Can Deal with Homophobes   195

Bibliography   207
Index   213

Preface

These days the subject of homophobia is both much mentioned and little understood. What prevails is the sociopolitical view of homophobia as an unfortunate mean-spirited attitude toward gays and lesbians, to be condemned and overcome. What is missing is a scientific theory of homophobia that goes beyond criticizing homophobes, deploring their disastrous effects on the gay and lesbian community, and calling for a stop to the discrimination. What is needed, as Colin Spencer (1995) in *Homosexuality in History* says, is an understanding of the "deeper roots" of homohatred (p. 400). For, as Marshall Kirk and Hunter Madsen (1989) in *After the Ball* suggest, "to solve [the] problem you must first understand it through and through" (p. 112).

Yet few observers have made significant inroads into understanding homophobia. Those who have studied it in depth have done so primarily as a sideline of their interest in other bigotries. For example, Theodor W. Adorno, Else Frenkel-Brunswik, Daniel J. Levinson, and R. Nevitt Sanford (1982) in *The Authoritarian Personality* occasionally mention homophobia as part of their study of anti-Semitism. Others have focused on homophobia itself but only briefly and superficially. Spencer (1995), for example, devotes no more than a few pages to the topic, while Kirk and Madsen (1989) discuss the behavioral psychology of homophobia but say little to nothing about the psychoanalytic and interpersonal perspectives.

Gay and straight mental health professionals alike have contributed to the superficial manner in which we have come to view and handle homophobia, each in his or her own way. Gay (and straight but simpatico) observers view homophobia as a problem for gays and lesbians, but not as a disorder of straights. They describe what homophobia means to the gay and lesbian population without first understanding what it means to be homophobic, sparing homophobia from the withering glance of the trained analytic eye, in effect praising it with faint condemnation. Kirk and Madsen (1989) even say outright: prejudice is "not 'illness'; and can't be 'cured' by psychotherapy" (p 114), a point with which I and some of my more insightful patients most emphatically disagree.

On their part straight (and sometimes unsympathetic) mental health professionals have been generally reluctant to handle the topic at all. For example, the term "homophobia" is completely missing from the *American Psychiatric Press Textbook of Psychiatry* (1988). It is not in the index and I cannot find it anywhere in the body of the text. And the *DSM-IV* (1994), the American Psychiatric Association's *Diagnostic and Statistical Manual,* fails to mention homophobia either in its list of phobias or, where it would seem to fit best dynamically, under paranoia.

This silence seems not only officially sanctioned but also golden. Mainstream "straight" psychology remains mum about homophobia because mental health workers know how dangerous it is to take on homophobes publicly. Simply put, they fear to tread because of potential political problems. Fearing professional stagnation, personal exile, and loss of earning power, they side with those, often homophobes themselves, who hold the administrative reins, and "man" the referral desk. They know that to do otherwise virtually guarantees them that place in hell reserved for individuals who enter emotionally heated frays armed only with good intentions, an open mind, and the kind of curiosity that in like circumstances "killed the cat." And they persist in their removal though they find that those who say nothing at all get into a second difficulty, one that follows from the first. They escape from the place in hell reserved for those who enter active frays unprepared. But they end up in another place in hell: the one reserved for those who remain neutral at times of crisis.

Part of the problem everyone has in understanding homophobia is that it is difficult to obtain information about homophobes. The main source of most clinicians' information about homophobes is "straight" patients being evaluated and treated for emotional problems of a general sort. Many of these patients are willing, perhaps too willing, to sound off negatively about gay and lesbian colleagues at work, gays and lesbians in the army, gay and lesbian marriages, and other timely gay and lesbian issues. But few can give more than a superficial answer to the question, "Why don't you like homosexuals?" The question startles them since no one has asked it before. Or it upsets them, and they happily avoid the matter, anxious to move on to another, less controversial, topic.

Another, and equally unsatisfactory, source of information about homophobia is from observing the homophobes we all run across in our daily lives. As an example from my personal experience, it took very little imagination on my part to recognize that of two men working out together in the gym, at least the one wearing the T-shirt that says, "Silly faggots, dicks are for chicks," might be homophobic due to problems with latent homosexuality. This man can be "analyzed," but only in a crude inexact way. (I cannot prove it, but my common sense tells me that a simple Shakespearean principle applies: "The lady doth protest too much, methinks.")

Another problem with understanding homophobes is that the few homophobes who admit to being homophobic either deny that their homophobia is a problem, or, if they admit it is a problem, show little interest in understanding it. Either they like it and do not want it interfered with, or they are ashamed of it and do not want it criticized. They view their homophobia not as disorder but as order. They see it not as an intruder, but as a guest, and not as a symptom of a character problem, but as a sign of strength of character. Typically they argue, often passionately, that they have not an illness, which needs to be cured, but a mission, which needs support; a preference, which needs to be respected; and a credo, which needs (1) dissemination, and (2) no apology. As they see it, they have not a symptom but a system—of preferential, rational, conscious, unassailable, social, and religious values and beliefs—beliefs that are, as they might say if they were psychologically sophisticated, "ego, not id."

They say they prefer heterosexuals to homosexuals like some people prefer country to classical music or representational to abstract art. They deny gays and lesbians threaten them. They deny their homophobia is a way to resolve inner conflicts over being homosexual themselves. They insist that they are merely responding to bad experiences they previously had or are currently having with gays and lesbians. They claim they are not paranoid, for their so-called paranoia is just an appropriately negative reaction to reality. They say, in effect, that while true symptoms of an emotional disorder have the purpose of self-reassurance, to overcome something unacceptable in the individual, they as individuals are not self-reassuring to influence themselves to overcome "evil" within, but influencing others to overcome evil without in the world. They argue that they are not hiding something about themselves that they do not want to see, but rather that they are saying something about themselves that they do want others to hear.

They deny that it is prejudicial to dislike gays and lesbians, or discriminatory to harass them, either covertly, by holding them back, or overtly, by knocking them down. They reserve their right to shun gays and lesbians, if not in an open space, such as in a restaurant, then in a closed space, such as in the company for which they work. For their mission, they claim, is not one of bad, but one of good. Analyzing them as neurotic, they conclude, is at best unnecessary, and at worst an unwelcome invasion of their privacy, an intrusion into an area that is, or should be, off-limits—except to those similarly inclined: their secret sharers, and all others who silently or vocally acquiesce in and support their worthy views and endeavors. And, they strongly suggest, those who deem it otherwise, including their therapists, are common scolds, wagging their fingers at them, when they should instead be retroflexing those fingers, and wagging them at themselves. If they accept treatment at all it is only for another problem: paranoia in many, obsessionalism in some, and depression in more than we think, or they care, to admit.

ABOUT THIS BOOK

I view homophobia as an emotional disorder and use depth psychology to analyze it the way I would analyze any other emotional disorder. I am hardly the first person to view prejudice and discrimination as a symptom "worthy" of standing beside such other well-known and highly "respected" symptoms as delusion or obsession. For example, Daniel J. Levinson and Nevitt Sanford (1982) say in the preface to *The Authoritarian Personality*, speaking of the psychological origins of anti-Semitism in terms equally applicable to homophobia, that we have to understand "an adult's [bigoted] social outlook or ideology [as] an aspect of her or his personality [really, personality *disorder*]" (p. vi). And James H. Carter (1996) speaking about racism in mental health professionals in his article "Racism and Mental Health Professionals," also in terms equally applicable to homophobia, says that racism is not an "attitudinal" issue, but "a defined medical or psychological condition," not merely a psychological disorder, but, as the psychiatrist Chester Pierce says, "a lethal disease—a public health hazard—and [one that] must be fought as we would any other disease" (p. 23).

Because homophobia is a symptom/disease structurally akin to a psychopathic act or a paranoid delusion, to handle the problem we have to do more than merely condemn it as an attitudinal perversion and try to jawbone it into submission. Instead we have to deal with it as one deals with any other deeply rooted emotional problem that is in turn part of an entrenched emotional disorder. Homophobia requires the same clinical understanding and therapeutic care we might lavish on any other manifestation of abnormal psychology. It may be impractical to therapeutize the world, but we can apply the therapeutic method to understand and even influence the masses.

Part I of this book describes the "illness homophobia." I open with a description of the general attributes of homophobia, emphasizing the traits that all homophobes tend to have in common. In Part II I describe the different homophobias, each of which I view as a symptom of a different larger syndrome. For example, one homophobe, the kind some gays, lesbians, and straights alike stereotype as the red-neck bigot, was, as aptly described by Alan Stoudemire (1988), in another context, "poorly educated, rural, fundamentally religious, ethnic," from a lower socioeconomic background and "too lacking in psychological insight" (p. 535) to express himself abstractly, and so was only able to think about gays in concrete terms—that is, representationally, so that they were either men in tight blue jeans with a handkerchief in their back pocket waving a fairy wand or one "man" in tight red pajamas with a forked tail grasping a pitchfork. In contrast another was a more contemplative, obsessive, homophobe who could not concretize for being too abstract. Instead of simply seeing gays and lesbians as the devil and shunning them, he brooded about the difference between homosexual evil incarnate and homosexual evil deliberate, unsuccessfully trying to determine if there were any possibility of absolution for homosexual sin.

In Part III I discuss some possible causes of homophobia. My theoretical view is an eclectic one, as I analyze homophobia from the psychoanalytic, interpersonal, cognitive, behavioral, and biological perspectives.

In Part IV I develop a treatment approach to homophobia, based on the insights developed in Parts I–III. I begin by suggesting some ways to treat homophobes themselves, recognizing that they can suffer as much from their homophobia as gays and lesbians suffer because of it. One could hope that after treatment these homophobes will learn enough about their homophobia to distinguish what is their reasonable need, like the one many of us have, to distance themselves from others unlike themselves, from their neurotic compulsion to despise anyone who is at all different.

Next I apply what we have learned about homophobia to help gays and lesbians deal with homophobes. I suggest gays and lesbians "know their enemy" as a way to deal with the enemy more intelligently and effectively. For example, gays and lesbians must learn that different homophobes require different responses. To illustrate, paranoid homophobes are more dangerous than schizoid homophobes. It is, as a general rule, unwise to confront and cross paranoid homophobes, for they tend to be delusional and possibly dangerous. On the other hand, it is usually not particularly dangerous to cross schizoid homophobes. But here the problem is that it is usually a waste of time, having as it does no, at least no discernible, effect, positive or negative. Because the plan I develop for dealing with homophobia is based on understanding what it means to be homophobic, it goes beyond the sociopolitical approaches recommended for handling homophobes in vogue today, such as activism believed to be a panacea, to hit homophobia in the midriff using magic bullet antidotes that are precise because they are directed not to homophobia's sociopolitical facade, but to its psychopathological core.

Certain difficulties present themselves throughout this book, and rather than mention and try to handle them each time they occur, I will try to anticipate them all here. I refer to all homosexuals as gays and lesbians except when I use such familiar expressions as "gay bashing," where I feel substituting "gay and lesbian bashing" though more accurate is extremely cumbersome. When I speak of straights, homophobes, or homophiles in this book, though I sometimes forget to emphasize it, or do not do so adequately for stylistic reasons, I am referring specifically not to all individuals of a particular class but only to those in that class who suffer from gross psychopathology. For example, when I speak of religious homophobes, I am speaking not of an ordinary worshiper but of morbidly, pathologically religious individuals whose religion is emotional, not devotional.

Also when I quote certain individuals as saying something that seems to me to be homophobic, I am just expressing my own opinion, and I do not mean to imply that I really know what these individuals are thinking, or even that the secondary sources I used to get to know them are accurate and representative. I am not homophobic of homophobes. I am not out to call them names, to describe them pejoratively, or to make an ad hominem argument against being homophobic. I simply recognize certain patterns in homophobes that look very much like the patterns I find in patients with emotional disorders, and pass my observations on. While I speak of this resemblance frequently, I am not entirely sure if it signifies something meaningful—that is, I am not sure that homophobes who behave as if they were neurotic are actually suffering from an emotional disorder. I have learned (and wish that some homophobes would learn it too) that no one can draw a distinct line between sickness and health. Rather there is a continuum between the two, and healthy people resemble sick people, and vice versa, in many ways.

And finally, throughout I skirt, or try to skirt, what I consider to be two of the most controversial and difficult issues of them all. The first is, "To what extent is one individual entitled to separate him- or herself from, or even dislike, another individual based on perceived differences, identified flaws, or for any other reason?" Is prejudice ever really preference? And the second is, "Do victims of bigotry ever bear any responsibility for having provoked a degree of the prejudice/discrimination leveled against them?" Is there ever an ounce of truth in the pounds of distortion that characterizes all bigotry? Or, what is essentially the same thing, is all prejudice prejudice, or have, as Kirk and Madsen (1989) put it, "America's homohaters . . . like the proverbial blind pig, rooted up the truffle of truth: the gay lifestyle . . . is the pits" (p. 276). I do not answer these questions directly because I am not precisely sure what the answers are. Again I simply present what I consider to be clinically significant material, and try to analyze it scientifically—that is, both accurately and in a way that is as fair to all concerned as I can possibly make it. I

feel that by doing this, whatever limitations exist are those of my analytic process, not of my prejudicial distortions.

The discussion that follows is nominally about homophobes and homophobia. But it is also about other forms of bigotry, from anti-Semitism
to xenophobia. This is partly because I derive my theories about homophobia from others' theories about bigotry in general. But it is also for
another reason. Just as in phobics one phobia is rarely enough to express
the phobic condition, so that most agoraphobics virtually require other
fears besides their fear of open spaces, and also fear dogs and heights, it
is the rare homophobe who can adequately express his or her "homophobic condition" exclusively in homophobia. Additional symptoms are
needed, ones like anti-Semitism or racism, to express and resolve their
pressing emotional problems. As a result, few, if any, homophobes are
specialists who limit themselves to homophobia. Unfortunately, most, or
all, of them are in "general practice," as they invest all forms of bigotry
with equal interest, then express all their bigoted ideas with equal fervor.

PART I

General Characteristics of Homophobia

1

How All Homophobes Are Alike

In this chapter I will describe some of the cognitive and behavioral characteristics many or all homophobes have in common. Most homophobes tend to be *dereistic*. They live in a world all their own, where reality consists of myths substituted for facts and maintained in the face of evidence to the contrary. Some become convinced that all gays and lesbians are child abusers. Others think that because some gays have feminine and some lesbians have masculine traits, all gay men act like women and all lesbians act like men.

A homophobic psychiatrist equated homosexuality with feminine gender identity and that with weakness and passivity. He added that all gays and lesbians were infantile not only because of the "primitive sex they had in bed" but also because they refused to run their lives like heterosexuals. According to him, not only did gays and lesbians not get married and have children like responsible heterosexual adults, they were as irresponsible professionally as they were personally. But if he were right at all it was only in his private little world. For though he referred to all homosexuals at large, he was basing his beliefs on a limited sample of homosexuals: the small group of homosexuals who were his patients, many of whom came to therapy because they had relationship problems. This gave him a skewed version of what relationships were like in the homosexual community at large. In particular his belief that homosexual relationships did not last came about because he rarely heard from his patients about the ones that did last. While there are no good statistics available, so that no one knows for certain how homosexual relationships compare in stability to straight relationships, stable relationships are quite common in both gays and lesbians, and perhaps more so than generally presumed. Gays and lesbians do often stay together, are monogamous, and cheating may be no more frequent among homosexuals than among heterosexuals. Gays and lesbians stay together for the same reasons straights stay together. They stay together not only for sexual gratification but also for companionship, and to share living expenses. As with straights, some have interests in common, while in others the attraction is one between opposites, as when a calm partner quiets a nervous one, who in turn healthfully tones the other up if he or she is too laid back.

This analyst needed, but didn't have, the input of therapists who knew homosexuals personally in the general population. They could have given him a realistic, sober view of homosexuals who were not patients and, functioning just as successfully as the vast majority of heterosexuals, had no need to seek psychological treatment.

In cases like this, dereality breeds further dereality because homophobia flourishes in the climate of ignorance bred by the homophobia itself. It is the rare bigot who seeks to discover the truth about his or her subject. Indeed being bigoted virtually requires avoiding the objects of one's bigotry, so that eventually there is no first-hand knowledge of the subject anywhere to be found. While there are myths or stereotypes about straights—for example, the myth of the hypersexual construction worker, or the hyposexual nerdy intellectual—at least some of what most straight people know about other straights is based on direct observation. But for homophobes often the only information they have about gays and lesbians is from newspapers and other secondary sources. As a result what they know about gays and lesbians they get from tabloids, which speak only about the things gays and lesbians do that are considered to be newsworthy—which is, thankfully, behavior that is atypical for most gays and lesbians.

Grandiose and narcissistic homophobes are know-it-alls who think they have all the answers, even in situations where the experts disagree. For example, they are certain that homosexuality is an illness, though while a few experts believe it to be an illness, most believe otherwise and see it as a lifestyle variant, a personal preference, an alternative biological predisposition, or even part of a sociopolitical movement. As the unattributed article, "Activists Are Targeted in Bishop's Excommunication Order" (1996) puts it, here referring to bishops who discriminate against gays and lesbians, grandiose people "exercise monarchal authority in a democratic society [and] lay claim to possession of a singular and universal truth in a secular age rife with religious and cultural diversity" (p. A9).

Another homophobe type is the *Unoriginal/derivative*. As one gay activist in essence put it (personal communication), "homophobes tend to see themselves as clever, perceptive, original thinkers whose observations about gays and lesbians in specific and human nature in general are to be taken seriously and to heart, at the very least aired on talk-show radio or printed in a Letters to the Editor column of the daily newspaper, or even enshrined in a leather-bound volume destined to live through the ages." But in fact most homophobes are amateur, not professional, students of human behavior who, though they present their thoughts as original with them, are mostly derivative thinkers who steal ideas from others. Because they all tend to steal from the same few people simultaneously, they regularly throw the same platitudinous darts at their targets: depressingly uniform, predictable ideas that merely echo homophobic ideas and opinions currently in vogue. These days they all seem to think in terms of "but where will it end"—and simultaneously hold the one-thing-leads-to-another semidelusional belief that if you allow gays and lesbians their rights then you have to allow them to get married, and if you allow gays and lesbians to get married, then you will have to allow polygamy and marriages between adults and children. Or they all speak at the same time of how homosexual marriage will weaken the moral fabric of society, and lead to social chaos and disorganization.

Other homophobes are *prone to reason implicitly.* While many homophobes have (knowingly or unknowingly) met a homosexual personally, few have gotten to know one well, so that their ideas about gays and lesbians rarely come from experience with actual gays and lesbians. Instead, what information homophobes do not get about gays and lesbians from secondary sources such as newspapers and television (featuring rumors and myths of the moment), they get implicitly, as they reason through to without ever checking their conclusions out.

Homophobes can be *simplistic/stereotypical* in their attitudes toward gays and lesbians. They take a complex subject and oversimplify it. As Daniel J. Levinson (1982) might say about gays and lesbians, though he is speaking of anti-Semitism, homophobes make "general [prejudiced] statements about [all gays and lesbians though gays and lesbians are a] heterogeneous [people who] belong to every socioeconomic class and represent every degree of assimilation" (p. 57).

Homophobes are often *histrionic/prone to excessiveness* and blow the "homosexual problem" up out of all proportion and lose all perspective about it. They get overexcited about homosexuality because it touches one of their nerves like phobics get overexcited about dogs biting or bridges collapsing because dogs or bridges incite one of their personal fears. Or they are afraid of gays like phobics are afraid of flying because they have only read stories whose headlines speak of planes that have crashed. Then their anxiety feeds on itself and spreads, anxiety breeding further anxiety until panic supervenes. Now, for the homophobe, gays and lesbians become frightening creatures, and everything about them becomes monstrous because everything they do is seen as the start of something big. For such homophobes the mere fact that gays and lesbians have different lifestyles means that the gay/lesbian lifestyle is about to spread and undermine the entire straight social fabric.

The *New York Times* in an unattributed article, "Zimbabwe Leader Condemns Homosexuality" (1995 d) reports a typical example of what I consider to be antihomosexual hysteria:

> Officials in a foreign country go beyond "argu[ing] that homosexuality is foreign to [that country's] tradition [to]support laws making it an offense." Their president excitedly "delivered a stinging attack on homosexuals today" calling "homosexuality a repugnant offense against nature by 'sodomists and sexual perverts'" and added that "if the nation accepts homosexuality as a right . . . 'what moral fiber shall our society ever have to deny organized drug addicts or even those given to bestiality the rights they might claim under the rubrics of individual freedom and human rights? . . . I don't believe they have any rights at all. I hope the time never comes when we want to reverse nature and men bear children'" (p. A7).

The idea that homosexual marriage will lead to undermining the fabric of society is hysterical in the extreme. As one gay activist put it, again in a personal communication, this idea is "in its own way the equivalent of the idea that the practice of religion today will inevitably take us back to the bad old days of the Inquisition."

Homophobes are often *generally bigoted* and rarely if ever limit themselves to being homophobic. Like an anxious patient with a mixed neurosis who, when internal or external factors require, can readily substitute obsessions for phobias, homophobes substitute racism, ageism, anti-Semitism, and xenophobia for homophobia. That I can almost verbatim adapt the general characteristics that Adorno, Frenkel-Brunswik, Levinson, and Sanford (1982) attribute to anti-Semitism as salient characteristics of homophobia makes this point without needing further elaboration.

> For example, a man who was at odds with his own homosexuality, and felt inferior and hated himself because of it, criticized gays and lesbians to make himself feel better about his own presumed sexual transgressions, and the feelings of inferiority these invoked. But he did not stop there. He also tried to enhance his self-image by becoming an ageist who condemned old people as defective, a sexist who condemned all women as inferior, an anti-Semite who abhorred all Jews, and a racist who abhorred all blacks and Asiatics. This man's various bigotries were at bottom little more than different characters in the same play, each saying his or her own lines, but with all the lines part of the same old story.

Even when homophobes seem to be talking about gays and lesbians they are really being *self-referential,* talking about themselves. The homophobic idea that gays and lesbians are all sinners is as much a statement about the homophobe's own sexual guilt as is the paranoid's idea that "others are watching me" a statement about the paranoid's own sexual shame. (Self-reference also makes for the self-aggrandizement described above. The idea that the blue-collar work I do is more masculine and so more admirable than the sissy work most gays do is an example. Another is the belief that, as Jon K. Meyer [1988] puts it, my heterosexuality is "the standard against which other modes of sexual expression should be judged" [p. 1056]. So is the belief held by many people that every American should be judged by the standard of the blue-collar worker married with children, a belief that is narcissistic and grandiose in the extreme because it in effect says that everyone should conform to *me* because I am the *greatest.*)

Because homophobes, like most bigots (and like most every one else), when they speak of others are really speaking of themselves, in effect substituting object for subject, their every statement about gays and lesbians originates with and in turn amounts to a self-statement. For example, as Levinson (1982) says about anti-Semites, "when the belief that Jews possess financial power out of all proportion to their numbers persists in the face of overwhelming evidence to the contrary, one is led to suspect not only that the individual holding this belief has an unusual preoccupation with power but also that he might himself wish to assume the kind of power which he supposes Jews to have" (p. 57).

In particular, if we listen carefully to what homophobes say, we soon discover that (1) Every criticism of gays and lesbians is a self-criticism. For example, male homophobes who dislike gay men because they act like women really are downplaying and disavowing their feminine side by criticizing and condemning the supposed femininity of others. (2) Every criticism of gays and lesbians is a self-compliment. As a result we often do not know if homophobes are complaining about gays and lesbians or bragging about themselves. For example, accusations of homosexual sin are often disclaimers of individual guilt, and exclaimers of personal innocence.

(Homophobes are often really speaking *about* the person they are speaking *to,* displaced onto gays and lesbians. While it is stretching a point to call some homophobes polite, in fact homophobes will often displace personal criticisms away from the person they are with and onto a distant, remote stranger who is a stand in for their immediate audience. When they say, "I hate queers," or the like, to someone they are with, the person listening should always think, "he or she suspects me of being queer, or something similar, and hates me for the same reason.")

As I stress throughout the text, there are aspects of homophobia that are *symptomatic*, which closely resemble aspects of emotional disorder, so that homophobia is in many ways as much like a mental illness as some homophobics say homosexuality is like one. For example, many homophobes reason like patients with paranoia vera reason. Like these paranoids they elaborate an illogical initial hypothesis logically. They make the flat assertion that gays and lesbians are sick, an incorrect premise, then elaborate it, correctly (I am speaking only of the elabora-tion), to conclude "and they should be treated" (or, even, "quaran-tined"). While it is true that the conclusion follows logically upon the ini-tial premise, the flaws in the initial premise make the conclusion invalid. It is the same with my patient who felt that Pablo Picasso's "Guernica" was staring and jeering at him, then concluded that he should stick a knife in it, and proceeded to do so. What he did made sense in light of what he thought. Only what he thought was delusional from the start.

Too, homophobes feel that gays and lesbians are out to seduce them like paranoids feel that enemies are singling them out and persecuting them. And like these paranoids, homophobes stay perfectly calm and unflustered until their "favorite subject" comes up—persecution in the case of paranoids, homosexuality in the case of homophobes—at which time all concerned become equally overwrought, hysterical, panicky, and defensive. Many homophobes experience the same feelings of *wel-tuntergang* (delusion of world decay) that severe depressives and schiz-ophrenics experience, with all concerned suffering from the false belief, based on very little evidence, that the world, as one homophobe put it, is "going to hell in a hand basket," and all because of what gays and les-bians do in bed, or because gays and lesbians want to get married legally.

Homophobes, like others suffering from an emotional disturbance, are individuals in conflict, and they are in conflict about the hidden wishes that drive their manifest fears. William McGurn (1996), writing for *The Wall Street Journal*, recognizes one of these conflicts when he says in another relevant context, that behind "traditional fire and brim-stone" we find "pinched eroticism" (p. A18).

For example in saying, speaking about a gay lecturer, "I was afraid he would blow me a kiss," a homophobe was likely expressing three forbid-den wishes in the form of a fear. First he was expressing two erotic wishes: (1) the wish to be more attractive than he actually was, and (2) the wish to be more attractive to homosexuals than he could ever allow himself to be. Then he was expressing one hostile wish: (3) the wish to condemn his own transgressions by noting, and condemning, similar "transgressions" in others.

Another typical conflict is the one between a wish to be and a fear of being passive.

> A Vietnam war veteran said, "Fags don't belong in the army because they are cowards. Under fire in the trenches all they would do is their nails." This man criticized homosexuals as a way to handle his guilt over being a coward reluctant to enter into battle. He felt that being a coward was the same thing as being a woman. So he bashed gays as disgustingly feminine as a way to distinguish himself from them, to make himself feel like more of a man.

Homophobes are *preoccupied,* caught up in the homosexual problem like paranoids are caught up in the "persecution problem," or obsessive-compulsives are caught up in the "dirt problem." Homophobes are over-involved in homosexual life, however little it is any of their concern, like phobics are overinvolved with Friday the 13th, however much it is just another date on the calendar.

It is as *masochistic* for homophobes to bring their own political parties down at convention time, never to win the election, or to jail and ulti-mately kill Oscar Wilde, never to have the beautiful things he could have written, as it is for borderlines (patients who tend to be impulsive and have unstable relationships) to kill off relationships only to find they have de-prived themselves of the pleasure and satisfaction that the relationships they destroyed could have brought had they been allowed to prosper.

Sadistic homophobes are not simply individuals in conflict about their own guilty erotic wishes. They are also simply mean, nasty people looking for an outlet for their hostility. As Levinson (1982) says about anti-Semites, they have "*negative opinions*" (for example, that gays and lesbians are sick); "*hostile attitudes*" (for example, that gays and lesbians "should be excluded, restricted, [and] kept subordinate to" straights); and negative "*moral values* which permeate the opinions and justify the attitudes" (p. 58)—for example, that gays and lesbians are sinners. In a typical scenario, homophobes who have been abused in their own lives take it out on the next person to come along, making gays and lesbians a scapegoat for the anger they feel about having been rejected by their family and society. They handle feeling like outcasts from society by casting others out in turn.

As is often the case, hostility translates to depression. And all depres-sives feel better, at least temporarily, when they get their anger out and make others suffer along with them. As a result, many cases of homo-phobia are in effect a depressive misery that loves company.

A fear of all things sexual, originating in *sexual guilt,* is behind a fear of all things homosexual. Why sex, though a biological function, should be so intimately associated with guilt, as if it were a bad thing to do, is a question that is beyond the scope of this text. But it is so associated, and in the fantasy life of sexophobes homosexuality occupies, as a colleague who wishes to remain anonymous put it, the same place wherein lies any form of sex that is not in the dark, in the missionary position, and for the purpose of making babies.

Homophobes *envy their victims*, which explains why they not only bash but also imitate them at the same time. They bash gays and lesbians because they are jealous of them for being able to do what they want to do sexually. And they imitate them for the same reasons: because they desire to have what they have—their sexual freedom, and sometimes high status in life, and with it the high level of disposable income of people they call "dinks" (double-income-no-kids). This is why gay bashers so often take their fashion cues from gays and lesbians (rarely acknowledging the source), or move into the neighborhoods gays and lesbians have established (rarely acknowledging their debt).

> A blue-collar homophobe took on the superior airs that gave him the same "elitist" look he saw and envied in gays and lesbians, differing only in the details. His was a reverse chic. He did not act superior by driving a classic foreign car. Instead he acted superior by driving a classic truck which he elevated on big wheels and in the back of which he put a labrador retriever. He did not watch shows on the Public Broadcasting System. Instead he only watched football games and mud wrestlers. He did not read and quote the pithy sayings of La Fontaine. Instead he read and quoted the pithy sayings of the bumper stickers on the cars in the road. Though the means differed, the end result was the same. Though about different things, he was just as smug, holier than thou, superior, and pretentious as the gays and lesbians he knocked for doing exactly the same thing.

All of this said, of course not all homophobes are exactly alike. There are shades and subtypes of homophobia over and above the syndromal differences I will describe in later chapters. We might say that some homophobes are orthodox while others are reformed. Paraphrasing Frenkel-Brunswik (1982), orthodox homophobes make no "exceptions to the general rule" (p. 254) that all gays and lesbians are bad, while reformed homophobes allow of some exceptions. For example, again according to Frenkel-Brunswik, sometimes homophobia is "general" so that "all outgroups are rejected" (p. 253), while at other times it is confined more to specific subgroups or outgroups. Some homophobes, church people and psychoanalysts among them, accept gays and lesbians who are in the closet, in conflict about being homosexual, and sexually inactive. They reserve their condemnations for gays and lesbians who are out of the closet, accept their homosexuality, and are sexually active. Some extrude even close relatives who are homosexual, while others feel that there are some good gays and lesbians in the world. And for some, as Frenkel-Brunswik points out, homophobia is "'essential.'" These homophobes feel that gays and lesbians' "faults" can never "be eliminated" (p. 253). But for others homophobia is nonessential. These homophobes feel there is hope for gays and lesbians. There are also, according to Frenkel-Brunswik, differing opinions as to "whose responsibility is it to make the change[s]" (p. 253) that homophobes feel gays and lesbians need to make. Some feel it is the responsibility of the church, or psychotherapists, while others feel it is the responsibility of gays and lesbians themselves, who should, at least as far as they are concerned, meet their "helpers" halfway.

The aggressiveness that is present in all homophobes also takes different forms. Some homophobes merely dislike gays and lesbians—that is, they are "merely" prejudiced. Others discriminate against and persecute gays and lesbians, as Frenkel-Brunswik points out, either by "segregation (with 'equality') or [by] exclusion" (p. 253).

In some cases homophobia is conscious while in others it is unconscious. And sometimes homophobia is overt and sometimes it is covert. Homophobes vary in how openly they express their homophobia to others, and also to themselves—that is, how much there is what Frenkel-Brunswik calls a "pseudodemocratic facade" (p. 253). Madhusree Mukerjee (1995) says that "women are less homophobic than men" (p. 24), but I doubt it. At least in my experience, women are just as homophobic as men, but their homophobia is less conscious and less overt, either because they are more subtle about it or because they are simply hypocritical. For example, one woman often preached but less often practiced her nonhomophobic philosophy. She would not ski in Colorado because the state would not give homosexuals equality. So she skied in Utah instead. (At the time Utah was considered to be less homophobic than some said Colorado was.) That was easy to do, and required very little self-discipline or self-sacrifice. But closer to home, in the condominium in which she lived, she rarely trampled on the rights of straights like she did on the rights of gays and lesbians, especially when it was a question of either their rights or hers.

Homophobes also vary in how conflicted they are about their homophobia. For some more than others, as Frenkel-Brunswik puts it, "rationality, respectability or in-group feelings, [and] Christian antiaggression" (p. 253) are forces that oppose prejudice. And finally, as Frenkel-Brunswik says, homophobes are also divided on questions of influence. Some think gays and lesbians are a "menace," about to take over the world, while others think them "just a nuisance" (p. 254) to be suffered somewhat gladly.

It would seem as if there are mild and severe homophobes. But this does not mean that there are good and bad homophobes. I do not buy the theory that homophobes can minimize the extent and seriousness of their homophobia by claiming that they are not as bad about their homophobia as they could be because their homophobia does not go far and has no practical implications, or because they have second thoughts or even guilty conflicts about it. If only because bigotry tends to start small and spread, any degree of homophobia is as unacceptable as it is inexcusable.

2

Homophobia as a Manifestation of Sexophobia

Many homophobes are basically "sexophobes," who have a negative feeling about all sex, gay or straight. Sex makes them anxious, or they find it revolting. To a degree, sexophobia is not abnormal. Many people seem to find at least some aspects of sex inherently anxiety-provoking, or even "disgusting," especially after their sexual excitement is over, taking with it the alchemy that turns physical dross into emotional gold. They explain their anxiety and disgust in a number of ways. Some see the sex act as inherently unrefined, and for them anything unrefined is crude, and anything crude is disgusting. Others are bothered because the genitals are anatomically close to the excretory organs. Still others are in conflict about sex, with their disgust, quoting Otto Fenichel (1945), a defense against forbidden "sexual, especially oral and anal drives" (p. 139). And finally others say that, being only human, they are horrified as a predictable and understandable response to gay or straight sex that is meant to shock. For example one straight woman, not by any means a homophobe, felt she was being reasonable when she complained that she "found it just too much to be strolling down Christopher Street in New York City's Greenwich Village, only to suddenly espy a go-go dancer performing in a store window, for all to see, wearing a small bikini, and a large erection" (personal communication).

But some individuals, straights and gays alike, are abnormally sexophobic. They find all forms of sex much more frightening/revolting than they actually are. Among these are, as Fenichel (1945) calls them, anal prudes whose "anal prudishness is a reactive cleanliness" (p. 177), and who are only comfortable when sexuality is refined to the point where it becomes "not dirty" (as described below). There are also hypocritical prudes, who demand others be of the cloth as a way to handle guilty behavior of their own that, as they see it, would easily qualify them for the blacklist. These prudes, and others like them, are uncomfortable not only with sexuality itself but also with any of its manifestations, including blue jokes, depictions of things sexual on TV or in the movies, dogs having intercourse in full view, and even the healthy developing sexuality of their own children.

Many go beyond being merely prudes easily shocked to become proselytizers who expect, or demand, others be as shocked as they are, to fall into line, and to treat sex, as they do, as a bad thing, something that should only be suffered gladly, and reluctantly, when it is strictly intramarital/procreative, and part of a traditional, loving relationship. Some of these proselytizers are polite and refined. They limit their prohibitions to symbolic ones. They "merely" do what some call a "pecker check" on gays, as when a neighbor peeps through her keyhole into the hall of her apartment complex to learn what time a gay man is coming home, and with whom, then, after seeing what she is afraid of seeing, and getting over the shock, warns him, the next morning, based on her research of the night before, of the dangers of staying out late at night, cruising, being promiscuous, and bringing home strangers.

Other proselytizers go beyond trying to spread their own brand of "morality" to others and actually try to prohibit others from indulging in certain forms of sex entirely. These individuals include (1) those church members who advocate general celibacy for gays; (2) those politicians who vote for laws that discriminate against gays as their way to cast a vote against all forms of sodomy; and (3) those psychoanalysts who make their patients into the equivalent of priests or nuns, in effect insisting that if they are to undergo therapy they must take the vow of "poverty, chastity, and obedience." (As one lesbian put it, poverty was the result of her analyst's high fee; chastity the only possible response to her analyst's rule of abstinence—no sex for the duration; and obedience required because of the need to slavishly submit to the basic rule of the psychoanalytic process, which is to free-associate and talk about, without acting-out, fantasies.)

Few sexophobes actually admit to being sexophobic. Some instead rationalize their sexophobic behavior on religious/moral grounds. They say they condemn sexuality because the Bible commands them to do so, though in fact they are really quoting the Bible because they condemn sexuality. These individuals read the Bible, quote it selectively, and fail to find the ways around its prohibitions that occur readily to their less sexophobic cohorts. Still others rationalize their sexophobia in specious practical terms such as a parent's desire to protect young children from being exposed to sex prematurely. (Up to a point parents have a responsibility to protect their children from undue sexual input/stimulation. But some of my colleagues feel it is reasonable to become suspicious of parents' true motives when they overprotect older children who are in fact one step ahead of them when it comes to grossing out about sexual matters.)

Developmentally, sexophobia can originate in oedipal guilt—that is, guilt a child has over incestuous fantasies directed toward the parents. This can later take the form either of a general sexual guilt, or a specific sexual guilt such as guilt over masturbation. As Fenichel (1945) says, some adolescents have an

> unconscious interest in believing that masturbation is a dreadful thing. Analysis, as a rule, shows that a guilt feeling arising from the tendencies of the Oedipus complex has been displaced toward the activity that serves as an outlet for these unconscious fantasies (the conscious mas- turbatory fantasies being a distorted derivative of the unconscious oedi- pus fantasies); this displacement serves as a safeguard for the repression of the Oedipus complex. If the patients were to believe that masturba- tion as such is harmless they would not be rid of the guilt feeling; they would have to look for its source and might become aware of the re- pressed; thus they prefer to feel guilty "because they masturbate" [or for anything sexual] (p. 76).

Sexophobia can also start with actual prohibition of masturbation. The child is warned, "Don't touch yourself down there." This is duly noted and rolls around in the child's unconscious during the latency pe- riod like ideas roll around in people's heads while they are asleep. Then when the latency period is over the child tries to masturbate, and experi- ences overwhelming guilt. He or she swears, "I will never do this again," then becomes tyrannical to the self and others about this, and some- times all other, manifestations of sexuality.

Sexophobia can also originate with the viewing of the primal scene, especially when the experience involves a high or intolerable level of ex- citement and incest guilt combined.

Sexophobia can also originate in guilt over incestuous fantasies be- tween siblings. Speaking of Arthur Schopenhauer's reaction to depiction of brother-sister love in Richard Wagner's *The Ring of the Nibelungen*, Karl S. Guthke (1996) notes in his article "The Deaf Musician" that when the curtain falls on Sigmund and Sieglinde's "turgid infatuation" Schopenhauer comments in the margin of the score (which Wagner had given him as a gift, hoping for his evaluation of the poem), "High time, too" because, as Guthke says, Schopenhauer was "unable to let pass such unbridled abandon to what he called the 'will.'" (p. 48).

Sexophobia can also derive from sexual excitement itself. Here distress appears because of what Fenichel calls the ego's inherent unfriendliness to the instincts. As Fenichel says, "innate tendencies [can] exist to suppress or inhibit sexual or aggressive impulses, besides externally aroused feelings of anxiety, guilt, shame, and disgust, tendencies that might operate even without frustrating experiences . . . [a kind of] primary hostility of the ego to the instincts" (p. 140). The result is that the sexual instincts, having no access to discharge, boomerang on themselves, and do so in the form of guilt, so that the more sexually excited the individual becomes the guiltier he or she feels.

Sexophobia can also represent a sexualization—often a homosexualization—of nonsexual guilt, where guilt about sex, gay or straight, is a convenient and comfortable spokesperson, sacrificial lamb, and scapegoat combined for guilt of another sort, such as guilt about one's anger, or about one's selfishness.

Finally sexophobia can have a biological basis. It may be regulatory—that is, a message from the brain saying "enough is enough," much as the brain says to the hungry person "you are full." Speaking teleologically, the purpose of guilt may be to prevent sexual excess; to keep individuals from being so active sexually that they have little time or energy left to do anything else with their lives. Or, speaking teleologically again, its purpose may be to prevent overpopulation within the tribe, or in the world; to avoid, as Desmond Morris (1967) puts it, the overcrowding that can fragment society, produce chaos, and require that we "reduce the breeding rate without interfering with the existing social structure" (pp. 99–100).

3

Models of Homosexuality—I: The Homophobic Medical Model of Homosexuality

In this chapter I shall discuss the homophobic medical model of homosexuality, where homophobes view homosexuality as a sickness. In the next chapter I shall discuss the homophobic religious model of homosexuality, where homophobes view homosexuality as a sin; the homophobic criminal model of homosexuality, where homophobes view homosexuality as a crime; the homophobic social model of homosexuality, where homophobes view homosexuality as a deviation from the norm; and the homophobic political model of homosexuality, where homophobes view homosexuality as a useful tool for politicians trying to seize or maintain power by making gays and lesbians, as Frank Rich (1996) puts it, "political fodder in an election year" (p. A17).

DESCRIPTION

Two broad groups of individuals see homosexuality as a sickness and call gays and lesbians sick. The *first group* consists of laymen, who use the term "sick" pejoratively. For example, Eugene Narrett (1995) reports that one layman, a black politician, used the term "sick" in this fashion (in a nonhomophobic context) when he said: "Whites are 'sick' and . . . 'I've got to operate on your head . . . what makes you like this? You're not well'" (p. A19). In the unattributed article, "San Francisco Station Ousts a Blunt Host" (1995) the *New York Times* reports that another layman, J. Paul Emerson, a right-wing talk show host, used the term "sick" in this fashion (this time in a homophobic context) when he said: homosexuals are "'sick and pathetic'" (p. 14). The *second group* consists of profession-als, who can in turn be subdivided into *two subgroups* and *one crossover subgroup*. Members of the *first subgroup* use the term "sick" in what they consider to be a scientific manner. According to them, they use it cor-rectly, and with detached neutrality. (According to others they use it in-correctly, pejoratively, and prejudicially—i.e., homophobically.) In the view of these professionals, heterosexuality is normal and homosexual-ity is, as Peter Steinfels (1995) quoting Andrew Sullivan puts it: "compa-rable to an illness or a disability," "analogous to an addiction, like alco-holism," "morally neutral in itself but potentially destructive to the individual [and to others in the individual's life]" (p. 9).

For example, some psychoanalysts believe that heterosexuality oc-curs when psychic development has progressed normally—from the most primitive, or oral, to the most mature, or phallic/oedipal stage, without incident or complication. They feel that homosexuality occurs when there is a developmental lag or reversal—that is, when normal progression is thwarted so that the patient's sexuality remains undevel-oped (and primitive), or, having developed to a mature, phallic/oedipal stage, backslides to the immature "pregenital" phase (of anality or oral-ity). For example, Charles W. Socarides, Harold D. Voth, C. Downing Tait, and Benjamin Kaufman (1995) believe that gays and lesbians are "vic-tims of certain intrapsychic processes that have subverted their hetero-sexuality and made for profound disturbances in their lives" (p 23). Sig-mund Freud, though assuredly no homophobe, according to Ernest Jones (1957) felt homosexuality was not an illness. Yet even he consid-ered it to be a "variation of the sexual function produced by a certain ar-rest of sexual development" (p. 195).

Two psychoanalysts, both former colleagues of mine, consider them-selves to be objective and nonhomophobic even though they do view homosexuality as an illness.

> The first colleague, a psychoanalyst who wishes to remain anonymous, said, in a personal communication, "I agree with Socarides and with all those psychiatrists who call homosexuality an inversion, or see it as com-parable to a neurosis. I see homosexuality as comparable to a physical or a psychological illness because: (1) being homosexual interferes with the ability to function effectively since it keeps gays and lesbians back both professionally and personally, just as a paralyzed limb keeps people from walking; (2) being homosexual is a substitute gratification, since com-pared to heterosexuality it is more like foreplay than like intercourse, and like foreplay it is not an alternative but a lesser form of sexuality. It is at worst a narcissistic form of loving (because gays and lesbians are having sex with a mirror image of themselves); and at best an oedipal form of lov-ing (because gays and lesbians are having sex with their parents); and (3)

being homosexual is a deviation from the norm, partly because it is so much less common than heterosexuality, and partly because it serves no natural reproductive function.

Another psychoanalyst, who also wishes to remain anonymous, said, in a personal communication, "I am not hostile to gays and lesbians because of something in me. I am not a latent homosexual who criticizes homosexuality in others to get myself off the hook for being gay myself. I am not a homophobe who uses psychiatry to put gays and lesbians down. I am a scientist who uses psychiatry to understand gays and lesbians. My gay and lesbian patients would like me to deny that their homosexuality is an illness. They frequently argue that it is not an illness to distract me from analyzing them, and cite my presumed "homophobic attitude" to avoid having to take me seriously. But my beliefs are rational, not prejudicial. For homosexuals do have sexual and characterological problems, and both the sexual and the characterological problems are caused by the same factors, since both are a manifestation of the same neurotic conflict, or a product of an attempt to resolve that conflict.

For example, I have treated many gays and lesbians who are very hostile people. Either they are passive-aggressively hostile, with their hostility couched in politeness and civility, as when they on intellectual grounds challenge the Freudian dynamics I apply to them, or they are openly hostile, as when they attack me personally for even suggesting they have emotional problems. They are hostile when they give parties and seem more gratified by whom they *didn't* than whom they *did* invite—whom they *excluded*, rather than whom they *included*. And their homosexuality is another manifestation of their hostility—for in men, homosexuality is due to a hostility to women as sex-objects, and in women homosexuality is due to a hostility to men as sex-objects.

Other gays and lesbians are excessively shy. They don't relate to others, me included. And they are homosexual for the same reason. They are too shy to relate to members of the opposite sex, but they can have same-sex relationships because they find those less interpersonally threatening.

They are also superficial people with a skin-deep value system that assigns the most importance to the least important aspects of relationships with other people. For example many gays I know live and die according to whether or not others flattered them by inviting them to certain key social events. And their hosts live and die according to whether the ones they invited accepted proffered invitations.

Both gays and lesbians are narcissistic and exploitative as well. At times they are off-putting in their selfish exclusiveness. For example, I live in Greenwich Village in New York City and as a straight man wouldn't even think of trying to enter a lesbian bar. It makes lesbians feel good, and important, to reject me. (I have feelings just as they do, and even I, who have no real interest in joining in, feel a bit rejected by some of these women's more exclusionary practices.) Also I spend my summers in a semi-gay resort. Here I overhear gays' and lesbians' conversations, and see them in action. It seems as if gays' and lesbians' personal needs, particularly their need for sex, always come before the needs of others. They certainly come before their friends' and family's need for affection. I still remember the time a gay friend of mine (I have some) left me in the middle of a brunch celebration because he was so self-preoccupied that when an old lover he was still sexually interested in happened to come along, off the two of them went, leaving me literally with egg on my face. A lesbian dental hygienist was similarly selfish and self-centered. She spent an entire hour reminding me of how disgusting my mouth was when I first started coming to her. She unloaded her hostility on me. She didn't care how I felt, and that I had to listen to her, defenseless, while strapped into her chair. And worse, there is the ultimate selfishness of committing murder for one's transient pleasure. One of my patients says he has AIDS in one breath and in the next, constantly cruising and promiscuous like many gays, he speaks of his conquests, from his cleaning person to strangers in a gay bookstore, conveniently forgetting that he is contaminating every one around him, like the tar baby did to Br'er Rabbit.

The same narcissism that appears in gays' and lesbians' nonsexual behavior also explains their need to make a homosexual object choice. Gays and lesbians love members of the same sex simply because they love themselves. Gays and lesbians choose love objects as close to themselves as possible. Gay men don't like women and lesbians don't like men, and vice versa, because they aren't what they hope and expect to find when they look in the mirror. It seems that Fenichel (1945) was right when he said that "homosexuality represents, so to speak, a state between the love of oneself and the love of a heterosexual object. In a regression to narcissism, the level of homosexuality is an intermediary step, where the regression may temporarily stop; and a person who has regressed to the level of narcissism, in striving to recover and to return to the objective world, may fail to get beyond a homosexual level" (pp. 427–428). It seems that Fenichel would agree that homosexual sex is like kissing yourself.

So I think Dr. Socarides has a point when he says that gays and lesbians are warped developmentally, and need analysis to help them become mature. True, some analysts have done bad things to gays and lesbians. But that is a function of how critical all analysis is, noting as it does only the flaws in people, while rarely acknowledging their virtues. These analysts are no harder on homosexuals than they are on others they treat. They criticize and blame gays and lesbians for being homosexual, just as they criticize and blame depressives for complaining too much. They generally use insight not as an instrument for learning but as an instrument for torture. But this is not analysis, but analysis poorly done. For it still remains true that, as George Santayana said in "The Life of Reason" as quoted in The Macmillan Dictionary of Quotations (1989), "Those who cannot remember the past are doomed to repeat it" (p. 499). And gays and lesbians must understand their pasts, not so that analysts can come up with even more reasons to criticize them, but so that analysts can cure them of their homosexuality, and so relieve them of the life's suffering that being homosexual invariably entails.

In sum, if I am antianything it is antipsychiatric illness. Even correcting for my limited experience with gays and lesbians, a personal queasiness about things sexual in general, and a low tolerance for too much overt hostility from anyone, I am as liberal and understanding as they come. So, if I am hard on gays and lesbians it isn't because of their sexual orientation. It is because I consider myself the Will Rogers of psychiatry, who "never met a symptom I didn't like (to analyze), or a neurosis I didn't like (to cure)."

Pro-gay mental health workers strongly believe that most or all "scientific" theoretical sets proposed to explain the development of homosexual orientation are homophobic simply because they suggest that something went wrong somewhere along the line—one definition of abnormality, disorder, or illness. For example, Judith V. Becker and Richard J. Kavoussi (1988) propose

> (1) psychoanalytic theories [that] have suggested that unresolved oedipal conflicts are critical, (2) learning theories [that] contend that early homosexual experiences or fantasies which do not have negative consequences are reinforced through sexual behavior and masturbation; (3) genetic theories that view homosexuality as a genetically inherited trait; and (4) biological theories that suggest adult homosexuality is a response to individual hormonal levels or hormonal factors during the patient's mother's pregnancy" (p. 601).

Does Morris' theory, advanced to explain the development of homosexuality in apes, suggest that homosexuality in humans is the product of a pathological parenting, the same kind that has been implicated in illnesses ranging from hysteria to schizophrenia? Morris (1967) says:

> If, in the parental situation, the offspring are exposed to an unduly masculine and dominant mother, or an unduly weak and effeminate father, then this will give rise to considerable confusion. Behavioural characteristics will point one way, anatomical ones the other. If, when they become sexually mature, the sons seek mates with the behavioural (rather than the anatomical) qualities of the mother, they are liable to take male mates rather than females (p. 98).

Of course, not all "scientists" call gays and lesbians sick and then claim scientific objectivity and neutrality. Members of a *second subgroup* of "scientific homophobes" come close to admitting, or simply admit, that they call gays and lesbians sick prejudicially and homophobically. For example, Dennis Altman (1987) quotes a physician's editorial in a medical journal in 1984 as saying, "Perhaps, then, homosexuality is not 'alternative' behavior at all, but as the ancient wisdom of the Bible states, most certainly pathologic" (p. 66). And Robert Paul Cabaj (1995) contends that the "World Health Organization's refusal to remove homosexuality as a mental illness from its *International Classification of Diseases (ICD)* until the most recent revision" (p. 13) was motivated by homophobia, the same homophobia noted in an APA [American Psychiatric Association] survey of international psychiatric organizations that found that the "majority of their psychiatrists view homosexuality as pathological" (p. 13).

Finally there is a *crossover subgroup* of professionals: those who give lip service to scientific neutrality, though their actions suggest they are anything but neutral. As some have pointed out, Socarides belies the temperate, even reasonable, medical model he at times seems to espouse by the way he actually behaves toward gays and lesbians, giving evidence that his is not a reasonable position but a cover for something sinister. Some have even stated that Socarides' antihomosexual politics seem to suggest that he is rationalizing his homophobia scientifically, or, if he is not, then he is at the very least saying one thing to pro-gay groups and another thing to anti-gay groups. Jack Drescher (1995) thinks that Socarides is using "the rationalization of 'illness' to perpetuate the historic discrimination against lesbians and gay men. . . . [This view is suggested by] NARTH's [National Association for Research and Therapy of Homosexuality] rejection of privacy rights and its active embrace of sodomy laws and other discriminatory legislation" and its "support of traditional 'family values,' traditional sex roles, and religious traditions condemning homosexuality" all of which in turn "are consistent with a 'treatment modality' that encourages social opprobrium of homosexuality" (p. 16). As Drescher concludes, the "transparency of [NARTH'S] rationalizations, combined with the insubstantial scientific underpinnings of their developmental and psychological theories, make it difficult to take their claims of scientific neutrality seriously" (p. 16). John A. Gosling (1995) puts it even more strongly: that Socarides can say that "'the very fact of AIDS is the same-sex movement's terrifying contribution to this terrific century' [means to me that Socarides] does not belong on the faculty of any medical school worth its reputation" (p. A14).

A number of core fantasies are associated with and responsible for the belief, in laymen and scientists alike, that homosexuality is an illness. Here are some of them:

1. Illness as punishment. In this fantasy gays and lesbians are ill because they have been struck down for being homosexual. Throughout

history naturally occurring diseases have been viewed as punishments for moral transgressions. Victims of AIDS like victims of other dread diseases suffer twice—first from their illnesses and second at the hands of those who believe that they are simply getting what they deserve. Dennis Altman (1987) quotes a physician's editorial in a 1984 medical journal as saying: "We see homosexual men reaping not only expected consequences of sexual promiscuity, suffering even as promiscuous homosexuals the usual venereal diseases, but other unusual consequences as well" (p. 66).

2. Illness as self-created. In this fantasy the "homosexual illness" is a self-induced one. Gays and lesbians are often compared to addicts who refuse to stop being addicted though they could, if they would, quoting a familiar phrase popularized by Nancy Reagan, "Just say no." In this fantasy, gays and lesbians could, if they only would, modify their behavior, be celibate, and remain disease free. For example USA Today reports in an unattributed article (1995) that Jesse Helms said that "most people with AIDS—homosexuals and intravenous drug users—could have avoided it by modifying their behavior" (p. 8A).

3. Illness as abhorrent and reprehensible. In this fantasy an illness is something dirty and disgusting. Gays and lesbians are beyond sick; they are "repulsive lepers" who, as an anonymous writer of a New York Times (1995c) editorial entitled, "Who's Being Disgusting on AIDS?" reports, again quoting Jesse Helms, have contracted the disease through their own "deliberate, disgusting, revolting conduct" (p. 14).

4. Illness as criminal. In this fantasy the "homosexual sickness" is a crime. (The criminal model of homosexuality is discussed further in Chapter 4.)

5. Illness as defect. In this fantasy gays and lesbians are defective humans much as in ageists' fantasy old people are defective adults.

6. Illness as diathesis. In this fantasy illness is broad-based, not encapsulated; metastatic, not static. It invariably spreads to affect all areas of functioning, not only gays' and lesbians' sexual but also their professional and personal lives.

7. Illness as infectious. In this fantasy gays and lesbians are infectious in one of two ways. First, being homosexual is believed to be "catching," for gays and lesbians encourage others to be homosexual or actually recruit them into being gay. And second, gays and lesbians not only catch but pass on physical illnesses venereally, spreading them to innocent others, gays and straights alike.

In an unattributed editorial in the New York Times (1995b) entitled "White House Inhospitality" the writer reports that several uniformed Secret Service guards "donned rubber gloves to greet a delegation of gay elected officials" (p. A 26).

According to Dennis Altman (1987) "a letter from the American Family Association soliciting signatures for a petition read in part: Dear Family Member: . . . If you want your family's health and security protected, these AIDS-carrying homosexuals must be quarantined immediately. . . . These disease-carrying deviants wander the streets unconcerned, possibly making you their next victims. What else can you expect from sex-crazed degenerates but selfishness" (p. 67).

8. Illness as something that *can* and *needs to be* treated. In this fantasy the illness of homosexuality can, and needs to be, treated with psychotherapy, or its equivalent, much as illnesses caused by bacterial infections can, and need to be, treated with antibiotics.

For example, according to the unattributed article, "Doctors Urged to Stop Trying to Change Homosexuals" in the *Asbury Park Press* (1994), in its old position the American Medical Association reasoned, "there are some homosexuals who would like to and probably could change their sexual orientation. . . . Because some homosexual groups maintain, contrary to the bulk of scientific evidence, that preferential or exclusive homosexuality can never be changed, these people may be discouraged from seeking adequate psychiatric consultation. What is more important is that this myth may also be accepted by homosexuals" (p. C9).

Socarides et al. (1995) believe that in select cases there is a possibility of sex-preference reversal. They note that some "individuals believe that homosexuality is completely contrary to their value system." They say that they "acknowledge that many homosexual men and women do not wish to change their psychosexual adaptation, and . . . respect their wishes not to seek therapy." However, they "believe that treatment should be available, encouraged, and affirmed for those who voluntarily seek help [and that] in its public health mission, APA should work to protect the rights of patients who seek treatment as well as the rights of the therapists who treat them" (p. 23). [Socarides recommends reparative therapy. Linda Ames (1995) denies rumors that there is a "link between electric shock therapy and reparative therapy" (p. 5), which its proponents say is just a short-term psychotherapy based on analytic principles.]

9. Illness as something that *must* be treated. In this fantasy homosexual illness is a menace to public health, just like TB (tuberculosis). As TB must be treated with quarantine or antibiotics, "homosexual illness" must be treated by isolation, or castration. For example, we often hear that, on average, gays have more partners during their lifetime than straights, and that changing gays to straight is not homophobic but a

way to save lives. Jeffrey Burke Satinover (1995) says that "epidemiolo-gists estimate that 30% of all 20-year-old gay men will be HIV positive or dead of AIDS by the time they are age 30" (p. 4).

As a contrast to the homophobic medical model of homosexuality, I present the views of some scientists who strongly deny that homosexuality is in any way comparable to an illness.

A colleague of mine says that homosexuality is no more an illness than is having red hair or being left-handed. She views the specific choice of geni-tal for sexual gratification as of no special psychological significance be-cause it does not reflect an individual's developmental level—that is, his or her level of psychological maturity.

The AMA's present position on homosexuality as described in its new policy paper obtained from the *Asbury Park Press* article "Doctors Urged to Stop Trying to Change Homosexuals" (1994) differs from the old one pre-sented above, as follows: "Homosexuals may have 'some unique mental health concerns' related to negative social attitudes regarding homosexu-ality. However . . . most of the emotional disturbance homosexuals may feel about their orientation 'is due more to a sense of alienation in an un-accepting environment.' For this reason . . . 'aversion therapy'—such as showing a gay man nude pictures of men and then administering electric shocks or a substance to induce vomiting—'is no longer recommended for gay men and lesbians.' 'Through psychotherapy, gay men and lesbians can become comfortable with their sexual orientation and understand the so-cial responses to it'" (p. C9).

Daniel W. Hicks (1995) says that "Socarides has been obsessed with pathologizing homosexuality for over 30 years." He denies homosexuality is pathological, and suggests instead that it is "innate, either genetically, anatomically, or hormonally" determined (p. 16).

John A. Gosling (1995) says that "homosexuality has been one of the diverse manifestations of human sexuality since time immemorial. . . . There is nothing to 'fix' in homosexuals because there is nothing broken" (p. A 14).

The unattributed article "Origins of Homosexuality Debated at Annual Meeting" (1995) quotes Richard Isay as saying that homosexuality is not an illness but a "sexual orientation" (p. 5), a "biologically determined and probably inherited trait" (p. 5), and that most "theories of homosexuality's origin have been proffered by 'heterosexual males who have had no expo-sure to gays'" (p. 5).

Terry Stein (1994) agrees that homosexuality is not an illness. He says that "homosexuality has not been demonstrated to represent a form of mental illness in terms of any measurement of functioning or adaptation" (p. 24).

Stein denies that homosexuality is a "damaged heterosexuality" and mentions the harm resulting from efforts to "repair what is labeled a damaged heterosexuality in gay and lesbian persons" (p. 24). That psychiatrists think being homosexual is an illness means that "prejudice against gay men and lesbians continues to exist in many countries of the world and . . . this prejudice is reflected in the psychiatric organizations of those countries" (p. 24).

DISCRIMINATION AS THE RESULT OF THE MEDICAL MODEL OF HOMOSEXUALITY

Calling homosexuality an illness is troublesome for more than semantic reasons. For homophobes use the medical model to discriminate against homosexuals. Anti-gay discrimination that uses the medical model as its basis takes a number of forms:

1. Anti-gay law-making. As Judd Marmor (1994) points out, Socarides used his homophobic medical theories as an excuse to sign an anti-gay petition favoring eliminating the laws protecting homosexuals in Colorado, "submitting strong statements in support of its outrageous constitutional Amendment Two that would have deprived all homosexuals in that State of their civil rights! Such bold and errant hypocrisy boggles the mind" (p. 24).

2. Limited professional opportunities, or doors quietly closing. As Cabaj (1995) says, "Until very recently, gay men and lesbians were refused entrance into psychoanalytic training programs based solely on their sexual orientation—unless, of course, they promised to try to 'change' it through analysis" (p. 13). (In the old days, and probably in many cases still today, they might not be admitted even then.) From personal contacts I know that the Boston and San Francisco (!) Psychoanalytic Institutes in the 1960s flatly refused to admit homosexuals for analytic training. A gay psychiatrist who was, for reasons I cannot mention here, in a position to eavesdrop on the private conversations of members of the Boston Psychoanalytic Institute swore that he regularly overheard them making homophobic statements. I also know firsthand that psychoanalysts functioning as hospital administrators tried to keep gays and lesbians from joining the medical staffs of the departments that these psychoanalysts headed. Cabaj says that homosexual psychiatrists are still refused "admission to psychiatric residency based on the idea that homosexuality is pathological, a mental illness that would interfere with their ability to deliver competent psychiatric care" (p. 13).

One such psychiatrist reasoned (personal communication) that psychiatrists who cannot heal themselves cannot heal others. It is not, he reasoned, as if gays and lesbians are trying to be dentists though they have cavities of their own, or physiatrists though they themselves are in a wheelchair. According to him, homosexuality thoroughly and significantly both directly and indirectly corrupts the ability to analyze because it is one manifestation of a serious personality disorder in the healer that makes the healer too brittle to tolerate the stresses inherent in doing analysis, too corrupt to maintain neutrality, and even too sexually preoccupied to resist seducing patients. He also thought that because gays are by nature too passive to make good authority figures, they make bad psychiatrists because all patients need a firm, guiding hand; and that because lesbians are by nature too aggressive and authoritarian to be patient listeners, they make bad psychiatrists for most patients have already been pushed around too much in their lives to tolerate more of the same in their therapy.

According to an article by Brian McCormick (1994), a poll of doctors revealed that: homosexual doctors "got the message that some specialties such as surgery were less open to them than others, such as psychiatry" [but see below]. . . . "About 56% of the doctors [and 67% of the medical students] reported experiencing some sort of social or economic discrimination from colleagues. Ironically [the poll found that] psychiatrists as a group reported the highest levels of discrimination. . . . The forms of professional discrimination faced by gay and lesbian doctors varied in degree and subtlety. . . . Nearly one in five said that they experienced some sort of job-related discrimination, and a similar number said they had been denied referrals. About one in 10 said they had been discouraged from a residency or denied a slot because they were gay. . . . [Then there] is 'social' discrimination—verbal harassment and ostracism by peers. . . . A . . . physician said he was told by a fellow resident that he 'deserved to die of AIDS'" (p. 6).

I know a gay psychiatrist who had his medical school appointment removed because he was inactive; and he was inactive because he was not given a teaching assignment with the medical school, in spite of his considerable abilities and his many requests for one, because he was gay. One time they actually assigned him a class, then, two days before he was to begin, administration called him to say, "We have enough people already, so we don't need you."

3. Doctors discriminating against patients. According to McCormick (1994), the "American Assn. of Physicians for Human Rights polled 700 of the group's 1,300 members [and found that] more than two-thirds of the respondents—mostly gay and lesbian physicians—said they had seen evidence of homosexual or bisexual patients receiving substandard care. About half said they had witnessed gay or lesbian patients being denied care. And 88% reported hearing colleagues make disparaging remarks about homosexual patients. . . . [A surgeon even says that] 'sometimes punitive measures are good for fags'" (p. 6).

Homophobic psychotherapists can be subtly sadistic to their gay and lesbian patients. They distance themselves from them by offering interpretations when support is needed. They put them down in a number of ways. In one case whenever a patient tried to make a point about himself by comparing his behavior to rumored similar behaviors in household names both living and dead, his analyst ignored the thrust of his remarks to instead stress his presumptuousness in making them. For example, when the patient compared his poor spelling to Agatha Christie's poor spelling, his analyst told him that he was being narcissistic and grandiose in comparing himself to such a great author. Homophobic psychoanalysts can be unforgiving as well. They set impossible standards for gays and lesbians to follow, then reject them when they cannot meet these standards. For example, I know of some cases where when patients persisted in having homosexual sex in spite of the analyst's "orders" to the contrary they were thrown out of psychoanalysis, even when the patients themselves wanted to continue. Then these analysts rubbed salt in the wounds of rejection by telling the patients that they provoked their own dismissal.

One gay patient, celibate for his psychoanalysis, could take no more than five years of sexual deprivation, after which time he resumed having gay sex. His analyst threatened that if he continued to have gay sex she would summarily terminate his treatment. In so doing she reminded him of how his own family rejected him when he was young, and for essentially the same reasons. He became extremely anxious, and handled his anxiety by becoming sexually promiscuous, as a way to convince himself, "Nobody doesn't love me." In retaliation she diagnosed him as borderline based on his inability to develop a stable positive transference relationship to her. Then she suggested terminating analysis, and further suggested he continue with another therapist, in psychotherapy, not analysis, because analysis "is for healthy patients and you have serious characterological problems."

(A year later he ran across his analyst in a public place, and something inside of him kept him from acknowledging her hello. He simply stared ahead, unresponsive. For years afterward he regretted *his* rejecting *her* this way, forgetting that she had in effect rejected him first.)

He could not resist commenting to me that her heavy smoking was a more deeply rooted "oral" fixation than his "oedipal" fixation. And when she died of lung cancer he commented, through his sadness, that she was no less self-destructive than gays who "supposedly bring AIDS on themselves by their evil indulgences."

One homosexual author complained that she was depressed because a book she wrote did not bring her a contract. Her therapist, emphasizing her depression, suggested fluoxetine (Prozac), when instead he should have emphasized her real problem—rejection, and suggested she solve it by trying harder to get a publisher. The patient's hopeful message was, "See I'm no different from anyone else." Her therapist's critical reply was, in effect, "As a lesbian you are too sick to resolve your problems in the same way straights resolve theirs."

Homophobic psychotherapists routinely allow their dislike of gays and lesbians to influence their diagnostic judgment, and their misdiagnosis in turn to dictate the terms of their treatment. In effect they express their personal prejudice in their psychiatric diagnoses and subsequent mistreatment. They misdiagnose as a way to say, "Gays and lesbians are not just sick; they are *really* sick." The vagaries of psychiatric diagnosis offer them ample opportunity to stigmatize gays and lesbians as both personally and professionally disabled, even when they are essentially healthy.

As they sometimes do with heterosexuals, homophobic therapists use specific cognitive errors to bend science to their will. Failing to differentiate between healthy and pathological or superficially similar pathological behaviors, they make diagnostic errors that are the equivalent of the one a medical doctor makes when he calls a viral sore throat a strep throat because in both cases the throat is red and raw. And the resultant mistreatment is the rough equivalent of a medical doctor's giving penicillin for a cold caused by a virus.

One analyst misdiagnosed a lesbian as suffering from a borderline personality disorder (and said that there was a relationship between her being borderline and being homosexual). The analyst thought that the patient was unreliable, unstable, and promiscuous, because she fell in and out of love quickly, one day overvaluing, and the next day devaluing, her significant other, because she was afraid, like other borderlines, of being first engulfed and overwhelmed then rejected and abandoned. For example, once the patient became anxious when her lover was late coming home from work. Though she knew the lover was held over at work, she became suspicious, and feared that the lover was cheating on her with a co-worker. When the lover got home the patient started a fight over her supposed cheating, and threatened to leave her. Then the patient, fearing she would be lonely, admitted her part in the problem, reconsidered, and forgave her lover. The night after one of these fights the patient had a dream: my lover is running around with another woman and all my friends know it. They are all making fun of me, saying, "She'll just have to look for another lover."

But her fear was not the typical borderline one of losing a dependent relationship. It was the more hysterical one of running afoul of a rival. She feared an interloper, not a maternal rejection. She was angry and jealous, not afraid of being abandoned. And she could ask herself throughout, "Am I imagining this?" and reassure herself, "If we part, I will survive without her, and find someone else." She lacked the typical borderline's intense and primitive feeling of impending doom. She never felt she would be entirely and forever alone on earth. She feared that her relationship was over, but she did not feel that her life was over as well.

A true borderline in equivalent circumstances dreamed, "My lover died, and I am all alone, I don't know anybody, everyone I call hangs up because they don't know me, or is dead, the world is like a graveyard, no one moving, no one speaking, no one to help me."

The homosexual woman was an adult afraid she was losing a lover to the competition. The borderline woman was a baby afraid she was losing a mother to death.

Homophobic psychotherapists misinterpret/overinterpret the significance of a given behavior in gays and lesbians. If gays and lesbians have more than one partner, homophobic therapists accuse them of compulsively, frantically, and promiscuously searching for a forbidden mother, or see them as suffering from a disinhibition state indicative of an ego disorder, when they are merely overage adolescents at a time in their lives where the pleasure principle temporarily holds sway over the reality principle, and they are no sicker than teenagers on their way to a (delayed) maturity, hoping that they can hang on a bit longer to a life that is an ongoing vacation, while knowing that sooner or later they will want to move on, and develop a serious and strictly monogamous relationship.

Homophobic psychotherapists see gays' and lesbians' problems, but overlook their strengths. For example, few homophobic psychotherapists I know have commented on how being homosexual, which can to some extent cut across the lines of class distinctions, opens up interpersonal opportunities not usually otherwise available, and not as often available to straights.

Homophobic psychotherapists overlook how the behavior they cite as being "due to gay pathology" also exists in straights, where they ignore it, or call it normal. For example, all people, straights and gays alike, are somewhat sexophobic, narcissistic, and even, at certain times in their lives, promiscuous. Here is a case of a straight man who is just as narcissistic and at least potentially just as promiscuous as some homophobic psychotherapists accuse all homosexuals of being:

An older straight gymnast who condemned gays for outrageous camping himself made loud braggadocio show-offy comments in the gym meant to be overheard, call attention to himself, and inflate his self-esteem, all to convince himself that he was not as defective as he feared he was. He made leering remarks to young women, had them feel his legs for hardness, and announced in a loud voice that he was flying to Italy because "that is the only place at this time of the year with snow." He did these things so that he could let others know he was a wealthy man, and a skier. No homosexual was more promiscuous than he could have been, at least if his wishes had come true.

Here is an excerpt from Douglas Martin's (1996) article, "Summertime, and the Living Is Single" that would seem to suggest that at least some straights are just as promiscuous as all gays are accused of being, and have as many partners as all gays are accused of having had:

"When the cat's away the mice will play," said a derivatives trader. . . . She spoke of having often heard male counterparts boast, during 19 years on Wall Street, about their summer flings. . . . The women are not above occasional mischief themselves . . . friends who thoroughly enjoy their weekly ladies' night out at the local taverns [are] "very flirtatious, and what happens, happens," she said, "It's usually a one-night kind of thing" (p. 9)

Homophobic psychotherapists fail to separate the homosexuality itself in their patients from any emotional issues, or disorders, with which it may be associated by coincidence. Gays and lesbians have problems, but these can have little if anything to do with their being homosexual. One psychologist saw lisping and swishing as common gay behaviors that reflected, according to him, the same pathology that made his patients gay. With little in the way of substantiation, he said one gay swished like a woman as a way to reassure his father that he did not envy, and was not competing with, him, and moved like a femme fatale to caricature the seductive pose to satirize sexuality, as a way to convince his father not to take his oedipal sexuality too seriously. And he said that this gay lisped as "a manifestation of his infantilism, specifically his inability to get his mother's breast out of his mouth."

Homophobic psychotherapists confuse endogenous disorder (due to innate illness) with exogenous disorder (due to the real problems homosexuals face in life.) Too many therapist-diagnosticians deliberately overlook exogenous and favor endogenous causation so that they can minimize how badly straights treat gays and lesbians. If there is a higher incidence of character pathology in gays and lesbians than in straights, it is almost certainly because gays and lesbians are as a group more mistreated by the world than are straights. Paranoid gays and lesbians do exist, but as often as not gays and lesbians are not paranoid but reacting appropriately to a world they size up correctly as being a cruel dangerous place, at least for them. As Edward L. White (1994), writing about the exogenous versus endogenous controversy, says, "The existence of prejudice and opprobrium provides a rich field for the expression of character pathology, which, in a more tolerant society, might need [and take] a different outlet" (p. 29).

One therapist said, "Gays groped each other in the standing room section at the old Metropolitan Opera House because they are all infantile, impulsive, and out of control," while her colleague disagreed, saying that they were "huddling together as protection from a homophobic society." The first therapist told a gay patient that he was too fond of the superficial things in life because he suffered from a narcissistic personality disorder, citing as evidence that he named his Cherry Grove, Fire Island house "Instant Elegance," reflecting less what it was than what he wanted himself to be. But the second therapist countered that the patient was not a skin-deep narcissist but a depressive suffering from that low self-esteem that affects those gays and lesbians who have been too long ignored and abused, a class of which the patient was most certainly a member. He was merely using the elegant house as a way to deny a presumed personal inelegance, a feeling he distilled about himself from his inability to get any real respect from others. The first therapist also insisted that all gay men are naturally fey, and pretentiously hysterical. He cited as an example how a gay man threw his lover out of a house he had just purchased in Fire Island Pines, saying, "I want this to be a house of happiness." He called his behavior typical gay "emptiness" or "phoniness," part of gays' supposed "regressive inability to form meaningful and substantial relationships." He overlooked how this gay man, like most gay men, use behaviors like camping as coping mechanisms, wish-fulfilling denials they bring into play to deal with harsh reality, especially the loneliness that comes from being excluded professionally by colleagues and personally by family and friends.

The first therapist overdiagnosed psychopathy in all his gay and lesbian patients. Some gays and lesbians, like some straights, are psychopaths. He was right about the one who synthesized and sold drugs from his Florida house and sent them through the mail to a distributor in New York, and stole from chain stores in Florida, then returned the goods as an unwanted gift to branches in New York, all to maintain a lifestyle otherwise beyond his means. And he was right about the one who told young men he was a famous builder, or entrepreneur, or shipping magnate, to impress, so that he could seduce them. But he was wrong about the many scrupulous gays and lesbians he treated who did not take advantage of the system any more than straights. For these gays and lesbians, what psychopathy there was was less a character flaw than a desperate act.

The first therapist also overdiagnosed obsessive-compulsive disorder in all his gay and lesbian patients. For example, he noted that one gay individual spent all night on the meat-rack in Fire Island Pines doing "dirty" things, then went to an elegant restaurant on the pier and spent all morning abusing the waiter and the restaurant for serving him a water-stained glass with a speck of dirt on the rim. The first therapist saw the patient as an obsessional who first enjoyed anal pleasure then cleaned up his act out of a sense of guilt (a commonly cited dynamic reason for obsessive-compulsive disorder). But the second therapist countered that this man was neither more nor less anal than many normals, noting that many normal people find sex a bit disgusting, after it is over, and have to wash it off, both actually and symbolically. And if he were anal at all it was not a psychic but a physical thing, because for him, as for all homosexuals, anatomy, not psychic fixation, is destiny.

The first therapist diagnosed another gay as obsessive-compulsive because he cleaned off the light bulbs he got from the store before putting them in the light fixture. However the gay man did this not because, as his therapist said, he was an obsessional but because he felt he was floating in a world that did not want him. He was creating order and cleanliness around himself to give himself a mooring in the chaotic sea of a life of rejection he felt everywhere. This gay man acted cheap, another characteristic of obsessionals. For example, he soaked a sponge in bleach to get it clean so that he did not have to buy a new one. But a few quirky behaviors of this sort aside, he was not primarily cheap, and so not primarily obsessional. Down deep he was saving money to be somebody in a world that treated him like a big nobody.

In another case the first therapist called a gay patient a sadomasochist because he cheated on his partner to hurt him. Overlooked was how his cheating was the result of his homophobic gay partner's abusing him for being gay, a self-defense the patient had learned out of necessity. For, having been rejected by society and his family, and, having no children, he was hungry for people whom he could collect and cling to as a way to relieve his fear that he would be left out in the cold, without a place to go, and without something to fall back on, should he lose this lover.

One lesbian felt her lover was about to convert, go straight, and run off with a man to get married. Her therapist diagnosed her as paranoid, but she was not paranoid. She was not projecting her latent heterosexuality onto her lover, and condemning the lover for doing something that the patient wanted to do herself but was too guilty to try. The patient was in fact reading the signs right, and responding correctly and appropriately.

A straight landlord/therapist had gays for tenants. He said about his tenants, "You can do little better than complain about everything, blame me, and demand immediate resolution of your problems even when that is impossible. You seem to prefer to complain over having your needs met." And to ice the cake he added, speaking to one of them in words thick with implication, "you are defensive because you just had your name cut out of a research paper because the main author didn't want to be associated with the likes of you." In fact the landlord/therapist would do nothing for his tenants that he did not have to do. He deliberately let them writhe by delaying solving their problems. As a consequence their "sadism" was not innate, but an understandable reaction to their being oppressed.

A gay Jewish psychiatrist was depressed because he did not have the fame or fortune of his straight non-Jewish colleagues, the result of both homophobia and anti-Semitism on the part of his superiors at the time, including some of the psychoanalysts of the day, who, though Jewish themselves, were as anti-Semitic as they were homophobic. (At the prominent New England hospital at which he worked, the informal name for the physician who first saw patients in the emergency room, and whose job it was to refer them on to the appropriate specialist, was gauleiter—a name that was sometimes used to refer to the man in Nazi concentration camps who triaged the inmates into the gas ovens!) His therapist blamed him for his failings, though the real culprits were lack of opportunity and ego-quashing discouragement.

Two gays had a particularly difficult time in finding work because they were, as one potential employer put it, "over a certain age." They looked schizoid and withdrawn but they were simply unemployed and floundering. Two waiters/lovers at a successful restaurant, they never quite got their lives together after the restaurant failed. Instead, unable to find another job, they took to their attic apartment, with their four cats and rotting furniture. They saw no one, slept all day, and stayed awake all night, watching old movies. Eventually their relationship deteriorated. Now, because they had only one bed, they slept in shifts, one by day, and the other by night. To one therapist they looked completely bizarre. But their bizarreness was due to their isolation, and that was created and enforced, at least in part, by a society that did not have jobs for them.

One bisexual was diagnosed as suffering from a multiple personality disorder, and thought to be gay only in an alter ego. However he was just responding to homophobic criticism by confining his gay behavior to a "not me" state. He also looked like a gay promiscuous Don Juan character. But his promiscuity was out of a desperation to be loved by other gays, because he felt, and was, unloved by most straights. Nor was he the self-interested narcissist his therapist said he was. Instead he related to the only person left to relate to after the world abandoned him: himself.

A lesbian was diagnosed as exceedingly dependent though her dependency was little more than an intense need to belong that was in turn a reaction to her constantly having been rejected. She was so desperate and lonely that she threw herself at people who did not want her, and tried to fit into places where she was not wanted, like homophobic small towns. Once she begged her father to love her after he rejected her for living with another woman. He "caught her doing this" after she moved with her lover from Chicago to New York, ironically, mainly to be closer to her father. She, like other lesbians and gays, was no different from normal straights. When rejected by one person she tried to get accepted by another. She looked and was dependent, and desperate, but no more so than most straights would be if they had to live under similar, unloving, conditions. Desperately begging for love from people is hardly a behavior confined to lesbians.

Patients in their turn also discriminate against gay and lesbian professionals, such as gay or lesbian doctors. One, though he had many gay experiences himself, fired his psychiatrist when he ran across him in the street wearing a leather jacket and walking next to a much younger, similarly dressed man. In a Veterans Administration clinic where I once worked, a few bigoted veterans virtually ran all the gay and lesbian workers out of the clinic, regardless of their professional qualifications, and despite their considerable ability to help them get well.

DYNAMICS

Some homophobes create and use the myth that gays and lesbians are sick to condemn gays and lesbians as a way to maintain their distance from them, and to avoid condemning themselves for the same thing. For others the same myth is the product of the sick mind's seeing itself in the minds of others. For still others the myth is a manipulative ploy to quash the competition when that is good for business. Finally mythmaking may be simply part of a plan for sadists to attack gays and lesbians, whom sadists routinely tend to welcome as the readily available, easy target of their dreams.

HOMOSEXUALITY AS A WELLNESS

Homophobes who subscribe to the homophobic medical model of homosexuality regularly overlook how there can be *less* pathology in homosexuals than in heterosexuals. Theoretically at least, and in my experience, practically too, homosexuality can heal. I have seen some schizophrenic, asthmatic, and psoriatic teenagers get better both emotionally and physically when they become openly homosexual. To me this suggests that, at least in these cases, the problem is not with the homosexuality itself but with the individual's inability to express it in a healthy fashion.

In conclusion there is disagreement among experts as to the exact nature of homosexuality. Some call being homosexual an alternate lifestyle, while others call it an illness—if not in their official pronouncements then in their underground comments to each other.

The official view of the American Psychiatric Association is that homosexuality is not an illness. If we accept this view, then we also have to accept that scientists who see homosexuality as an illness are by definition homophobes.

Many scientists conclude that homosexuality is an illness after picking the one theory out of many that best suits their homophobia. They tend to favor the psychoanalytic theory of unresolved Oedipus, which they use to explain homosexuality the same way they use it to explain conversion hysteria. Or they conclude it is an illness after defining illness the way they want to. The terms "illness," "sickness," or "disease" can be stretched to fit their inclinations, for they are relatively broad terms encompassing phenomena ranging from coronary artery disease to mortal greatness. [As Herman Melville said in Moby Dick, "Be sure of this, O young ambition, all mortal greatness is but disease" (1851/1981, p. 77).]

I think the confusion between homosexuality and illness arises when the similarities between homosexuality and physical and mental illness are stressed but the differences overlooked. These differences make the homophobic medical model of homosexuality inapplicable, an uncomfortable procrustean bed in which to confine homosexuality. One difference is that sex comes from a different part of the brain from conscience and conflict, making it as difficult to apply psychoanalytic principles to sex as it is to apply them to creativity. So, paraphrasing what Freud (1957) said about creativity, "before the problem of homosexuality analysis must, alas, lay down its arms" (p. 222).

Sexuality may be an unceasing marvel, or a constant curse, but sexuality, including homosexuality, is more elemental than even unconscious ideation. Being an instinct it inherently lacks the conflictual basis of symptom formation. What conflicts appear are often not part of the homosexuality itself but a reaction to having thought about, or actually having done, something homosexual. For these and other reasons, homosexuality is in many respects no more like a neurosis than "love sickness" is in fact an emotional (or physical) disorder.

Some medical-model theories of homosexuality are more mythical and more homophobic than others. The most mythical, and homophobic, are the psychoanalytic, behavioral, learning, and biological theories of homosexuality that state that those who traverse the road to becoming homosexual are on a path that has deviated from the ones normals presumably take. Less homophobic, but still qualifying, are the theories that describe a deviant process but minimize its pathological nature. They note that homosexuality is different from heterosexuality but soft-pedal any pathological stigma. In effect they view homosexuality as the equivalent of extrasystoles of the heart that give the heart a different, but not necessarily an abnormal, rhythm (because the arrhythmia, while present, neither signifies the presence of cardiac disease nor actually makes the patient sick). An example of such a theory is that gays and lesbians become homosexual by being imprinted on the parent of the same sex because that is the more loving parent.

Not homophobic are those theories that argue against heterosexuality being the standard and homosexuality the deviation, with straight the order of things, and gay the disorder, instead suggesting that there are two standards, not one. These theories do not call gays and lesbians inverts, perverts, regressive narcissists, oedipally fixated neurotics, or even suggest they have the equivalent of an arrhythmia or are pathologically imprinted. Instead they view gays as they view left-handed, or red-headed people: as simply healthy variants of normal, each traveling the legendary different road. One such theory compares homosexual humans to lone gorillas or homosexuality in humans to homosexual behavior in animals. Another compares humans to bees or ants, and suggests that humans are specialized like them, so that, as with bees or ants, some humans are there to reproduce, while others are there to do other, just as necessary, but different, things—in the case of gays, the creative work of the world.

I think a scientist's homophobia is revealed by which causal theory of homosexuality he or she buys. In unresolvable controversies like "what causes homosexuality," theories tend to be accepted when they represent prejudices that express an emotional set already in place. It is the same with theories of the cause of depression that say as much about the scientist creating or adopting the theory as the patient under observation. Just as the mental health practitioner who says to the depressive "You have a chemical imbalance" sometimes wants to say "I don't like complainers, so don't bother me with your whining," mental health practitioners who subscribe to the homophobic medical model of homosexuality do so as a way to say something equally self-revealing, and negative, about gays and lesbians. When they say "gays and lesbians are sick," they really do not mean "I am so sorry and I will do what I can to help you reverse your chemical imbalance." They really mean "I think of you as a leper, and the sooner you get out of my sight, the better."

4

Models of Homosexuality—II: Other Models

THE HOMOPHOBIC RELIGION
MODEL OF HOMOSEXUALITY

In the homophobic religion model of homosexuality, homosexuals are viewed not as sick people but as sinners. As Peter Steinfels (1995) says, quoting Andrew Sullivan, in the view of individuals who see gays and lesbians as sinners "homosexuality [is] comparable to the evil inclinations that Christian tradition attributes to original sin" (p. 9).

Description

This discussion of the homophobic religion model of homosexuality is not applicable to all religious people, for many religious people are not homophobes:

As Margaret O. Hyde (1994) suggests in her book, *Know About Gays and Lesbians,* not all religious people are morbidly prejudiced against gays and lesbians, or use the homophobic religion model of homosexuality to express their homophobia. For "the subject of homosexuality causes tremendous controversy in many religious groups. These feelings run deep, and many faiths are in turmoil about whether or not homosexuals are sinners, may be ordained as leaders in the church, or be accepted only if they refrain from sex" (p. 52).

Similarly David W. Dunlap (1996) notes that there is a "stark division in Judaism over the place of homosexuals in society. Orthodox rabbinical groups believe that homosexual relationships violate Jewish law. The Conservative group of rabbis, known as the Rabbinical Assembly, has not taken a position on civil marriage but disapproves of rabbis officiating at same-sex commitment ceremonies. [On the other hand,] rabbis from the smaller, liberal Reconstructionist branch have been performing such ceremonies for years, with the support of their movement" (p. B9).

And Gustav Niebuhr (1996a) notes that while some religious people cite "specific biblical verses, like Leviticus 18:22, that have traditionally been used to condemn homosexuality . . . others appeal . . . to the example of Jesus Christ, saying he put aside old laws and prejudices to preach salvation to all people" (p. A16). This last group might agree with Sullivan, as quoted by Steinfels (1995), when he says: the "church [teaches only] two values . . . : to witness to the truth and to love one another" (p. 9).

The following discussion is applicable only to what I call "morbidly religious homophobes"—individuals for whom religion is not theology but psychopathology—that is, less a reflection of sanctioned official religion than of personal emotional conflicts. Certainly the Bible passages morbidly religious homophobes cite to show that homosexual relations are sinful do exist; but it is just as true that morbidly religious homophobes emphasize these passages to express their homophobia. In particular they overlook the general loving tone of much of the Bible. Instead they repeat its specific negative messages so that they can ignore its positive message as a whole. They read the scriptures as if they were inkblots on a Rorschach test: they take out only what they put into them. In short, while they say their homophobia is based on religion, their religion is based on their homophobia, because it is used to justify a homophobia already in place: to make it official, so that amateur gay bashing can look professional, and so that homophobes, many of whom would otherwise suffer from secret pangs of guilt, can gay bash with abandon, with few or no qualms, and (they at least hope) with a minimum of consequences.

Parents, church leaders, laypeople, and even gays and lesbians themselves are to be counted among the ranks of morbidly religious homophobes. Here are some specific examples from these different subgroups:

From parents:
    Renee Graham reports in her book review, "A Grieving Mother Faces Up to Her Homophobia" (1995), that before Bobby Griffith (a 16-year-old gay adolescent) killed himself because he was gay, Mary, his mother, warned him that "You can't love God and be a homosexual" and that "he was bound for hell unless he repented, that homosexuality was a sin, [and] that God turned His wrath on sinners" (p. 35).

From church leaders/members:
    Hyde (1994) notes that "Southern Baptists [banished two congregations] for accepting homosexuals saying 'their actions were contrary to the teaching of the Bible on human sexuality and sanctity of the family and are

offensive to Southern Baptists.' One church had blessed a homosexual union, and the other had licensed a homosexual to preach" (p. 53). Gustav Niebuhr (1996a) notes that the Methodist Church adopted the statement in 1972 that "while the 8.5 million-member denomination officially holds that homosexuals are people of 'sacred worth,' . . . [they] do not condone the practice of homosexuality and consider this practice incompatible with Christian teaching" (p. A16). Lois M. Rogers (1996b) reports that "a 1979 [Episcopal Church] resolution [says that] ordaining practicing homosexuals was inappropriate" (p. 1) [though it later ruled that "there is no official prohibition against bishops ordaining practicing homosexuals" (p. 1)]. Niebuhr (1996b) reports that a homophobic church takes official action recommending boycotting "Disney Company stores and theme parks if they continue [their] antiChristian and anti-family trend" for having adopted a policy "extending health insurance benefits to the same-sex partners of employees" (p. A14). (The boycott was put into effect in 1997.) And according to Mireya Navarro (1993) "citing its moral imperatives [some churches resist] teaching prevention messages widely recommended by public health officials, like the use of condoms" (p. 1).

I reproduce here an anonymous flyer distributed in Greenwich Village and environs in New York City. I reproduce the flyer in its entirety because it specifically identifies and quotes key Biblical passages that some of us have only heard about, and in general well summarizes what is in my opinion less the biblical basis for religious homophobia than it is the homophobic basis for biblical religion.* [Readers of this flyer should take it with a grain of salt for many reasons. One of these is that, as Hyde (1994) says, "most biblical scholars now question the interpretation of many references that are used to justify negative judgments on same-sex orientation. . . . In some cases, an ancient word may have as many as forty different meanings" (p. 52).]

---

*Here is what Leviticus actually says: "And the Lord spoke unto Moses, saying: 'Speak unto the children of Israel, and say unto them: . . . Mine ordinances shall ye do, and My statutes shall ye keep, to walk therein: None of you shall approach to any that is near of kin to him, to uncover their nakedness. . . . Thou shalt not lie with mankind, as with womankind; it is abomination. And thou shalt not lie with any beast to defile thyself therewith; neither shall any woman stand before a beast, to lie down thereto; it is perversion. Defile not yourselves in any of these things; for in all these the nations are defiled, which I cast out from before you. And the land was defiled, therefore I did visit the iniquity thereof upon it, and the land vomited out her inhabitants. . . . For all these abominations have the men of the land done . . . For whosoever shall do any of these abominations, even the souls that do them shall be cut off from among their people.'"

HOMOSEXUALITY

Is It An Alternate Life Style?

Will This Bless Or Curse A Nation?

Is It A Sin?

Is It Wrong?

What Does The Bible Say?

Is This Practice A Perversion?

Is It Right?

Can Those Who Practice This Go To Heaven?

At the present time millions of people are infected with the disease called **AIDS**. Multitudes are being infected by this disease daily. It has been predicted that by the year 2000, every family in America will have someone infected by this terrible disease.

There was a time when **homosexuality** was not spoken of very much in the public. In the last twenty years this has changed. Vast numbers of people are coming out of their so-called closets. Christians have been silent too long. According to the Word of God, **HOMOSEXUALITY IS SIN.** It is not an alternate life style as many would have us to believe. **Homosexuality** is contrary to nature and the Bible.

This sin is found in the first book of the Bible.

But the men of Sodom were wicked and sinners before the Lord exceedingly.
Genesis 13:13.

God revealed to Abraham that He was going to destroy Sodom.

And the Lord said, Because the cry of Sodom and Gomorrah is great, and because their sin is very grievous; Genesis 18:20.

God sent two angels, who appeared as men, into Sodom to warn Lot and his family to flee the city. The angels spent the night in Lot's house. That night the men of Sodom surrounded the house and said:

And they called unto Lot, and said unto him, Where are the men which came in to thee this night? bring them out unto us, that we may know them. Genesis 19:5.

Then Lot offered to give the men of Sodom his two virgin daughters, but the men of Sodom did not want them, they wanted the men.

Behold now, I have two daughters which have not known man; let me, I pray you, bring them out unto you, and do ye to them as is good in your eyes: only unto these men do nothing; for therefore came they under the shadow of my roof. Genesis 19:8.

Because of this sin, God destroyed the city.

Then the Lord rained upon Sodom and upon Gomorrah brimstone and fire from the Lord out of heaven; Genesis 19:24.

The Word of God must be our guide book. God never intended for men to run with men or women to run with women. To do so is an abomination.

Thou shalt not lie with mankind, as with womankind: it is abomination.
Leviticus 18:22.

The Homosexual is called a Sodomite in the Bible.

And there were also sodomites in the land: and they did according to all the abominations of the nations which the Lord cast out before the children of Israel.
I Kings 14:24.

Churches, denominations, preachers, or anybody else who advocates, condones, or excuses **HOMOSEXUALITY** will have to give an account unto God.

Know ye not that the unrighteous shall not inherit the kingdom of God? Be not deceived: neither fornicators, nor idolaters, nor adulterers, nor EFFEMINATE, nor ABUSERS OF THEMSELVES WITH MANKIND, I Corinthians 6:9.

We are living in the last days, the Lord Jesus Christ is about to come for the saints of God. This sin of homosexuality just points to His return. God did not let Sodom and Gomorrah get by, neither will He let America get by. This nations will be judged for this sin.

But there is hope for the Homosexual, or any other sinner. The sinners hope is only through the shed **BLOOD OF JESUS CHRIST,** the Son of God.

For whosoever shall call upon the name of the Lord shall be saved. Romans 10:13.

CALL UPON THE LORD WHILE YOU CAN.

Dynamics

Stripped of their higher calling and theological trappings, morbid religious homophobes are just like other individuals with an emotional disorder, for they are:

1. Lacking in compassion: They are often biting, mean-spirited, aggressive individuals full of a desire for vengeance. They criticize and condemn gays and lesbians in a cruel, sadistic manner. They punish them both by beating them up physically, and by bashing them emotionally—by excluding them, banishing them, excommunicating them, and thinking of them as dead when they are in fact still alive. They are "citizens" of what some gays and lesbians, referring to Colorado (a state that passed antihomosexual ordinances), call the "hate state."

2. Hypersensitive to rejection: Some morbidly religious homophobes at first form deep, intense relationships with gays and lesbians, only their loving feelings are expressed in control (conversion) fantasies. Then they perceive the gays' or lesbians' refusal to go along as a personal rejection, and seek vengeance. In such cases their homophobia, which is reactive, sounds uncomfortably like the pain of a lover scorned, with homohatred the response to what they perceive as having been ignored by a significant other.

3. Controlling: Morbid religious homophobes are controlling because they attempt to run gays' and lesbians' lives for them. They impose their own rules on them, using the carrot of salvation and the stick of damnation.

4. Submissive and suggestible: As Morris (1967) says, "the extreme potency of religion [and religious bias] is simply a measure of the strength of our fundamental biological tendency, inherited directly from our monkey and ape ancestors, to submit ourselves to an all-powerful, dominant member of the group" (p. 180).

5. Unreasonable: Homophobes make unreasonable demands on gays and lesbians. For example, they put them in an impossible position when they assert that the only morally correct way to prevent AIDS is by practicing fidelity within heterosexual marriage and abstinence outside. As Steinfels quoting Sullivan (1995) says, a church that "insists on the dignity of the homosexual person and the blamelessness of homosexuality in itself, but teaches that 'if this blameless condition was acted upon'" and these "emotional and sexual longings . . . manifest . . . in physical intimacy and a lasting companionship" "'it would be always and everywhere evil'" creates an "impasse [that gays and lesbians ultimately find] spiritually destructive, choking off [their] ability to love either [them]selves or others" (p. 9).

6. Narcissistic: Narcissistic morbid religious homophobes condemn gays and lesbians for self-serving reasons: simply because they do not produce the babies they need to create the new parishioners that they want to fill their churches. They are also narcissistic in that they preach to gays and lesbians, and try to convert them, as if they, the preachers, alone know what is right. The fantasy that they are God often underlies their self-certainty and with it the utter conviction of the truth of what they have to say, and their sense of the righteousness of their personal mission, a sense that is so entrenched that they even expect complete strangers to agree with and yield to them though they don't know them, or anything about their qualifications, if they have any. As Morris (1967) says, "religion has . . . given rise to a great deal of unnecessary suffering and misery . . . whenever the professional 'assistants' of the god figures have been unable to resist the temptation to borrow a little of his power and use it themselves" (p. 181).

7. Perfectionistic: Morbid religious homophobes see gays and lesbians in terms of either black or white. The "gay sin" makes the complete sinner, so that the "imperfection" that is being gay or lesbian makes gays and lesbians entirely defective.

8. Dereistic: Morbid religious homophobes, in viewing homosexuals as the devil—not merely the apotheosis but the actual instrument of evil—are indulging in a kind of autistic irrational thinking that closely resembles the thinking of schizophrenics. (This illogical thinking is described further in chapter 16, which discusses the cognitive errors that contribute to homophobia.)

9. Ambivalent: Many morbidly religious homophobes do and undo, practice and regret, their homophobia until their overwrought struggles uncannily resemble the ones between good and evil that are the core of the weaving rituals of obsessive-compulsive neurotics. This was the case for a minister who alternated between condemning gays and lesbians, then, believing himself too harsh, forgiving them, then, believing himself too soft on sin, condemning them again—behavior that reminded me of some of my patients with a cleaning compulsion who always managed to soil what they were cleaning so that they had to restart the cleaning ritual, once more, from the top.

10. Hypocritical: Homophobes proclaim the Judeo-Christian ideal of love while forgetting how their cruelty to gays and lesbians is incompatible with this ideal. They also disregard some of the tenets of the Bible they quote, as when they feel free to cast the first stone, even though they themselves are sinners.

In conclusion I present two contrasting views of religion. Some gays and lesbians who have been victims of religious persecution take comfort in Freud's (some say realistic, others say degrading) view of religion.

Others take more comfort from Hyde's view, because, as they say, she offers hope and solace in her softer, more forgiving tone.

Freud, in *The Future of an Illusion* (1927) asks if we should believe the Bible (and by implication the passages that homophobes use to justify their homophobia). He then suggests some reasons we should not believe the Bible. He says that

the dogmas of religion . . . claim to be believed . . . based . . . [on] three answers, which accord remarkably ill with one another. They deserve to be believed: firstly, because our primal ancestors already believed them; secondly, because we possess proofs, which have been handed down to us from this very period of antiquity; and thirdly, because it is forbidden to raise the question of their authenticity at all. Formerly this presumptuous act was visited with the very severest penalties. . . .

The third point cannot but rouse our strongest suspicions. Such a prohibition can surely have only one motive: that society knows very well the uncertain basis of the claim it makes for its religious doctrines. If it were otherwise, the relevant material would certainly be placed most readily at the disposal of anyone who wished to gain conviction for himself. . . . [As for the idea that] we ought to believe because our forefathers believed . . . these ancestors of ours were far more ignorant than we; they believed in things we could not possibly accept to-day; so the possibility occurs that religious doctrines may also be in this category. The proofs they have bequeathed to us are deposited in writings that themselves bear every trace of being untrustworthy. They are full of contradictions, revisions, and interpolations; where they speak of actual authentic proofs they are themselves of doubtful authenticity. It does not help much if divine revelation is asserted to be the origin of their text or only of their content, for this assertion is itself already a part of those doctrines whose authenticity is to be examined, and no statement can bear its own proof (pp. 43–45). . . . [The] utterances of their spirits are merely the productions of their own mental activity (p 47).

Hyde (1994) notes that

theologians and scholars who have studied the Bible for many years in efforts to learn its true meaning have a variety of opinions about how these passages relate to homosexuals. They tell us that, in some cases, an ancient word may have as many as forty different meanings. Most biblical scholars now question the interpretation of many references that are used to justify negative judgments on same-sex orientation. Some controversial passages that are used to condemn homosexual acts deal with sexual behavior that is unloving and exploitative, such as prostitution. Even here, the Bible's message is one of forgiveness and healing. . . . An increasing number of religious people agree that a few passages cannot override Jesus's central message of love and reconciliation. Christianity is not a cause; it is a way of life. They feel that the Bible should not be used to try to convince people that their way is right or wrong. The purpose of the Bible is not to prove something. It is a love story, teaching people to love one another. (pp. 52–53).

[Hyde concludes] Many religious people accept homosexuals as church members because they believe that God forgives sins, including heterosexual sins such as child abuse, incest, adultery, and so on (p. 53).

These days many churches are moving in the direction of inclusiveness, and will even support the ordination of noncelibate homosexuals.

THE HOMOPHOBIC LAW ENFORCEMENT OR CRIMINAL MODEL OF HOMOSEXUALITY

In the homophobic law enforcement or criminal model of homosexuality, gays and lesbians are not sinners but criminals. The *New York Times* in an unattributed article, "Excerpts from Court's Decision on Colorado's Provision for Homosexuals" (1996) quoting Justice Scalia reminds us that in the case of "Bowers v. Hardwick we held that the Constitution does not prohibit . . . making homosexual conduct a crime" (p. A21). The law enforcement or criminal model of homosexuality is based on circular reasoning: being homosexual is a crime because it is against the law; and being homosexual is against the law because it is a crime. It contains another fatal logical flaw: those who see gays and lesbians as sick are often the same individuals who see gays and lesbians as criminals. As such they are in the untenable position of recommending we punish people for being ill.

The issue of pedophilia is beyond the scope of this text. K. Robert Schwarz's (1994) description of the arrest of the composer Henry Cowell "in 1936 on charges of having sex with a minor" [According to Schwarz he "served four years in San Quentin" (p. 24)] may or may not provide us with an example of the homophobic criminal model of homosexuality at work.

THE HOMOPHOBIC POLITICAL MODEL OF HOMOSEXUALITY

In the homophobic political model of homosexuality, gays and lesbians are not sick, sinful, or criminal but, as Frank Rich (1996) put it (as also mentioned in chapter 3) "fodder in an election year [as politicians] play . . . the gay card . . . [when they] turn same-sex marriage, hardly the year's most pressing issue, into a flashpoint for a polarizing culture war in which gay people become the Willie Hortons of '96" (p. A17). Freud

(1927) said essentially the same thing, but in another way, when he noted that people such as politicians conveniently use "the strength of . . . differences [such as being homosexual] to claim . . . the right to despise the rest" (p. 18). And Colin Spencer (1995) put it this way: "fears of homosexuality are authorities' means of manipulating the masses into submitting" (p. 401). Spencer specifically cites how "McCarthy bent homosexuality to his own ends when he link[ed] homosexuality with communism as both enem[ies] of the state" (p. 402) and further notes how other politicians believe they can relieve economic hardship by encouraging "kicking and spitting at the underdog" (403). According to Todd S. Purdum (1996), David B. Mixner, "an old friend of [President] Clinton's who has raised money for his campaigns among gay supporters" says that the statement that gay marriages will undermine straight morality is "a ridiculous statement" that must be "extraordinarily political in nature." He argues that this is so because "no one in the White House can make a cogent argument about how gay people committing themselves to a life-long relationship threatens the American family" (p. B9).

THE HOMOPHOBIC SOCIOCULTURAL MODEL OF HOMOSEXUALITY

In the homophobic sociocultural, or small town, model of homosexuality, gays and lesbians are not sick, sinners, criminals, or convenient political tools/subjects for political manipulation/assassination, but eccentrics—deviates who do not belong and should on that account be banished. Small towns tend to be family-oriented. This is partly a state of mind and represents an ideal. But it is also partly a reality, because in many small towns the family is still intact and is physically there to enforce the traditional roles with which it is associated. And in the traditional small-town family, gays and lesbians are the black sheep—isolated from the rest of the family without regard for their actual behavior and accomplishments—that is, their actual and potential value. In effect, at least in some of the blue-collar small towns I know, the most unaccomplished citizens condemn the most accomplished, ignoring or even banishing some of their best-qualified and high-level people—precisely those who are most able and so most likely to do the town, and its individual inhabitants, some good.

THE HOMOPHOBIC BIOLOGICAL MODEL OF HOMOSEXUALITY

There are three forms of the homophobic biological model of homosexuality. In the first form, homophobes view gays and lesbians not as sick,

sinners, criminals, objects of convenience, or deviates, but as biologically defective mutants. For example, one straight homophobe (personal communication) cited how gays and lesbians emit unpleasant
odors, explaining that "they don't even *smell* right to me, especially
when they are in heat."

In the second form, straights view gays and lesbians as interloping
strangers, with gay bashing, as Kirk and Madsen (1989) put it, serving
"some evolutionary purpose" or having a "survival advantage" (p. 113).

For example, many homophobes see gays and lesbians as generic
outsiders, distinctly not of a feather, who threaten them as insiders who
belong to a defined, structured, sanctified entity such as the "nuclear
family." Kirk and Madsen speak of "approach" and "avoid[ance] . . . emotions" (p. 116) in "baboons . . . band[ing] together into tribes" (p. 117).
They compare homophobes who dislike gays and lesbians to baboons
who find other baboons to be a source of stranger anxiety, and who
throw bananas at those who don't belong to their own tribe because they
see them as invading their turf. They refer to the baboons' ability to

> discriminate . . . between members of their own tribe and members of
> other tribes . . . [and afterwards] having discerned the strangers at a glance
> *flee* . . . or . . . *fight*. . . . 'the baboon reaction [is] see the stranger, fear the
> stranger, hate the stranger, kill the stranger!'. . . . [With] humans [who]
> feel . . . exactly the same sorts of things as baboons do . . . a rewarding
> sense of relief from fear and anger [comes] when they avoid or destroy
> outsiders, and [obtain] an equally rewarding sense of pride, self-righteous-
> ness, and the respect and approval of their own 'tribe'—their parents, their
> family, their neighborhood, their 'set,' their class, their nation, and their
> race (pp. 118–119).

One homophobe said gays and lesbians reminded him of the plant and
animal that was in him as his evolutionary inheritance. He spoke of and
treated gays and lesbians as if they were all competing trees in a forest and
if he were to survive he had to grow tall to maximize the limited light available so that he could dwarf the gay and lesbian competition. He spoke of
and treated gays and lesbians as if they were runts of the litter whose survival benefited nobody; as if they were crippled individuals who had to be
destroyed so that they didn't waste the precious resources of the strong;
and as if they were old people who had to be put out in the cold to die to
preserve the limited supplies for younger, reproductively active members
of his tribe. He added, continuing this line of thought, that gays and lesbians should be relegated to the bottom of the pecking order, and the food
chain. And after comparing his homophobia to an antibiotic secreted by a
good bacterium to destroy the bad bacteria, he compared himself to a spi-
der who caught gays and lesbians in its web—simply because it was hungry, and needed something good to eat.

In the third form, gays and lesbians are viewed as individuals who threaten the homophobe's internal homeostasis—that is, their precarious emotional balance and need for internal control. They are seen as primitive people who, as Spencer (1995) says, are pagans, "barbarians . . . at the gates" who arouse a fear of "pagan worship" and "pagan wastrels" who like "masturbators" can dissipate the "life-force of humanity for the sake of a passing sensual thrill" (p. 401).

5

Homophobia in Gays and Lesbians

Gay bashing is not confined to straights. Gays and lesbians bash both themselves and other gays and lesbians. For example, one lesbian noted how her sisters kept gay men out of lesbian bars, and one gay man complained about gay men who "outed" other gay men to embarrass them or destroy their careers.

MANIFESTATIONS OF HOMOPHOBIA IN GAYS AND LESBIANS

Self-Homophobia

William W. Meissner (1985) defines *inhibition*, one reason for celibacy, as "an unconsciously determined limitation or renunciation of specific ego functions, singly or in combination, to avoid anxiety arising out of conflict with instinctual impulses, superego, or environmental forces or figures" (p. 389). This definition applies to gays and lesbians who self-closet, renouncing homosexual relationships/homosexuality to avoid accepting themselves as they are, as a way to win a struggle they are having with themselves about being gay.

According to Samuel Hynes' (1994) book review of a biography of E.M. Forster, the novelist "came to realize he was a homosexual, but saw his condition only as a crippling and isolating misfortune; . . . he had no full sexual experience until he was in his late 30s, and even after that lived a nearly celibate life for many years . . . until he was 45, just at the point where his novel writing ended" (p. 7).

While promiscuity can at first glance seem to be the opposite of inhibition/celibacy, in many cases it is instead just another one of its manifestations. So often gays become promiscuous to master the conflicts that make them inhibited by denying these conflicts even exist.

Self-homophobic gays and lesbians act out their self-homophobia by *distancing* themselves from friends, lovers, and family in a self-abnegating way. They may avoid developing close relationships or abandon close relationships they already have, tiring of them too easily, and after finding some excuse or other giving them up and going on to the next relationship. Many of these gays and lesbians distance themselves from their lovers by fighting with them. For example, one gay man fought with his lover both while awake and in his dreams. A dream he had one night suggested the reason for the fights:

> I am taking a train with my lover and the two of us are fighting. The train I wanted to take ran from up north down to Manhattan, while the train I was actually on ran across upper Manhattan to New Jersey to the cemetery where my parents were buried. I thought in the dream that I am fighting with my lover because he is gay and I hate gays just like my parents, when they were alive, hated me, and all gay men as well.

Some gays and lesbians cheat and turn to anonymous sex less as a way to express continuing hope that there is something better out there than as a way to make a negative statement about being homosexual, in effect saying, "I would not want to have a serious relationship with anyone I know well because once you get to know gays and lesbians well you find they all have something wrong with them." The ultimate expression of this attitude is a homosexual's refusing to have sex with other homosexuals because of what homosexuals do to their bodies during sex. So they become specialists in "straight" men or women, which they rationalize as "I like married men or women," when they really mean, "I like 'straights,' because I despise gays and lesbians."

Self-homophobia can be manifest as sexual or nonsexual *self-destructive behavior.* As for sexual self-destructive behavior, many gay men describe having unprotected sex when they are depressed and are, like all depressives, full of self-hate. The following case illustrates what I mean by nonsexual self-destructive behavior:

> One gay intern flirted with danger by bouncing checks the hospital cashed for him, thinking, "They deserve it, because they pay me such a small salary, one that does not adequately cover my living expenses." Sometimes he stole food from the cafeteria, having discovered a way to get past the cashier without paying. He regularly drank and cruised all night and came

back to the dormitory obviously drunk and too late to get enough sleep to be sufficiently alert to function properly the next day. And when he was assigned to two different medical services, tired from cruising the night before, he told one he was busy with the other, then disappeared from both, went to his room, and took a nap.

Camping is a self-effacing joke on one's self and on one's own kind.

An example of a campy homophobic joke one gay made on himself and other gays is the one he told about the grandfather clock, related in order to make fun of gays' exhibitionistic tendencies. In brief the joke told of a gay man who, having just purchased an antique grandfather's clock, was carrying it home on his back when he was hit by a car, and both he and the clock were knocked to the ground. He is okay, but the clock is damaged beyond repair. A straight man passing by notices the gay man's predicament, and comments, "This wouldn't have happened if you hadn't been such a queen and worn a wrist watch like the rest of us."

Self-homophobia can take the form of a preference for *pornography* and *onanism*. As for onanism, as one gay put it, the use of a legendary auto-jac, a mechanical masturbator on the market some years back, and possibly still on the market today, doesn't say much about what gays think about the wonders of relationships in general, or the wonders of gay relationships in specific. "All the latter does," he continued, "is put a new, and not very flattering, spin on what people mean when they speak of the 'relationship between man and machine.'"

Homosexual *hustlers* sometimes do it for the money, believed to be acceptable, to convince themselves that they are not doing it for the sex, believed to be unacceptable.

A gay hustler denied he was in business for the sex, saying he was only in it for the money. He broadly hinted to a man who took him in, "We are having a good time but I am not any richer these days than I was before I met you." And yet after the inevitable break up the gay hustler kept coming around, inviting himself over for dinner, and telling the other man his problems with life. So it was not only money after all—for him money was, as it is with so many "straight" hustlers, just another excuse to have sex guilt-free, a way to say, "I am not having gay sex, which I abhor, I am just doing a job, trying to earn a living."

Gays and lesbians express their self-hatred by avoiding self-fulfillment. They often do this by *wasting time* in such substitute gratifications as compulsive cruising. These are substitute gratifications because they do not tap their real capacities, and they divert useful energy from potentially more rewarding and satisfactory pursuits.

Suicide is the ultimate expression of self-hatred, and the most serious one to grow directly out of self-homophobia.

Other-Directed Homophobia

Some gays and lesbians *abuse* their lovers in the belief that the lovers are defective because they are homosexual, and what they want is a nonhomosexual homosexual, the homosexual equivalent of "a virgin mother." They might *cheat* on their lovers in a way that is destructive to all concerned. They say they cheat on their lovers for sexual variety, but they cheat less for the sex than to hurt their lovers (and themselves). This is often why they see to it that their cheating gets back to the one they are cheating on.

> A lover once put four asterisks as an entry in the checkbook of his and his lover's joint account, calling attention to how he had written a check in secret. He knew his lover would become suspicious and look for the original check when it came back from the bank. And sure enough, there for him to see, was a check that was written for a weekend's stay at a well-known gay resort, dated on a day the lover was supposed to be visiting his brother.

Threesome arrangements, however much two people agree to have them, and deny that cheating is involved because they do it together, are always homophobic because they always imply a put-down of the steady partner's worth.

Like cruel adolescents humiliating a peer who wears glasses, or like hooligans defiling old ladies, some gays and lesbians *dish (a campy badmouthing) or condemn* other gays and lesbians, often for the same things, and in the same ways, straights condemn them.

> For example, one gay activist "dished" (bad-mouthed) other gays and lesbians, who as a result found they could not win with him. He condemned gays and lesbians who came out of the closet for being indiscreet, while he condemned gays and lesbians who stayed in the closet for being dishonest and nonassertive. He criticized gays and lesbians with a certain degree of sophistication for being too snotty. For example, he made fun of what he called "pretentious East Hampton," a semigay resort on eastern Long Island, calling it variously "East Hamptoon" and "The Tampons" to "burst the bubble of the self-love rife among the pretentious queens there." On the other hand he criticized gays and lesbians who were promiscuous for not being snotty enough, that is, for "whoring around with low-rent people." He accused gays and lesbians who picked companions/lovers who were

younger than they were of "robbing the cradle," and accused gays and lesbians who picked companions/lovers who were older than they were of favoring "geriatric cases." Male gays who swished he called "femmes," while those who swaggered in what he considered to be an excessively masculine fashion he dubbed "just too butch for her [sic] own good."

Some gays and lesbians resort to back-stabbing. One man got a call from a friend of his lover, telling him that the lover was cheating on him, behind his back, and citing the evidence. He said, "I do this because I respect you and don't like to see you treated that way." But he really did it because he wanted to humiliate his friend and mistreat him by rubbing his nose in all the goings-on.

Combinations of Self- and Other-Directed Homophobia

Some activist gays and lesbians argue that gays' and lesbians' *outing* of other gays and lesbians is a useful thing to do when the means justify the end. Others argue that outing is perhaps the ultimate in gay bashing as well as in self-directed homophobia, because in suggesting that one can embarrass gays and lesbians by exposing them as being homosexual, one is admitting that being homosexual is inherently an embarrassment.

Some *name-calling* is both self-destructive and hurtful to other gays and lesbians. As Steinfels (1995) puts it, Act-Up, a gay activist organization, offends gays, lesbians, and nonadversary straights alike when it "brands as murderers those who disagree with its view of homosexuality" (just as "Operation Rescue does the same to those who disagree with its view of abortion") (p. 9).

DEVELOPMENTAL ASPECTS

Gays and lesbians become self-homophobic when they go along with/identify with hostile or actually homophobic parents, introjecting their critical nonaccepting attitudes toward them, accepting these attitudes as their own, and in turn treating themselves, and other gays and lesbians, just like their parents treated them. Often they incorporate their parents' negative values in order to proclaim their love for their parents and to tell them how sorry they are for having turned out homosexual. Particularly at risk are gays and lesbians who were abused by their parents and think they deserved the abuse because they were bad people. (In such cases self-homophobia often becomes especially acute later in life when gays and lesbians lose their parents, and deal with the loss by abusing themselves even more to identify with the lost object—their parents—and their parents' negativity—as a way to maintain the relationship after the loss has occurred.)

Often a homosexual homophobe's parents were also sexophobes who criticized the child for masturbation and heterosexual behavior as much as they criticized him or her for having homosexual tendencies or for actually doing homosexual things. Such gays and lesbians become self-homophobic as part of a global self-sexophobia, and compulsively criticize themselves not only for being homosexual but also for all sexual and loving feelings. In such cases the self-criticism originates in a rigid punitive conscience which is composed of an intrapsychic parental database that, like digital sound, consists, figuratively speaking, only of ons and offs, goods and bads, 0s and 1s: a noise that is shrill, harsh, unforgiving, and unloving because it contains none of the nuances that make for what stereophiles call "the warmth of vinyl."

Here are some cases where fathers and mothers who criticized a child's sexuality and withheld love on that account created a stain that spread over their children's lives until the children could neither give themselves a vote of confidence nor confidently vote for other gays and lesbians in turn.

A mother and father put their son's masculine tendencies and sexuality down by curling his hair like a girl's and complaining when he tried to straighten it out. They regularly humiliated him for his loving feelings. For example, once they beat him for what turned out to be his last heterosexual venture, playing doctor with the little girl next door, saying that "nice little boys don't play that game." Then they made him steer clear of all little girls "so that you don't contaminate them with your germs or screw up their lives in even worse ways."

An overpossessive father repeatedly made the point that he did not want his teen-age daughter "talking to those dykes and faggots on the Internet." Then he forbade her to go on-line at all. Then he declared that she should not date men until she was 30 years old. Then he forbade her to have any women friends staying overnight at the house because "I can't tell what you two might do when I leave you alone together."

A father beat his son and threatened to cut off his funds if he did not see a psychiatrist to be cured of his "promiscuity," which, according to the father, consisted of his having relationships with more than one girl at a time. Later in life when the son became openly gay, the father was so ashamed of him that he regularly spirited him and his lover out of a restaurant where they were having family dinner together before any of the father's cronies could arrive and see the son and his lover there together.

Once he would not let the son bring his lover to a birthday dinner the family wanted to give for the son, and when the son bridled, the father simply had the party canceled.

A girl's parents punished her for being promiscuous by selling her their house, knowing, but not telling her, in advance, that a building project across the way was going to block the ocean view. To rub salt in the wounds, they built a new and better house, gave it to her brother, and gave him a large business they had built up over the years as well. Not surprisingly, when their daughter grew up a lesbian she became a self-destructive self-homophobe remote not only from friends and family, but also from gay men and lesbians, because she felt too undeserving to enjoy the company of good friends, and too worthless to allow herself to have a good life, especially one that included her gay version of a happy family.

A man played with girls when he was young. His father, becoming concerned that he would grow up to be "a sissy," abused him personally to get him to change, calling him "faggot" and the like. Later in life when he became openly gay the son himself demeaned anything he enjoyed doing short of chopping wood and playing ball as "faggots' work." Eventually he attempted suicide "because I cannot stand being such a fag."

However, not all homosexual self-abuse is due to the introjection of negative family messages. Gay bashing is innate as well as acquired, for gays and lesbians can bash themselves before others bash them, mistreating themselves even before they have had a chance to be mistreated. When not a symptom of the self-hate that is part of depression, this innate self-gay bashing is part of the universal guilt that all sexuality provokes in gays and straights alike—part of that universal negative attitudinal mind-set that makes all sex into something wicked, and sinful, at least when the sex is something other than what my colleague, previously mentioned in Chapter 1, called "missionary-position-in-the-dark."

SYNDROMAL ASPECTS

Descriptive Considerations

In the following discussion I illustrate how self-homophobia in gays and lesbians can be just as much a symptom of emotional disorder as homophobia in straights directed toward gays and lesbians. The examples that follow also illustrate how self- and other-directed homophobia tend to go hand in hand.

Self-homophobic *paranoid* homosexuals are suspicious, jealous individuals who bash other gays and lesbians as a way to condemn them for doing the very things they are guilty about doing themselves. Guilty about their own promiscuous wishes, they hold their lovers to an unfulfillable standard of what they define as fidelity, such as "don't even think about it," then put them down when predictably the lover cannot meet that standard.

Depressed gay and lesbian self-homophobes, like all depressives, see the world not as a pleasant place to live in but as an arena for conflict resolution, transference demands for absolution, and perceived or actual trauma recurrence. Those who do not like themselves use their homosexuality to explain and justify this self-dislike. They also treat other gays and lesbians as if they were their own "ugly reflection in the mirror," and attack them as a way to attack themselves, giving others the black eye they feel they deserve to have themselves. They devalue lovers as they devalue themselves—openly in fights, or covertly by cruising with their eyes, as a way to say, "That one has what you do not have." Like all depressives they are picky and unforgiving in their flaw-finding. One depressed lesbian ended every relationship because she heard a little voice saying to her something like, "You can do better, with someone bigger, stronger, richer, and less-queer appearing. After all, this lover of yours smokes constantly, and has such a deep voice that you would think you are talking to a man."

Depressed homophobic gays and lesbians caricature themselves in their dress, mutilate their bodies, or indulge in self-deprecating behaviors like campy graveyard (melancholy, romantically gloomy) humor, all to say "kick-me" to the world. This makes them even more the victims than they already are, and have to be. Some are masochistic in the way they come out of the closet, which they do not do to be free and open, as they think, but to be annoying and get themselves into trouble. They often deliberately engineer their own nonacceptance by baiting others who do like them, inciting bigotry by acting like rebellious sadomasochistic adolescents who play annoying adolescent games. (In this they resemble those adolescents who regularly play music whose main virtue and purpose is its ability to grate on others' nerves.) Others are masochistic in their preference for lovers who do not like them. (Males who do this sometimes have had a sadistic father whom they tried, unsuccessfully, to convert, to become a more ideal father.) Though they say they are looking for love, they deny the problems and risks involved in throwing themselves at the feet of unrepentant sadistic homophobes so that they can conveniently forget that their kind of object choice forms an unworthy basis for the lifetime relationships they claim to be seeking. They often like lovers who are rough because that way they can be involved in a sadomasochistic saphrophytic relationship where each member of the dyad feeds on the other, each going to sleep at night with the assurance that the other will not fail them, and will be there the next morning, to brutalize them further. Their specific sexual preferences like "fisting" (anal insertion of a fist) or water sports often have a self-sacrificial aspect. So can a preference for thin-as-a-board juveniles who look like women when the so-called preference is really a self-punishment for liking "real men."

Hypomanic gays and lesbians self-destruct by cruising frantically for new lovers. Their compulsive barhopping becomes addictive, and takes its toll on their lives, partly because they ultimately crash when later in life they realize how much time they wasted and how many good people they passed by. In the professional sphere many are constantly on the lookout for new jobs, thinking themselves dissatisfied with the old ones, even when the old ones are good, or good enough. They also favor "graveyard camping," which can carry over into their work. Instead of fully participating in work in a positive way, they devote their time and effort to what amounts to little more than making good jokes on their bad self, until neither colleagues nor superiors can any longer take them seriously.

Dependent homophobic gays and lesbians say they hate other gays and lesbians as part of a plan to pass as straights, which is in turn part of a plan to get straights to accept them. These gays and lesbians are ultimately self-destructive because they play into the hands of straights who select a few homophobic homosexuals as friends just to deny they discriminate against all homosexuals.

Psychopathic gays and lesbians attack other gays and lesbians less to deal with their own guilt than to throw their homophobic persecutors off the scent. These attacks have the reverse effect, because ultimately they are seen for what they are: little more than attacks on the self.

Avoidant gays and lesbians deliberately use their remoteness to hurt themselves. They keep to themselves, isolating themselves, just so that they can remain lonely and personally ungratified. Someone cruises them and they purposely (though unconsciously) think about something or someone else, to deny the other is interested. They might say, "He or she is not cruising but staring at me," and then retreat. Or they might subject someone interested in them to ridicule. (Many gays and lesbians can attest to having had the following experience: when they cruise one of two homosexuals who are together but available, the other one moves in and ridicules the one doing the cruising, for cruising.)

Avoidant gays and lesbians often self-destruct by abandoning their real family because they do not feel worthy of having one. If their avoidance is not too severe, they look to make a new family out of one-night stands held over. This can work, but it is ultimately unsound practice when it is a way to neglect their real family even more.

Younger gays and lesbians often miss out when they avoid older gays and lesbians because they see them as defective. Instead of relating to them, they make fun of them, calling them such things as "old aunty." Instead of developing friendships with them, they use them. If they have anything to do with them, it is for their own selfish purposes, as often happens when a younger, less-established gay man needs the older gay's apartment to "shack up" in. Dynamically they avoid old people because they symbolize all the defects they see in themselves, and because they remind them of the loneliness and physical deterioration that they fear awaits them around the corner. Being old is also a wound that attracts the shark, inspiring the more sadistically inclined, gays and straights alike, to move in for the kill.

Narcissistic homophobic gays and lesbians miss out because they hurt other gays and lesbians even more than they hurt themselves when they bash other gays and lesbians for not being just like they are, however much their self-standard is not necessarily the only or best standard. Anyone, straight or gay, cut from a pattern at all different from theirs is condemned, and precisely for these differences. The two messages are "I am the greatest" and "what I know, stand for, and exemplify is what is best, and right." Many such gays and lesbians view other gays and lesbians as too butch or too femme, too rough or too elegant, compared to themselves, as unempathically and as hurtfully as their straight counterparts view them, as compared to straights.

When narcissism hides low self-esteem, gays and lesbians reject other gays and lesbians to enhance their own self-image. One had a friend over regularly except for the holidays, when he had everyone over but him, just so he could deliciously contemplate how the friend was alone for Christmas and Easter, and how lucky he was, in comparison, to have company.

Narcissistic envy, where what you have automatically becomes what I do not have, provides another reason for gays and lesbians to reject other gays and lesbians. Narcissistic envious homophobic gays and lesbians put others down as sour grapes, just to make their own grapes seem sweeter.

Narcissistic gays and lesbians are selfish people who ask only what other gays and lesbians can do for them (and even become vengeful against their own kind when they feel they have deprived them of what they need). Such gays and lesbians become house guests who do not write thank-you notes and who do not return invitations. When the time comes to return a favor, they offer instead a slap in the face. One gay man put up friends every summer but never got a return invitation, even though he asked for one repeatedly. He asked a friend, a travel agent who stayed at his house all summer, for a travel brochure, but the friend was always too busy to get it for him. Such gays and lesbians send the message to other gays and lesbians that "You make a good mother when you give on demand, but make an off-putting child when you insist on getting something in return, to be taken seriously, and to be shown the respect and consideration every one, straights, gays and lesbians alike, deserves to have."

Histrionic gay men miss out because they are neurotically homophobic of lesbians because they imagine lesbians, as they imagine all women, to be castrators of gay, as well as of straight, men. And histrionic lesbians are neurotically homophobic of gay men because they imagine gay men, as they imagine all men, as having the penis they envy. All concerned criticize each other to exclude each other, to see to it that there is nothing anywhere about to be found to remind them of what they fear the most.

Posttraumatic stress disorder gays and lesbians miss out when they devote their lives to traumatizing other gays and lesbians as they were themselves traumatized in the past. Those who were beaten by their mothers or fathers after being caught "in flagrante" for playing sexual games often symbolically repeat their trauma by tempting fate, say by exposing themselves/masturbating in public places, hoping not to be caught, and punished, yet hoping to be caught and punished at the same time.

Dissociative gays and lesbians have self-defeating fugue-like episodes or attacks of amnesia at the moment of triumph to assure the iron strikes cold, both because they need and want to win only the unwinnable games, and because they experience discomfort and panic when someone extends them a helping hand, or fully encircles them in their embrace.

Sexual *impotence* is a manifestation of self-homophobia when gays and lesbians cannot obtain orgasmic pleasure because they brood right through the sexual act about whether or not they are good enough to be entitled to have an orgasm, until they cannot have one, just for that reason.

Cognitive Considerations

Many gays and lesbians become self-homophobic when they make the same homophobic cognitive errors about themselves that homophobic straights make about them. Many gays undergo an interminable, self-punitive psychoanalysis because they feel that they are sick. They themselves argue that because certain aspects of homosexuality can be understood dynamically, that means that homosexuality is a neurosis. They also confuse understanding with curing. Even in those cases where there are discernible developmental and dynamic reasons for "selecting" homosexuality, this does not mean that it can be consciously/unconsciously unselected by gaining insight into its presumed cause. [According to Jones (1957), Freud said that he could not "abolish homosexuality and make normal heterosexuality take its place. . . . in a certain number of cases we succeed in developing the blighted germs of heterosexual tendencies which are present in every homosexual [but] in the majority of cases it is [not] possible." (p. 195).]

6

Is It Ever Rational to Be Homophobic?

Homophobes who do not deny they are homophobic usually claim their homophobia is natural and normal, citing several factors:

1. Culture: Some homophobes say in effect that they are good citizens in their hometowns. They say they function in a socially responsible way, or if they are religious, according to the dictates of their ministers, or of the Bible. In citing society they deny that theirs is a sick society or that they are buying into the intolerant faction of a society divided—picking those aspects of society that fit their own morbid needs. In citing the Bible, they claim that following its homophobic dictates is right, justified, and appropriate, and even say the equivalent of, "don't blame me, I didn't write it."

2. Human nature: Some homophobes say it is only human nature for straights to dislike gays and lesbians, for several reasons. They say it is normal to be suspicious of others who are different, and cite the following paradigms in self-justification: children play only with other children of the same age while excluding all others; scientists embrace only their own school of thought, while savaging all others; birds of a feather flock together while avoiding all others; ducks think baby swans are ugly; and gardeners call some flowers weeds just because they are in an unwelcoming garden.

The more scientifically inclined suggest that there is a primary taboo against homosexuality. In particular they postulate the presence of a taboo against anal penetration, and claim it is just as powerful and basic as the incest taboo and for some of the same reasons—that is, it is there to encourage reproduction of the species while preventing disease—genetic and psychological disease in the case of incest, venereal disease and physical trauma in the case of anal penetration.

3. Preference: Preferential homophobes claim that their homophobia is a matter of individual taste. They assert their dislike of gays is voluntary, not compulsive or prejudicial. They deny that it is the product of an unconscious resolution of personal conflict, such as conflict about their own homosexuality. They deny that they hate gays because they are in conflict about liking them. They say that their dislike of gays and lesbians is the product of a conscious decision to dislike them, for at worst they are criminals who flout the sodomy laws, and at best they are unladylike women who cut their hair short or unseemly men who pad daintily about with tight jeans and codpieces. (However I have found that many homophobic men deep down actually do like feminine men. They find them pleasantly soft and seductive, and their passive ways make them feel more manly. But their macho male personal and social conscience forbids that sort of positive feeling, particularly when it involves gays, so they change these feelings over into their opposite to deal with their guilt and the social approbation they anticipate. Similarly, many men and women like masculine-acting women. They like them because they dislike women, and approve of anything that is manly in a woman. They like women who are go-getters and social accomplishers. But they squelch their liking for them because of their conscience, and demand they instead conform to their—as they perceive them—acceptable internal images and what they consider to be socially approved "feminine" standards of behavior.)

4. Healthy (mature) asceticism: Meissner (1985) says that asceticism is a healthy defense where individuals eliminate "directly pleasurable affects attributable to an experience" by directing their efforts "against all 'base' pleasures perceived consciously, [with] gratification . . . derived from the renunciation" (p. 390). Many homophobes, claiming that their homophobia is the product of healthy asceticism, say they dislike homosexuality simply because they prefer Spartans to Athenians, and moralists to immoralists (whores). They claim a line can be drawn between normal asceticism and sexophobia, even though they admit that this line is as difficult to draw as are other similar lines, such as those between health and disease, self-protection and paranoia, cleanliness and germ phobia, and appropriate concern and obsessive worry.

5. Nondiscrimination: Some homophobes admit that they are prejudiced but they deny that they discriminate, or worse. So they say their prejudice, having few real consequences, is of no significance, and so is in fact utterly harmless.

6. Provocation: Many homophobes say that they are merely responding in an expectedly negative way to gays' and lesbians' bad behavior. Some heartily agree with the author Dinesh D'Souza who, according to William McGowan (1995), speaking of racism in terms that are equally

applicable to homosexuality, does not deny that discrimination still exists but feels that

> taxi drivers passing by young black men, or shopkeepers barring them from stores, are not signs of the old racism, which was based on prejudice and ignorance. They are signs of "rational discrimination"—understandable responses to the realities of underclass black behavior, such as the shocking proportion of young black men in prison, on probation or parole . . . that can be eradicated only by getting rid of the destructive conduct that forms the basis for statistically valid group distinctions" (p. 20).

In a similar vein, many homophobes say they have suffered real pain because of homosexuals and homosexuality.

> One psychologist put it this way: "In fairness I had to consider the point of view of a mother who was saddened to find her only son was gay. Gays like to paraphrase a song title to make fun of such "homophobic" mothers, mimicking them by singing, 'I hate to see my only son go down.' But having an only son who is gay did present certain real difficulties for this individual. As she put it, 'I am human too, entitled to grieve for my child's being gay, and entitled to miss the grandchildren I will never have. My feelings are justified. It is cruel for gay men to make fun of me for having them.'"

One patient accused of being homophobic excused his homophobia as follows:

> Some people like a neat place; others are obsessively neat and clean. I dislike some gays and lesbians, but I am not obsessively homophobic. Some gay behavior is unpleasant, and provocative. Some gays and lesbians deliberately set out to shock, offend, or threaten me. My thinking gays and lesbians are elitists is not a symptom when gays and lesbians insist their sexuality is superior to, rather than the equal of, mine—that is, when gays and lesbians lord it over me deliberately, and not to get back at me for lording it over them, but just to see me writhe. It particularly threatens me to see people having sex out in the open, for example on the beach, or even displaying their sexual preferences publicly as they used to do years ago while walking the streets of the city wearing handkerchiefs in their back pockets to proclaim their sexual desires to strangers. I may be cranky, but I am no more homophobic because I cannot stand the transsexual prostitutes that hang around the street outside my door than I am heterophobic because I dislike the heterosexual prostitutes turning tricks in cars parked in front of my house.

Of course, just as paranoids are never 100 percent unjustified in their suspicions, homophobes are never 100 percent wrong in their homophobia. It is true that as Fenichel (1945) puts it, "projection is not 'hit or miss' but occurs in the field in which reality meets it halfway. The . . . paranoid sees the mote in his neighbor's eye . . . [and uses a] type of defense known as 'displacement to the minute'" (p. 433). In like manner, gays and lesbians do have problems, and some of these encourage homophobia. But what the homophobe forgets is that:

a. Many gays' and lesbians' problems are not directly related to being homosexual, but are the result of the same coexisting personality, neurotic, or psychotic problems that also plague straights. For example, just because a gay man is promiscuous does not mean that promiscuity is necessarily a homosexual problem. It is just as likely to be an hysterical (oedipal) problem (where gays and lesbians, like some straights, seek multiple partners because of conflicts relating to each relationship formed), or a depressive (oral) problem (where gays and lesbians feel as if their need for love is a bottomless pit that cannot ever be filled to capacity).

b. It is always difficult to tell who is doing what to whom when minor interpersonal provocations escalate to become pitched battles. Eventually many gays, like most people, will do the negative things homophobes accuse them of having done. Homophobes who criticize gays and lesbians soon find that their victims get angry and then do just what they have been accused of having done.

c. So often claims that gays as a group are dangerous have an overblown hysterical quality as homophobes make much out of little. For example, homophobes who feel that if they give an inch to gays they will then have to give a mile and gays and lesbians will take over the world may have a minor point: gains gays and lesbians make in one area quite naturally form the basis for further gains in another. But it is a long way from getting one's legitimate rights on the job to wanting, or being able, to take over the entire planet.

7

The Negative Effects of Homophobia on Gays and Lesbians

As children many gays and lesbians lived with homophobic parents. Now as adults they all live in a homophobic society. They live with homophobic individuals on the job, where they suffer professionally, and at home, where they suffer personally.

> Thomas Couser (1996), in an article on the effects of homophobia on gays, describes how he felt when someone thinking he was gay defaced his car by writing "fag" all over it. He says, "The possibility that I was being watched made me feel paranoid. Is this, I thought, a taste of what it's like to be homosexual in America—to fear random harassment by utter strangers. In the space of those few moments I began to appreciate that to be openly gay takes considerable courage. . . . how vulnerable I . . . felt. For several days I experienced shock and fear—fear that the incident might be repeated or that the violence would escalate. I felt violated, and I was angered by my inability to retaliate. . . . I felt as though I had been conspicuously branded. . . . gender stereotypes and homophobia diminish and dehumanize us all" (p. 56).

Homophobes seem to know how to produce the negative effect they intend to produce. They seem to know instinctively how to make gays and lesbians anxious and afraid. They know that people are most afraid when the enemy is unseen, their attack unpredictable, and the attacker elusive and difficult to apprehend and/or attack back. So they lurk in the shadows, hit when least expected, run too fast to be caught, then wait a while between attacks so that their victims develop a false sense of security that can then be shattered once again with a new attack, also when least expected. They know how to frustrate gays and lesbians. One gay says that the worst experience of his life was being repeatedly called a faggot by a child he could not identify because he or she was dressed in a halloween costume. And they know how to make gays and lesbians depressed. For example, some police used to raid gay and lesbian bars not merely to enforce the laws but also to search and destroy gays' and lesbians' comfortable retreats, so that they could deprive them of their home away from home by disrupting the one public place where they could be comfortable with their own kind.

Today homophobes seem to know instinctively when gays and lesbians need affirmation, support, and love, then withhold these from them. They will not let them march in identified groups in their parades, not only because they object to homosexuality on religious and moral grounds but also because they know that there is less pride where there is no recognition. They know that the best way to depress gays and lesbians is to put them down in a way that really hurts. A good way is to criticize them when they are wrong, while never complimenting them when they are right. Or they demoralize them, making them feel ashamed of themselves. If gays and lesbians want their homosexuality to be a source of pride to compensate for feeling low or depressed, homophobes counter by telling them: "Hide your face, God is looking down and condemning you, for, quoting Leviticus, 'you are an abomination, to be vomited up by the land.'" Or they tell them to be ashamed of what they do to their parents, warn them that they threaten the integrity of society, and suggest that they alone are the reason for the lack of peace in the world, and might even cause the world to erupt in flames, and consume us all. They also know how to get around gays' and lesbians' complaints about them and undermine their self-defense. When gays and lesbians complain that they are being treated prejudicially, homophobes counter that they are paranoid; and when gays and lesbians complain that they are being discriminated against, homophobes counter that the negative response to them is not a discriminatory but an appropriate one. Some even provoke gays and lesbians, in a carefully orchestrated manner, just so that they can justify bashing them, as they intended to do all along. For example, in the army straights ostracize gays and lesbians. Some gays and lesbians then get depressed to the point that they can no longer function properly, when the homophobes can justifiably say that they do not make effective soldiers.

A straight woman left her job with a gay boss, telling him she was leaving the very day he planned to start his vacation so that he had no opportunity to hire her replacement. She left her job this way because "I wanted to ruin his vacation." Throughout his vacation she deliciously contemplated how her resignation was festering in his mind while he was trying to have fun. She was paying him back for being "one of those queers I hate, who don't deserve any better." He wondered if he had mishandled her as an employee, and asked himself how he could have been a better boss. But he was suffering unnecessarily. He could have "reassured" himself that she did not see him as a defective boss. He could have "rested comfortably" knowing that she "merely" saw him as a defective person.

Some gays and lesbians do not recognize that they are being abused. They have integrated as part of their daily oppression the fish-eye from the garbage man, the silent treatment from the neighbor, the gas station attendants who fill their cars but do not wash their windows (as they do for every one else), the crossing guard who lets the cars keep going when gays and lesbians are crossing, and the police who come when called but are annoyed that they were bothered by a bunch of sissies, predictably take the straights' side no matter what the evidence, and do not do anything for the gays and lesbians, no matter what the crime against them.

In one case a gay tolerated his neighbor's dog barking for an hour. It was bothering him, and making his own dog bark. When he finally could not stand it any more, he asked the neighbor to stop the dog from barking. The neighbor told him, "Not for a faggot." So the gay man called the police. But when the police came the neighbor's dog had stopped barking. Alas, now the gay's dog, having been sorely provoked by all the goings on, was barking merrily away. The police knew that the neighbor's dog was a problem barker, for they had received many complaints about this dog in the past. But all they said to the gay man was, "I only hear your dog barking, not his"—that is, "I will take the straight man's side any time over yours." This is an example of what is usually dismissed as "small town justice." But it should really not be dismissed out of hand, as small town justice, but entered in the log books under the heading, "small town bigotry."

Two gay men complained to the code enforcement agency in their town that the street on which they lived was going downhill. The code enforcement inspector's loyalties, however, were to the straights, no matter how much they were destroying the neighborhood. So he made an excuse for every one of the straights' behaviors, however improper or illegal. For example, when the gays complained about an illegal apartment in the rental units across the way, the inspector defended the owner, saying that it was contiguous to the next apartment and so not an illegal separate at all. When the gays complained that the garages in the same house were rented out for commercial use in a residential neighborhood, with loading and unloading of trucks going on all day, their complaint was met with the excuse that it was not illegal to store something in a garage, even heavy equipment or industrial goods. When the gays complained that another house next door had installed an ugly jerry-built swing set in the front yard, their complaint was met with beside-the-point sophistry—that is, it had to be installed in the front yard because there was no back yard. And when the gays complained that the gas station next door was not a gas station but a junk yard piled high with scrap, their complaint was met with, "He is doing construction now, and I cannot distinguish construction materials from scrap," although in fact there should have been little difficulty in distinguishing spare tires, car seats, and the like from four-by-four wooden beams, and the like.

For these gays and lesbians, who are in denial, abuse is like a background noise that is unrecognizable until it stops. (If abuse stops they can contrast the good with the bad, and finally see what it feels like to be with people who like them, and who are supportive and kind, and who, if they do not accept them entirely, at least make homosexuality the nonissue that it in fact is.) Gays and lesbians in denial avoid a serious depression. But they do not avoid the limitations imposed on them by the depressing conditions in which they live.

Other gays and lesbians recognize that they are being abused. While some get used to it, in most cases they are constantly depressed as a result. They feel depressed because they feel as if they are being treated like second-class citizens both at home and at work, never really allowed to fit in, and more rarely still allowed to get ahead. One gay man's boss, for example, told him that he was wasting time from 8:00–8:30 A.M. having coffee when he should have been working, though she herself did not come in until 9:00 and she was due in, like him, at 8:00. Some are able to live with the depression. They accept it as the price of being homosexual, as part of the homosexual condition, and as an element in the necessary punishment of life that gays and lesbians, as one put it, "get from a world full of 'Sisters of No Mercy.'" They do not let their depression affect them, or if they do, they more or less successfully fight it with psychotherapy, antidepressants, or even hypomanic denial (such as promiscuity). But too often the depression eats away at them. It erodes their self-confidence, and lowers their self-esteem. They come to blame themselves, not their unfair treatment. On the job, siding with their oppressors, they criticize their own work performance, though it is their performance in bed that is really being criticized. They can no longer function creatively, or at all. Some even try suicide—indirectly, by having unsafe, unprotected sex, or directly, by slashing their wrists, or hanging themselves by the neck, until they are dead.

Many gays and lesbians, insightful or not, depressed or not, handle homophobes badly—that is, they handle them in one of two counterproductive ways: counterproductive because all they accomplish is making the homophobe's task easier, which in turn creates more, and more efficient, homophobia. First they try to fix what is not broken in their own lives, while letting what is broken stay that way. If they are being criticized as poor workers because they are homosexual, even though their work is up to par, they fix their work, which does not need fixing, but they do not fix their ill-deserved bad reputation, which needs all the work. And second they try solutions that actually aggravate matters. They abdicate when they should fight back. They let others take advantage of them when they should call a halt to being used and abused. They appease when they should protest. Instead they allow, in the vernacular, "the bastards to get them down." One, for example, used the excuse that a co-worker was homophobic to leave a high-paying 9–5 job with a short commute and excellent working conditions, on the grounds that "staying here just is not worth all the aggravation." They do these things for several reasons. First they hope to catch a few crumbs that fall from the feast of straights. Second they are afraid that standing up for themselves will only make matters worse. (In effect they model themselves on the lesbian who felt that suing a man who did not install her microwave oven correctly would ultimately encourage him to come back and write dyke all over her house.) And third, they are guilty and in a moral outrage with themselves over being homosexual, so they do not take adequate steps to assure their own comfort and success.

Gays are in conflict among themselves as to the best way to handle homophobes. Activist gays and lesbians handle homophobes by protesting loud and long, and often to some avail. They feel that they will not have to live with a bad situation if they can make it better. Nonactivist gays and lesbians find that accepting the world as it is and getting on with their professional and personal lives in spite of all is what works best for them. They feel that since they cannot change the world, they might as well live in and work around it. They realize that trying too hard to change what cannot be changed can ultimately cause them to feel even more like a failure. They recognize that gays and lesbians will never get the same love and approval that so often comes easily and automatically to straights, and that the gay life will always be harder than the life of straights. And they realize that the sooner they accept these things the sooner they can adjust to the inevitable and take steps to minimize its effects, instead of becoming depressed about their fate each day, as if they learned it anew each morning. And if they improve their self-esteem, using whatever methods they can, they can in turn make it harder for homophobes to devastate them.

Sometimes they can they improve their self-esteem by giving themselves a pep talk. But sometimes a short- or long-term therapeutic exploration of why the self-esteem is so low in the first place is required. At the very least, gays and lesbians with low self-esteem should join support groups ranging from mutual admiration societies to activist groups. These groups can help by countering homophobes' negativity in two ways. They counter gays' and lesbians' tendency to believe the bad things homophobes say about them, and they keep gays and lesbians from reacting to abuse by prostrating themselves in the hope of gaining a temporary advantage, although they can expect little more than a condescending friendship.

Activist gays and lesbians are at risk from carrying their aggression too far, while nonactivist gays and lesbians are at risk from carrying the moderation that is the order of the day too far. The last group might cut off their noses to scar themselves to appeal to those homophobes who suffer them gladly so long as they are deformed. Or they might tolerate abusive relationships with homophobes just because that reminds them of home. Or they might expect that homophobes can be converted into admirers, or even homophiles, even when they already know that no one has yet succeeded in getting love from a stone.

PART II

The Syndromes

8

Paranoid Homophobes

The term "homophobia" is a misnomer because while some homophobes are actually true phobics, most suffer from a nonphobic disorder, such as paranoia. As Terry S. Stein (1996) says, homophobia serves different psychological "evaluative, expressive, and defensive" functions (p. 39). For example, homophobia is phobic when homophobes view gays and lesbians as "bad luck" and avoid them "like the plague." But it is paranoid when homophobes view gays and lesbians as persecutors out to destroy their lives and the lives of their families. And it is obsessive-compulsive when homophobes primarily feel disgust with the dirty things (as they see it) that gays and lesbians do to each other sexually.

In my opinion most serious homophobes are paranoid—that is, they suffer from (1) paranoid schizophrenia, (2) delusional disorder, paranoid type, or (3) paranoid personality disorder. The more severely ill paranoids, those with paranoid schizophrenia or a paranoid delusional disorder, develop actual delusions and/or hallucinations about gays and lesbians. These may have an overt homosexual content, as in some of the delusions/hallucinations described below. Or, as happens with closet homophobes, the homosexual content may be hidden, sometimes to the point that it can only be inferred. For example, some closet homophobic men seem to be straight bashing. But what they are doing is straight bashing their wives after projecting their homosexual wishes and fears onto them until they develop Othello-like pathologically jealous fears that their wives are cheating on them. Or some closet homophobes, men and women alike, become litigious paranoids. First they become convinced that the world has condemned them as guilty for being homosexual. Then, displacing this guilt, they become litigious about some derivative matter as a way to prove to the world their "innocence" about being homosexual by taking the derivative matter "all the way up

to the Supreme Court," for exoneration and absolution. (Litigious paranoid homophobes are described further below.)

> A paranoid patient became convinced that "the Angel of Suck is sitting on
> my shoulder" and accusing him of doing homosexual things. He also de-
> veloped classical delusions of the influencing machine. He had delusions
> of being controlled, feeling that people were putting a computer chip in
> his head to manipulate him. Here the delusional "insertion" was seem-
> ingly a reference to anal penetration. He became suspicious of all technol-
> ogy, really fearing not technology per se but technologists, whom he be-
> lieved were out to use science to modify the gene pool of the world, their
> secret intent being to produce men, women, and a generation of children
> who were all queer.

The less severely ill paranoids, those with a paranoid personality disorder, do not become overtly delusional or hallucinate. Instead they
"merely" gay bash to handle the danger they fear from gays and lesbians.
The danger may relate to a fear that gays and lesbians will emasculate or
kill them personally. As Colin Spencer (1995) says, they "exhibit a paranoid fear that homosexuality will take over the world" (p. 402). Or the
danger may relate to a fear that gays and lesbians will recruit and seduce
them, blowing them kisses until they yield.

> A patient entered treatment because he was depressed that his mother
> had not given him her power of attorney, and he feared he would not be
> able to take care of her if she became senile, an event no more likely to oc-
> cur to her than to any other individual of her age. Soon it turned out that
> he was beset by a number of irrational worries, not just that one. One of
> them was that men were staring at him in the elevator, looking at his
> crotch, with "dishonorable intentions." He lived in Greenwich Village in
> New York City, which he reminded me was full of homosexuals, and he felt
> that he would be next to fall into their predatory path. He did not seem to
> consider that he was an older person who had never been physically at-
> tractive, and now had become completely unattractive—not so much be-
> cause of his age but because he did not take care of himself. He had be-
> come dilapidated because, though he had the money to buy new clothes,
> and he bought them, he would not wear them, fearing that they would get
> soiled and be ruined, for example, in the rain.
>   Soon this man became excessively preoccupied with the fear that he
> would be seduced by homosexuals. He spent an inordinate amount of
> time walking away from every gay bar in Greenwich Village so that "he
> wouldn't be cruised by someone coming out the door." But being in the
> Village made it likely that in walking *from* one gay bar he would merely
> be walking *to* another. Eventually he could hardly go out of the house at
> all for fear of being attacked by queers. Soon enough, and of course ex-

pectedly, he began to feel that I was one of them too, and became tortured by the possibility that I, like the others, would grab and seduce him against his will. Once he told me a joke and then spent days worrying if I would tell it to someone he knew who would recognize its source and connect him with me—revealing at best that he was seeing a psychiatrist, and at worst raising the possibility that he was not one of my patients, but one of my lovers. So he stopped going to his favorite restaurant because he knew I occasionally ate there. However, with the typical flair homophobes have for displaying their latent homosexuality, he instead began eating at another restaurant—this one right down the block from where (he knew) I lived.

He felt somewhat better after joining a loose-knit political group dedicated to taking symbolic antihomosexual stands. For example, he particularly favored one proheterosexual group that was in the business of suing the appropriate agencies to force them to allot more space in local building projects to sports facilities for the children of West Villagers. Now his symptoms improved because he felt as if he were part of a holy mission, as well as because he felt a sense of safety in numbers; supported and validated by those of like mind; and loved in a safe, at least manifestly nonhomoerotic, environment—if not for himself, then because of what he was doing—verbally bashing the "amoral conditions certain people create in the city we all live in."

A patient was an erythrophobic individual who feared being caught blushing. He believed blushing was a "sign of heat" that gave his homosexuality away. As a result he was unable to leave home to walk on the streets. He said, "I fear all the crime in the city." But the crimes he really feared were "those against nature."

True paranoid homophobia has to be differentiated both from manipulative paranoid homophobia and from homophobia that is part of what Grace DeBell might call Pollyanna paranoia homophobia (1960) (personal communication). As the examples I will give below illustrate, true paranoid homophobes have delusions or semidelusions, overt or hidden, with a homosexual content, the main purpose of which is to disavow their own homosexuality. In contrast, manipulative paranoid homophobes develop semidelusional ideas (or even frank delusions) with a homosexual content, but they have them for different reasons and to accomplish different things. They have them not to deny they love gays and lesbians by hating them to disprove a point about themselves, to reduce inner anxiety. They have them to deny they love gays and lesbians to prove a point about gays and lesbians in order to increase the possibility of real, often political, personal gain. And, as we shall see, patients suffering with Pollyanna paranoia homophobia of Grace DeBell are less paranoid than they are depressed. The message is also "I hate and fear you because you are queer." But here it really means, "Because you are queer you don't love me, but reject me. And I cannot get used to that, or take it lying down."

TRUE PROJECTIVE PARANOIDS

True projective paranoid homophobia was, at one time, considered to be the most common and familiar type of homophobia. I say was, for at the present time there is a tendency among laypeople and scientists alike to study homophobia without any reference whatsoever to clinical psychiatry/psychology, to overlook how many homophobes are actually mental patients, and so to describe homophobia entirely without reference to the emotional disorders that create it.

There are also circles of affectophiles whose main professional goal in life seems to be to reclassify all emotional illness, from schizophrenia to personality disorder, as an affective disorder. For them the diagnosis of paranoia is particularly unfashionable. So they call paranoid homophobes, when their emotional disorder is recognized at all, bipolar. [To an extent this was, at least until recently, when after 20 years or so a generation passed, a product of intergenerational rivalry, a form of bigoted ageism where "outmoded old fogies like you called every one schizophrenic" but "me, the bright, new, superior, upstart child, makes the diagnosis of patients in the modern way, calling them bipolar (manic depressive) instead."] The distinction between paranoia and affective disorder, while too rarely made properly, or at all, is an important one because the two disorders require different management. In particular, giving a paranoid homophobe a fluoxetine-like substance, especially when a covering antipsychotic medication is omitted, can make the paranoia worse and cause the homophobe to become violent, which in the case of homophobes can, and often does, entail picking up gays not for sex but to torture and kill them.

Third, these days paranoid homophobes are both generally aware of the homosexual content of their delusions and ashamed enough of it to clear the delusion up for presentation to the world. So they censor the homosexual content out of the manifest delusion, hiding their delusional homophobic thoughts or homophobic hallucinations.

Dynamics

Anxiety

True projective paranoid homophobia is a psychic self-cleansing and self-vindication. Unlike manipulative paranoia, which is a way to improve one's lot by increasing one's prospects, it is a way to improve one's prospects by reducing one's anxiety. This anxiety can develop in one of three ways:

1. It may originate in conflict. The conflict may be about latent homosexual desire which becomes vaguely apparent to an individual whose manifest sexual preference is heterosexual, or becomes all too apparent to an individual who tends toward bisexuality. Or it may be about a feeling of hostility toward gays and lesbians, or toward straights and gays alike for liking or having sex of any kind (sexophobic hostility). Anxiety appears when the sexual fantasies/hostility have become strong enough to overwhelm, and/or the conscience has become inflexible enough to become overwhelmed.

2. It may be due to a defect in the sorting capacity of the ego. For example, in some cases the homophobe can no longer distinguish a friendly from a sexual overture. This was the case for the patient who thought whenever anyone, gay or straight, greeted him, that "they were coming on to him," because he felt that the word "Hello" meant "Too much sex."

3. It may originate in schizophrenic (or depressive) *weltuntergang* fantasies, an excessively pessimistic worldview where the patient feels the planet is becoming a generally terrible place to live in, and blames that (potential or actual) problem on the gays and lesbians of this world. People suffering from *weltuntergang* tend to agree with the following psychological test postulate of Sanford, Adorno, Frenkel-Brunswik, and Levinson (1982): "Wars and social troubles may someday be ended by an earthquake or flood that will destroy the whole world" (p. 186).

Jerry Gray (1996) implies that Representative Bob Barr is afflicted with a kind of *weltuntergang* (as well as hysteria) because Barr says that "'The flames of hedonism, the flames of narcissism, the flames of self-centered morality are licking at the very foundation of our society, the family unit'" (p. 1). (Or perhaps Barr projects a personal feeling onto the world. Perhaps he is telling us how when he is in the presence of gays he feels that his unconscious sexual fantasies are licking at his ego, and threatening to overwhelm it, and him.)

As Joyce Purnick (1996) relates in her article "Recalling a Gay Rights Non-Crisis," after passing the gay rights bill in New York City in 1986, "lawmakers bickered and wept. Rabbis cited the Talmud, priests quoted from the Bible . . . and Mayor Edward I. Koch—sounding like an upside-down Chicken Little—intoned: "'The sky is not going to fall, the sky is not going to fall'" (p. B3).

The panicky dread of these individuals brings to my mind the paranoid-like worries of militia men that Timothy Egan (1995) describes in his article, "Men at War: Inside the World of the Paranoid":

To hear the[se] camouflaged leaders of these militia [groups] tell it, the nation is already under siege by troops hovering in black helicopters who have embedded interstate road signs with directional codes that only they can read. A few months ago, Yellowstone National Park received a flurry of phone calls from people who believed it had been taken over by the United Nations. [What was the proof?]: "What makes you think it hasn't?" (p. 1).

The First-Line Defense of Repression

The familiar defense of projection, described below, is actually a second-line defense, generally preceded by at least an attempt at repression. Repression, unlike projection, is an individual matter in the sense that it does not involve another person. There is no externalization of an individual's guilty sexual or angry impulses. Sex and anger are merely dismissed, by being suppressed.

Repression makes the homophobe into one kind of closet queen— the kind that is partly or completely unaware of his or her homosexuality (and anger toward homosexuals). This kind of closet queen is to be distinguished from a second, more familiar, kind, where a more or less overt homosexual knows he or she is homosexual, at least on some level, but is too shy or reserved to admit it to others and too afraid to admit it to him- or herself.

Repressing homophobes discover all too soon that repression works only incompletely to suppress their homosexuality/anger toward homosexuals. Not only will the closet door not stay closed, but the homosexuality, and the associated anger, come oozing out around the edges and seem to attract the most inner attention.

A homophobe who was trying to suppress his own homosexuality nevertheless found himself constantly preoccupied with what gays and lesbians do in bed. Each time he saw a gay man he found himself staring at his pudendum, wondering where it had been, and turning over in his mind what it had been doing there. And he reminded himself over and over to be angry at and disgusted with what he saw, and saw all too clearly. One day he attended a concert of American music. When a famous, and out-of-the-closet, homosexual composer appeared on stage for applause after a premier of his work, he could do no better than to imagine this man not writing at his desk but writhing in sexual positions. As he put it, he was, "turning him over in his mind," each time with a shudder over the possibility "that such complicated beautiful music could come out of such a simple ugly animal."

This oozing is particularly pronounced in homophobic men whose masculinity is challenged in real life, say after an attempted gay seduction, provoked or otherwise. Homophobia here, as Sanford et al. put it, [involves] "a strong inclination to punish violators of sex mores (homosexuals, sex offenders) [that is less] an expression of a general punitive attitude based on identification with in-group authorities [than a suggestion that] the subject's own sexual desires are suppressed and in danger of getting out of hand" (p 170). Such homophobes have a hypocritical ambivalent quality that results from their constant struggle with their homosexuality, so that one day they condemn close same-sex relationships and the next day they seem to be having something like close same-sex relationships of their own. On the one hand, it is "join the army to get with real men, and away from the queers," while on the other hand it is "join the army because that way you will be with people who are the same sex as you."

The simulated homosexuality that is often part of hazing (a recent image sticks in my mind of army men hazing each other by simulating anal insertion) is suggestive of this underlying homosexuality. That is why it is proper to raise the question with some homophobic recruits: "If you wanted to avoid everything homosexual, why did you decide to live with all those men in the first place?"

In prognostically unfavorable situations the second-line, or auxiliary, defense of projection becomes necessary.

The Second-Line/Auxiliary Defense of Projection

Projection is a second-line/auxiliary defense because those who use it are, if they are at all intact, generally aware on some level that it involves a break with reality, and they try to avoid taking such a drastic step whenever possible.

Projection ideally suits those homophobes who do not want to be attuned to the emotional subtleties of their inner world, for it allows them to perceive and react to their unacceptable inner impulses as if they were coming from outside themselves. Sanford et al. (1982) feel projection, or "projectivity" is typified by an attitude such as: "Most people don't realize how much our lives are controlled by plots hatched in secret places" (p. 186). They suggest it originates in an attitude of "anti-intraception" (p. 185) which they define as "opposition to the subjective, the imaginative, the tender-minded" (p. 185). According to them, people with anti-intraception tend to agree with certain postulates on the authors' psychological tests, such as: "When a person has a problem or worry, it is best for him not to think about it but to keep busy with more cheerful things." "Nowadays more and more people are prying into matters that should remain personal and private." "If people would talk less and work more, everybody would be better off." And "The businessman and the manufacturer are much more important to society than the artist and the professor" (p. 185).

According to Adorno (1982) another quality of projectivity is "the relative ease by which prejudice can be switched from one object to another" (p. 304). This is reflected in a passage in Pat Robertson's (1992) book *The New World Order* which vilifies homosexuals as part of a list of targets that also includes "drunkards, drug dealers . . . New Age Worshipers of Satan . . . greedy money changers [which I recognize as a sometimes code word for Jews], revolutionary assassins, [and] adulterers" (p. 329). As Adorno might put it, "this point[s] in one direction . . . that prejudice . . . is but superficially, if at all, related to the specific nature of its object" and is more a subjective experience, for example about "power fantasies" (pp. 304–305) "completely independent from interaction with reality" (p. 305).

Paranoid homophobes project not only sex, but also aggression and the feeling that they are decompensating:

Projection of Sex.   As we have seen, paranoid homophobes typically project onto and attribute their homosexual wishes to others.

> A latent homosexual patient when psychologically compensated insisted that his only interest in men was a platonic one. He admitted he admired men in uniform, but he said that that was only because they best represented the ideal man he wanted to be. Either things changed when he began decompensating into paranoia, or he began decompensating into paranoid when things changed. Now his interest in men in uniform became an adversary relationship with them, as if he were saying, "I cannot love them both because I hate them and because they hate me." For example, once when he decompensated psychologically he sued New York City, complaining that he was in constant pain in the groin because of something he was convinced happened when he rode a city bus. He insisted that when he fell asleep on the bus "the bus driver got up out of his seat, walked to the rear of the bus where I was sitting, took out his sharp pencil, and stuck it into my testicles."

Projection of Aggression.   The role of anger is generally downplayed today, for currently we seem more willing to call people latent homosexuals than we seem willing to call them latent or overt sadists. Nevertheless, teenagers who cruise in cars around a gay resort or "gay ghetto" yelling insults out of the windows, or individuals who pick up and murder gays, are not merely at odds with their own homosexuality. They are doing more than symbolically plucking out their own offending gay eyes and removing homoerotic stimulus in order to avoid homoerotic response. They are also simply mean people, the kind that would strongly agree with the postulate on Sanford et al.'s (1982) psychological test that "homosexuals are hardly better than criminals and ought to be severely punished" (p. 184).

We can appreciate how mean these individuals are when we compare them with other paranoids, such as the religiously grandiose, whose intent, at least manifestly, is to be helpful to man and mankind (even when the manifest kindly spirit of the thing only covers a latent hostility). For example, contrast the grandiose paranoid who thinks, "I am one of God's disciples sent here to cure the world of all the ills that afflict us" with the negative paranoid homophobe who thinks, "I am Satan, or at least his right-hand man, sent here to kill all the queers."

Often these individuals' anger shows in their appearance. As they speak, their facial expressions say it all. Their faces are pale, revealing the intense and constant sympathetic discharge that bombards. Narrowed, bloodless lips and tight facial muscles display their moral tenseness and rigidity, and they develop a feral look, exposing their teeth as if in preparation for sinking their fangs into their homosexual enemies.

Anger often appears in their tendency to demonize gays and lesbians, comparing them to Hitler or Satan. As Frank Rich (1995) notes in his article "Banned from Broadcast," Pat Robertson in a video clip says "'Homosexuality is an abomination. . . . Many of those people involved with Adolf Hitler were Satanists, many of them were homosexuals. The two things seem to go together'. . . . [And] a recent Christian Broadcasting Network handout lists homosexuality as an example of 'demon activity'" (p. 23).

Anger also appears in their behavior, which can be off-putting, or worse.

A homophobe displayed his anger at his homosexual neighbors by keeping his yard full of junk just so that he could cause them dismay. He picked fights with those who threatened him homosexually, as he once did with someone who brushed against him accidentally in the subway, and again with a man who merely walked in front of him in the supermarket as the homophobe was looking at a display case from across the aisle, "giving me a good view of his ass but blocking my view of the merchandise." He also fought with his wife, accusing her of paying too much attention to the gay neighbors next door, with her presumed interest, of course, being more his than hers.

One homophobe did not merely speak to God like many religious people do. God also spoke back to him, and indeed egged him on to "get his act together by handling the queer problem."

He replied to God by saying to Him, "Just hating them isn't enough. You have to *do* something that is a token of your hatred. I will prove myself to you, who are watching, and testing me, and to my buddies, and any strangers about."

Not one to actually assault anyone, except in his sleep dreams and daydreams, he confined himself to looking bullets at those he believed to be gay. For example, he haunted the local diner not to eat but to pick out groups of men eating together and stare at them, a withering murderous stare, "the kind one stares through a gun sight." He thought of his stare as a way to make a fist with his eyes, to visually beat up on his victims, even to burn them alive with the hot rays that were emanating from his head. His staring was a cleansing ritual meant to rid him of "rays of hatred" inside. It was also a way to alienate gays and lesbians to handle his guilt about being too close to them, as well as a way to deal with his inferiority complex by making nonverbal public pronouncements on the inferiority of others, implying that he was not like them in any way. Perhaps above all his stare was an erotic one, for as he stared he was taking, and getting, a closer look at the very thing he manifestly despised the most.

Gays and lesbians who try to pick up, argue with, or otherwise tangle with angry homophobes too soon and too often discover that their homophobia is the healthiest thing about them, actually one of their least unappealing characteristics. As one homophobe put it himself, he modeled his life on some of the more familiar examples of police brutality, and without individual homosexuals for him to have as enemies, he could easily have become an enemy of the entire state.

In many homophobes aggressive wishes tend to be projected in tandem with sexual wishes, as in the delusional idea that homophobes are out to *kill* me because I am *queer*, a homophobia of homophobes. One homicidal man confessed that he feared that the same forces that killed a gay serial killer were also out to get him. Of course, within the patient's psychotic scheme of things, this is not so preposterous after all—for it both allowed the first man to see himself, guilt free, as the victim of aggression, not the victimizer, and to admit, at last, if only in a roundabout way, that, in spite of all the protests, he was, after all, just "one too." (The grandiosity manifest in the conceit of being the center of attention, another factor in homophobia, is discussed in chapter 9.)

Perhaps to become a true paranoid homophobe it is necessary to be both a latent homosexual *and* an excessively angry person. There is some evidence that latent homosexuals who are not angry people tend not to involve others and strike out at them, but to withdraw and ruminate.

Projection of the Feeling That One Is Decompensating. Homophobes afraid that they are decompensating psychologically—their ego, their "castle," collapsing from an inner assault by the enemy homosexual "knights" of their id—project their feeling of decompensation onto the outside world, and call gays and lesbians crazy. As Rich (1995) says, Pat Robertson in his 1993 book *The Turning Tide* labels homosexuals "en masse" as "part of society's 'lunatic fringe'" (p. 23).

Projecting homophobes develop a wide variety of frank delusions, which may or may not contain, depending on the type, manifestly homosexual content. According to classical psychoanalytic thinking as set forth by Fenichel (1945), they may develop *paranoid delusions* when they defend themselves against the feeling, "'I love him' [by changing that feeling] to 'I do not love him, I hate him,' then project the hatred outward by turning 'I hate him' into 'he hates me'.... The persecution represents the homosexual temptation, turned into a fearful threat, threatening independently of the patient's will" (p. 428). Besides being a defense against forbidden homosexuality, paranoid delusions are also a way to rationalize hatred, so that homophobes can hate gays and lesbians as a second, not as a first, strike.

> According to John Darnton (1996) in his article "Scottish Inquiry's Focus: Why Strict Gun Law Failed," "Thomas Hamilton, 43, a loner with a history of bizarre behavior.... [before he shot 16 young school children showed neighbors] a collection of photographs of half-dressed boys" and sent "letters to politicians, the news media and the Queen complaining of a campaign to brand him as a 'pervert'" (p. A5).

Homophobes can develop *erotomanic delusions* when they deny that they love gays and lesbians by instead condemning them for loving (seducing, recruiting) them. (Sometimes instead homophobes become Don Juan figures proving their masculinity or, if women, femininity, over and over again in compulsive heterosexism, one manifestation of which is waving the marriage and family banner so that no one suspects them of marching under the gay flag.)

Homophobes develop *delusions of jealousy* when they accuse their wives or husbands of having the affair they want to have.

Homophobes develop *delusions of contamination* when they accuse others of doing the dirty things to them that they want to do to others. One of Sanford et al.'s (1982) prophetic psychological test questions asks if the individual agrees that: "Nowadays when so many different kinds of people move around and mix together so much, a person has to protect himself especially carefully against catching an infection or disease from them" (p. 186).

Homophobes develop *litigious delusions*, according to Fenichel (1945), when they "consider the outward establishment of their integrity and innocence as the most important thing in the world" (p. 433), and, after a "homosexualization" (p. 434) of the "spheres of guilt and punishment" (p. 434), verify their "innocence [as] an attempt to defend [themselves] against homosexual impulses" (p. 434).

Many of the above delusions are primary—that is, "I know it is so because I know it is so (and you do not know, and cannot prove, that it is not so)." Some gay activists, referring to the official antihomosexual stand of the Catholic Church, complain that what Thomas C. Fox (1995) in his article "Can the Pope Be Wrong?" refers to as the "infallibility declaration promulgated at the First Vatican Council" (p. 23) develops from a wrong-headed process similar to the process behind the primary delusion of the paranoid.

Projection of conflicts between homosexuality/hostility and guilt onto the outside world may result not in delusions but in pathological personality traits. Sanford et al. describe one such pathological personality trait: a readiness to "think about and to believe in the existence of such phenomena as wild erotic excesses, plots and conspiracies." They conclude that we can learn what is suppressed in the subject "by noting what attributes he most readily, but unrealistically, ascribes to the world around him." [In this case they feel the trait indicates strong "unconscious urges of both sexuality and destructiveness"] (p. 169). Or we may see the development of ideas of reference, false but not quite delusional beliefs that gays and lesbians are looking at or talking about the subject. Homophobes who develop ideas of reference after projecting their sexual interest in gays and lesbians and hostility toward them outward come to believe that all gays and lesbians are cruising them, or are planning a hostile attack on straight values, lifestyle, or straight society as a whole.

Associated Defenses

Identification with the Aggressor

Some homophobes gay bash to fight fire with fire. For example, paranoid homophobes who feel gays are castrating them, turning them into women, try to castrate gays back, both in subtle ways, by keeping them down, and in more overt ways, by beating them up.

Sublimation

In sublimation the latent homosexuality and homohatred are not discharged raw, but transformed into positive or negative social behavior. A homophobe can sublimate positively by changing forbidden homosexual desire into homoerotic bonding or laudatory charitable work with AIDS patients. Or a homophobe can sublimate negatively by changing forbidden homosexual desire into anti-gay proselytizing—for example, closing down shows by gay photographers (incidentally giving vent to his or her guilt about and hoped-for absolution from his or her own voyeuristic impulses).

Reaction Formation/Undoing

Homophobes in reaction formation in effect cover themselves by saying just the opposite of what they mean, and doing just the opposite of what they are tempted to do, all to deny what they really feel and to obscure what they really think. Like sublimation, reaction formation can go in either one of two directions. Homophobes who are erotically attached to gays and lesbians often handle their forbidden attachment by protesting too much that they hate them, while homophobes who hate gays and lesbians often one day preach homosexuality is an abomination then, the next day, feeling guilty about being so hostile, proudly change the bed pans of gays with AIDS. Some periodically shift positions between two immoderate stops, alternating between them without resting at a compromise middle ground. Then they come to resemble a swinging pendulum that pauses only at both ends, but never stops in the middle.

According to Adam Clymer (1996) in his article, "Bitter Debate, Then a Vote for Rejecting Same-Sex Marriages," Representative Barney Frank asks the question, "'How does anything I do in which I express my feelings toward another demean the powerful bond of love and emotion and respect of two other people?'" (p. A18). A possible answer is that it demeans the powerful bond because it gives married homophobes ideas, and they begin to demean what they have, because they secretly wish to have what gays and lesbians have. This makes them guilty and they handle their guilt by proclaiming, really protesting too much, that they are good people upholding the moral values of society by defending the sacred institution of marriage, and by demanding that all concerned do the same thing.

Intellectualization

Intellectual defenses are the specialty of contemplative homophobes who say, in effect, "do not hate, instead debate," and handle their passion (and try to handle that of others) by brooding about it.

In impersonalization, a form of intellectualization, personal antipathies are displaced onto impersonal institutions, such as the ballet or the Public Broadcasting System. These become symbols or stand-ins for individual highly charged emotional complexes as the homophobe tries to deal with a personal sexual/hostile threat by challenging an impersonal sociocultural institution. For example, with this in mind, homophobes complain of Public Broadcasting's elitist effeminacy and contrast it with the masculinity they associate with, and approve of, in the Sports Channel.

Control

Controlling homophobes believe that gays and lesbians could control their sexual impulses if only they would try hard enough to do so. They expect gays and lesbians to handle their instincts the same way they are trying to handle their own.

Associated Behaviors

Holding Grudges

Angry homophobia is like a Chinese finger trap—once caught up in it homophobes cannot get out. They become unforgiving, and they stay that way, and make no exceptions, for to do so becomes an admission that they are wrong.

Censoring What Others Say (Censoring Free Speech)

Unable to accept their own homosexuality as well as their own sexuality, homophobes develop a virginity complex which says in effect that the only good people in the world are asexual and celibate. Their goal of keeping everyone pure and chaste is of course part of their plan to control impulses of their own that push in the opposite direction. They censor literature and art not merely for the reasons given (to protect impressionable children from sex, and to protect women from violence), although these may be valid, and significant, but also to keep their own exhibitionistic, voyeuristic, and related impulses in check.

Alcoholism and Drug Use

Paranoid homophobes are often alcoholics as well. The answer to the question, "Why do homophobes (and many members of rightists groups) like talk radio?" is often given as "They like the opportunity to reach out, appeal to, and get approval from a wide audience." But alcoholism is another possible answer: the radio is the medium of choice for those who have been drinking, because in radio you can speak out from your hiding place, and nobody knows for certain if you are, or are not, drunk.

Paranoid homophobes often use alcohol to lyse their latent homosexual desires. They use alcohol in an attempt to live more comfortably in the queer world inside and out. Unfortunately soon enough alcohol becomes instead a way to churn these very same discomforting feelings. The following scenarios are typical: the "guys" get together and get drunk at a go-go bar, all the while concentrating on the fantastic dancers so that they do not have to notice each other. Or they attend a game and drink beer. Afterward they pile into a car. The drinking has already increased homosexual desire (and anger); desire increases even more when legs touch in the car. Now fantasies grow until previously adequate defenses are overwhelmed, and all concerned go into a homosexual panic. To relieve that panic they deny they are queer by shouting anti-gay slogans from the car at passing men believed to be homosexual. If this does not relieve the panic sufficiently, they may go on to develop homosexual ideas of reference or paranoid delusions where they feel seduced and attacked homosexually. In time some even begin to hallucinate that gays and lesbians are after them, or even that God for His own purposes is calling them queer. The hallucinations can be symptoms of acute alcohol hallucinosis, or delirium tremens (DTs). In such cases it is debatable if the homosexual fantasies promote defensive drinking, or if the drinking, and the closeness to buddies that accompanies it, promote the homosexual fantasies, or both.

The Return of the Repressed

As the repressed returns, some closet homophobes reveal their latent homosexuality in their appearance and behavior. They develop the same look they condemn in gays and lesbians. Homophobic men wear the same "badges" as male gays, such as earrings and ponytails, though they insist these signify different things. But, as one gay put it, under the skin, "the redneck covered with tattoos is not so different from the drag queen covered with feathers," and added, "one notoriously homophobic columnist's phony continental accent reminds me uncannily of the speech of some of my more piss-elegant pseudo-British gay friends."

MANIPULATIVE PARANOIDS

While projective paranoia looks mostly like a disease, manipulative paranoia looks mostly like a talent. Projective paranoids are relatively disinterested in worldly accomplishments. Social advancement is either a secondary matter or is entirely unimportant. The world that they are mostly concerned with is the internal one, where they suffer from and want relief from anxiety and guilt, particularly the anxiety and guilt about their own homosexuality. Unable to obtain this relief purely by altering the internal landscape—for example, by using defense mechanisms like repression—they alter the external landscape, bringing others into the fray, to struggle with them, or even to enlist them as aides in a common cabal.

In contrast homophobes who suffer from manipulative paranoia look paranoid and even use paranoid mechanisms, but they are not truly paranoid, for they do not primarily use these mechanisms for purposes of adjusting their internal economy. Rather they do so primarily for purposes of direct, palpable, personal—that is, interpersonal and political—gain. They employ these mechanisms so that they can use gays and lesbians when they need them, then abuse them when they are in their way, or no longer needed, or when it is time to give something in return for what they just got. They benefit somewhat from reducing their own anxiety. But that benefit is secondary to the one they get from improving their own lot.

A resort town accepts the money gays and lesbians bring in. It likes how gays and lesbians pay taxes but do not use the school facilities. It likes the class gays and lesbians impart to the town through the boutiques they decorate so enticingly. But when gays and lesbians ask to have a bar of their own in return and actually open one, the owners of competing (mixed) bars complain "the gay problem is getting out of hand—they are going to go after our children soon." Then they subject gays and lesbians to verbal harassment. They even gay bash on the beach at night—one motivation being to get gays off the beach: not to get them out of town, but to get them back into the straights' bars.

A straight individual expects a lesbian to give her a baby shower when her firstborn arrives, and baby-sitting services so that she can go to work. But when the lesbian's mother dies and the lesbian asks her to attend her mother's funeral, she decides "this lesbian is trying to seduce me" as a way to avoid inconveniencing herself.

Co-workers in the workplace gay bash in paranoid fashion chiefly to render gays and lesbians less the competition. Manipulative paranoid gay bashing was rife on a psychiatric service where I once worked. For example, a few workers were concerned, really convinced, that a gay mental health worker (who was innocent of the charges) was seducing patients in his office, after hours. The secondary purpose of this delusional idea was to deny individual latent homosexual trends. The primary purpose was to get the gay mental health worker out of the running, so that the straight mental health workers could get more of the pie. It was not primarily a complex intrapsychic matter. It could be simply put: "with a talented gay crippled/gone, there were more referrals for me."

Politicians who use gays and lesbians to fuel their campaign become delusional about gays and lesbians and put them down, less to feel psychically vindicated and superior than to promote intragroup cohesion in their ranks by creating a common enemy to rally around. In decrying how gays and lesbians are evil, they are not primarily ridding themselves of a feminine taint, or proclaiming their fidelity to blue-collar parents with similar ideas; rather they are proclaiming their identity with the majority of voters who are by birth, intellect, and inclination fearful of gays and lesbians. Males are not primarily out to deny the possibility of psychic castration—that is, demasculinization—but are primarily interested in denying the possibility of real castration—that is, the possibility that they will lose the election. Radio talk-show hosts who egg the audience on to condemn "queers" may incidentally be offering themselves and their audience of other paranoids the opportunity to get some "poison" out of their system. But in the main they are using the audience not to reduce their anxiety, but to increase their ratings.

For some newspaper columnists, gays and lesbians are "the hot topic" that sells.

A well known columnist is a manipulative paranoid of the gentle contemplative type, a pundit who uses butter (persuasive reasoning), not guns (threats of intimidation, or murder) against gays and lesbians. He is not mainly in business to prove that he is not himself gay. His primary purpose is to get a homophobic audience's attention. He is not mainly out to have a convenient scapegoat for his own sadistic feelings, to prove a favored philosophical or religious point to himself, or to find reasons to admire himself more, not less. If there is any admiration to be had, it is not from within but from without, not from his superego, but from his readers. He cites references (the Bible, certain homophobic psychiatrists) to prove that all homophobia (as he sees it) is understandable, excusable, predictable, justifiable, and inevitable because of what gays and lesbians are and do. By doing so he is not trying to verify the medical model of gays and lesbians as troubled sick people to prove himself well, or the criminal model of gays and lesbians as criminals to prove himself innocent. He is only trying to produce a daily column, and he needs to have something controversial to write about. He is not so much a closet queen as he is an overt opportunist.

Even a homophobic society recognizes, however covertly, that projective paranoids have emotional problems. But society regularly views manipulative paranoid homophobes not as ill but as rational, not your "usual neurotic homophobes." Society sees manipulative paranoid homophobes not as excessively homophobic but as appropriately antihomosexual. Society denies their homophobia is a mental disorder coming from below, from their id. Instead society sees it as coming from above, from their morality, or from God, and reminds us how the Bible backs society up. Society considers their dislike of gays and lesbians not to be a sign of mental disturbance, but:

1. a consciously determined legitimate preference for straights—a preference which is compared to a liking for classical rather than popular music—that is, a product of free will not determined for, but by, the individual. For example, homophobia is not homophobia but a respected religious belief or mainstream secular philosophical position or system on a par with existentialism, all in a free country where everyone is entitled to dislike gays and lesbians without being shamed or humiliated for it, or having their arms twisted until they feel otherwise.

2. a response to reality. As society sees it, gays and lesbians have real problems. They are difficult to get along with. Their sexual promiscuity makes them unreliable. For example, they keep late hours during the week because they cruise and so they cannot do their work the next day: part of their being self-destructive not only sexually but also occupationally.

Manipulative homophobes get away with their homophobia because they hold two trump cards: the king of being straight, and the ace of belonging to the ruling majority. They also get away with it because being manipulative by nature they can be manipulative about their manipulativeness. They know how to convince society to support them, for they know how to use the arguments and defenses just described for that invidious purpose.

COMBINATION DISORDER

Being a true paranoid is not at all incompatible with being a manipulative paranoid. There is every reason for individuals to want to reduce their anxiety about being homosexual themselves, *and* pick up a little advantage along the way. Most homophobes put gays and lesbians down for two reasons. First, they are paranoid and projecting forbidden homosexuality, and avoiding other feelings like feeling submissive and castrated. But second, in the sort of behavior we are familiar with from the *Wild Kingdom* shows we see on television, they want to establish dominance and seize control, vanquishing gays whom they perceive to be the competition so that they can win in a battle where, as they see it, gays and lesbians are the enemy, because they represent a threat to their own personal achievement and advancement, just by being there.

9

Mood (Affective) Disorder Homophobes

DEPRESSIVE HOMOPHOBES

Depressive homophobes bash gays and lesbians in order to relieve their personal feelings of worthlessness, which may appear when (1) depressive homophobes put themselves and their achievements down unnecessarily, as when a straight blue-collar construction worker feels inherently inferior because he is not a white-collar semiprofessional; or a white-collar semiprofessional feels inherently inferior because she is not a "real" professional. Or they may appear when (2) depressive homophobes put themselves down rationally, having recognized the truth: that they are troubled people who have in fact achieved little in life.

A large group of these depressive homophobes feels personally worthless in comparison to gays and lesbians because they envy them, and they envy them because they think they have it all. They handle the belief that gays and lesbians have it all by putting them down to even the score. They bash them for the same reason some fans bash their sports heroes when they lose. Manifestly they are booing them for being losers. But secretly they are just using the loss as an opportunity to express a simmering angry jealousy at the players for playing while they, the fans, remain on the sidelines.

> One straight man stared bullets at gay men who were in groups obviously enjoying each other's company. He envied their being together because their being together called his own loneliness to mind. When he railed against "faggots" he was in fact condemning them for having the fun he felt he could never have. The same man called all gays and lesbians elitists, condemning them in a way that sounded suspiciously like a compliment.

For he was really condemning gays and lesbians not for being bad but for being good. He hated them because they had the intelligence and sophistication he felt that he lacked.

A straight woman condemned gays and lesbians for flaws that were actually virtues. She called gays and lesbians elitists when she sensed they were smarter than she was; "dinks" when they had more money than she had; "swells" when she thought they were better looking and in better shape physically than she was; and "nerds" because they liked and understood the intellectual and artistic things that mystified her. Even being gay was something she envied them for, though she did not want it, except for the fact that she hated anyone who had something she did not have.

A homophobe liked to think all lesbians swaggered and all gay men were flighty, swishy, effeminate, superficial people only interested in money and sex, unable to do their work by day because they partied all night. This fantasy was facilitated by another one: the belief that all homosexuals had problems with gender identity. This was a wish-fulfilling fantasy because he had information to the contrary. He needed this fantasy, however, because it evened the playing field and the score. With it, he could make reassuring contrasts between himself and "them." He could self-congratulate for being straight. He could see himself as the superman he wanted to be, which he defined as someone without a feminine bone in his body. This is why no arguments to the contrary could convince him that while some gay men are transvestites, most gay men are not; that while some transvestites are homosexual, many are straight; and that gays who call each other "Jane" or "Mary" are camping, not in fact crossing the line that separates gender bending from actually breaking the gender mold.

A straight man condemned gays and lesbians as being sexually hyperactive to deny his forbidden desires to be promiscuous. He also perpetuated the myth that all gays and lesbians were sick as a way to delude himself into thinking that his having a roaming eye was not a sign that he was unhealthy. He also complained that gays and lesbians all behaved like lunatics. His evidence was that they all did obnoxious things in public, like being seductive at inappropriate times and in inappropriate places, as when teaching a class, attending family functions, on the beach, and even in private when according to him they discussed their sex lives too openly and in a vulgar way. He wanted to caricature all gays as being out of control, for the caricature reassured him, "I do not do crazy things like that." Even his bigotry became a source of self-pride. For he thought, "I have the good taste to discriminate, and my discrimination qualifies me as being discriminatory, which in turn makes me a member of the higher classes."

A straight neighbor demeaned gays and lesbians by evaluating their professional ability according to their sexual "disability." The predictable invidious comparisons helped him feel superior. For example, to humiliate a gay doctor he envied, he evaluated his personal doctors, to the gay man's face, according to the size and composition of their families. As the gay man put it, according to this neighbor a wife and two kids would be the rough equivalent of four years at Harvard Medical School.

A gay man's lover, one half of a wealthy couple, asked his boss's wife if she would do some of the couple's legal work for them. In reply she told them that she wouldn't take them on because they couldn't afford her. She said this without first making any attempt to determine how much money they actually had. Her response revealed her own need to be the queen, with all others her serfs—pretenders to her limited favors, to which only the most fortunate could legitimately aspire. She demeaned gays and denied any could have enough money to deserve her as part of her plan to make gays smaller so that she could grow comparatively in stature.

Gays and lesbians cannot argue envious depressive homophobes out of their demeaning homophobic myths. This only has the reverse effect, intensifying their homophobia. They see such arguments as a threat, because gays and lesbians are saying, "I am not bad like you need to think I am, but good, in a way you prefer not to recognize."

An equally large group of depressive homophobes feels personally worthless not because they envy gays and lesbians but because they are simply angry sadomasochistic people who hate everyone, themselves included. As sadists they are like piranhas who move in for the kill whenever they sense vulnerability, and homosexual "flaws" are the "wounds" that let first blood. As masochists they hate gays and lesbians as part of a plan to hurt themselves by depriving themselves of the pleasures of having homosexual friends and family. They want to hurt and deprive themselves both because they are guilty about their sadism and think they deserve to suffer for it, and because they are strict moralists who regret enjoying themselves in any way—"displeasure oriented" individuals who think that anything joyful is bad and that anything sad is good, with suffering the main qualification for being in a state of grace. They particularly hate gays and lesbians because, as they see it, gays and lesbians are pleasure-oriented hedonists who insist on enjoying themselves and their lives in a frenzy of immorality and corruption. They dislike hedonistic straights too, but their dislike is especially reserved for hedonistic gays and lesbians, especially those who are not suffering themselves but are, on the contrary, leading fulfilling lives. For these masochistic moralists the term "gay" is not merely a term of approbation with a deeper meaning. It is also a term of approbation that stands for itself.

Edward Gibbon (1776–1788/1980) describes a form of this displeasure orientation as follows:

> In their censures of luxury [such individuals] are extremely minute and
> circumstantial; and among the various articles which excite their pious in-
> dignation we may enumerate false hair, garments of any colour except
> white, instruments of music, vases of gold or silver, downy pillows (as Ja-
> cob reposed his head on a stone), white bread, foreign wines, public salu-
> tations, the use of warm baths, and the practice of shaving the beard,
> which . . . is a lie against our own faces and an impious attempt to improve
> the works of the Creator (pp. 287–288).
>
> These individuals impose whimsical laws . . . on the marriage bed
> [which] would force a smile from the young and a blush from the fair. It
> was their unanimous sentiment that a first marriage was adequate to all
> the purposes of nature and of society. The practice of second nuptials was
> branded with the name of a legal adultery; and the persons guilty of so
> scandalous an offence against . . . purity . . . soon excluded from the hon-
> ours, and even from the arms, of the church.
>
> [For] ascetics [of this kind] the loss of sensual pleasure [is] supplied and
> compensated by spiritual pride . . . the merit of the sacrifice [is estimated]
> by its apparent difficulty; and . . . in the praise of . . . chaste spouses [is]
> poured forth the troubled stream of . . . eloquence (pp. 289–290).

Other depressive homophobes feel personally worthless because they
have homosexual leanings themselves. This leads them to identify with
gays and lesbians, then to respond to the loneliness that they believe affects gays and lesbians and that they fear could affect them as well. After
putting themselves in the place of the homosexual, as one saw it, "cruising lonely hours among strangers, with no children to be my comfort in
my old age," they attack the lifestyle that they feel produces such an undesirable result, as a way to say, "there but for the grace of God go I."

Another group of depressive homophobes consists of the Pollyanna
paranoids of Grace DeBell (1960) (personal communication) first mentioned in Chapter 8. These individuals feel personally worthless because
they want to be loved by everyone, which can only lead to their feeling
rejected by everyone—not only by straights, but also by gays and lesbians. The rejection they feel may be a sexual or a nonsexual/imper-
sonal thing. As for a sexual rejection, some have tried to seduce gays in
the past, saying something like, "I just want to see how it feels," only to
be rejected by gays or lesbians who do not want to cross the line and
have relationships with bisexuals or who do but can see a problem coming down the road and have the good sense to avoid it. As for the non-
sexual/impersonal rejection, they take gays' and lesbians' desire to be
different personally, seeing it as a rejection of their own moral and value
system. When such homophobes say, "I hate gays and lesbians," we have
to add, "because gays and lesbians persist in being stubbornly individu-
alistic to the point that they will not accept my authority, go along with

me and my ideas, and be made over in my own image." Their so-called paranoid idea that gays and lesbians are the enemy is only persecutory in a general sense. It is not a question of assault, but of a failure to act, so that they feel not attacked by gays and lesbians who threaten them, but deprived by gays and lesbians who ignore them.

Developmentally their fear of rejection often starts in childhood, either with extreme deprivation or extreme overgratification. Those who were deprived in childhood carry the fear of deprivation over into adulthood. They expect disappointment, and they get it. Those who were overgratified in childhood carry the expectation of reward over into adulthood. They expect that the world will give them more of the same good things, and, expecting only gratification, are constantly, and sorely, disappointed.

A fifth and final group of depressive homophobes is those who feel personally worthless because they hate gays and lesbians because they see them as monstrous: fellow human beings who reflect badly on the human race as a whole. When paranoids murder gays it is because they feel that gays are seducing them. For paranoid homophobes, gay bashing/murder is mostly a form of homicide—a killing of oneself-become-one's-persecutors. In contrast, when these depressive homophobes murder gays, they murder them for the same reasons that some mothers with postpartum depression murder their children: they feel their children are bad seeds who need to be destroyed because they reflect negatively not only on them, but also on the human race as a whole. For such depressive homophobes gay bashing/murder is less a personal homicide than it is a miniature mass suicide, part of a general self-destructiveness, a desire to wipe everything human off the map. As such they bring about not so much the death of an individual by murder as they bring about the cleansing of the world by fire.

HYPOMANIC HOMOPHOBES

Hypomanic homophobes are homophobes in denial. They are in denial because they are homophobic as a by-product of an inappropriately elevated self-esteem, producing a euphoric state in which they believe themselves qualified to judge others, even though they have few qualifications to do so, and what qualifications they think they have are mainly self-conferred. Such homophobes use the very act of judging others to fool themselves into believing they have what it takes to judge them. It is as if they are saying, "the very act of judging others qualifies me to be a judge."

Homophobes with an elevated self-esteem tend to be narcissistic individuals who use the yardstick of themselves by which to judge others—as much a statement of self-love as we can ever hope to find. When they put others down, they do so for being the least bit different. Those who do not follow the male-female design and have the standard family are called immoral, not because they do bad things but because they do not replicate the fine qualities that the homophobes identify in themselves. In their scheme of things, perceived differences are not differences but flaws. In effect this kind of "morality" bears a close resemblance to the ego-expanding blood sport that locals in small towns/big cities play when they denigrate and exclude tourists for not being one of them, regardless of who and what these tourists are, and how much business they bring in. When these homophobes meddle in gays' and lesbians' lives, it is not so much to control them or to make them more moral as it is to remake them in their own image. Here the family standard looms large because it is their standard. They define marriage as an institution between a straight man and a straight woman for the purpose of having children, simply because that is what their marriage consists of.

They are also in denial because they do not admit to their own homophobia or to that of others. As for denying their own homophobia, they deny they are homophobic in an almost psychopathic way. (This denial goes "nicely" with the denial of individual defect and its projection onto others that characterizes the thinking of all bigots.) For example, speaking of a man he views as a bigot, Eugene Narrett (1995) refers to how he uses "superficial overtures to Jews and, over the heads of Jews, to the media . . . calculated to give . . . plausible deniability for his obvious hatred . . . [and after doing a] Jew imitation . . . says, 'We don't like this squabble with the Jewish community'. . . . smarmy insincerity . . . sugarcoat[ed] megalomaniac agenda and the race hatred at [its] core [is central to his bigotry]" (p. A19). Along the same lines, in his article "Youths on Racial Slurs: They're Only Words," Raymond Hernandez (1995) quotes students who sent an anti-Semitic note to the teacher as saying they did it because they did not like her teaching, and that they did not really mean anything by it. One student, for example, who was charged with sending a note which "had a swastika and included the words 'you bitch' and 'Hitler'" denies that he is anti-Semitic, saying "'It was just something stupid'" (p. B2).

As for denying the homophobia of others, a good model is the official denial of T. S. Eliot's bigotry by scores of critics. In Michiko Kakutani's (1996) review of a book by Anthony Julius, *T. S. Eliot, Anti-Semitism and Literary Form,* Kakutani says that Julius "points out in these pages, an astonishing number of critics have tied themselves into knots over the years, trying to rationalize or whitewash Eliot's prejudice" (p. C17).

They are also in denial because they deny their own homosexuality, using the following coping mechanisms:

Counterphobic Denial: Homophobes deny their loving homosexual wishes by protesting otherwise, and too much, that they love women, and hate queers.

Counterphobic Certainty: Homophobes make sweeping declarative statements like, "all gays and lesbians are disgusting" or "homosexuality is a sin," to be certain of where they stand, and to convince others of what they stand for.

Dissociative Denial: Homophobes, to be able to convincingly cite what they call "typical gay flaws" like promiscuity, virtually have to be hypocrites who overlook, conveniently forget, or comfortably dissociate away their own flaws. For example, homophobes who complain that gays and lesbians are always thinking and talking about sex have to conveniently forget what they said yesterday in the locker room. Those who condemn homosexuals for bringing AIDS on themselves neglect to mention that some illnesses of straights (like heart disease due to smoking) are also due to lifestyle indiscretions. Are gays and lesbians any more promiscuous, and self-destructive, than the straight doctor who shortly after his wife had a baby found his name listed in the newspaper for soliciting a prostitute in a run-down area of a Jersey Shore community? About these hypocrites we are tempted to say, "It takes one to know one" and "look in the mirror, and see your own flaws, before you criticize others."

Consensual Validation: Hypomanic homophobes join forces with others of like mind, "partners in crime" who help them feel admired and loved. Militia groups are in part mutual admiration societies. The more bigoted the group, the more external victims they have, the more love and approval they get from peers, and the less lonely, depressed, and guilty they feel as individuals.

Publicizing and proselytizing: Homophobes who find that their private denial defenses are inadequate to deal with their homosexual wishes or who want to deny how guilty they are about being homophobic often take the next step and proclaim their homophobia publicly as a way to enforce their denial (as well as to obtain the jus.-mentioned consensual validation they crave). They go public, hoping to hear something along the lines of, "Hey, buddy, I know where you are coming from"—loud, clear, and often.

Rationalization: Deniers rationalize their bigotry using the usual arguments. The basic ones are: "Some of my best friends are gay"; "I am not homophobic because I do not ski in Colorado" (or another trivial sacrifice that is less impressive than the individual thinks); "I am homophobic in my thoughts but not in my actions (such as my hiring practices)—that is, I am prejudiced which is okay because I do not discriminate"; "I am homophobic but I do not mean it personally and about you"; "there are worse homophobes in this world than I"; "everybody was doing it (being homophobic) at the time"; I was only following "'orders'"; and "I am only homophobic when sorely provoked by gays' and lesbians' bad, inciting behavior."

10

Phobic/Avoidant Homophobes

Almost all the discussions I have read about homophobia contain a statement to the effect that the term "homophobia" is inaccurate because homophobes are not really phobic. For example, Terry Stein (1996) says, "The term [homophobia] has been criticized as imprecise, too general, and inaccurate because it does not refer to a true phobia" (p. 39). And Richard Isay (1989) says, "I use the term 'homophobia' . . . reluctantly since it signifies the phobic avoidance of homosexuals, rather than the aggression that the anxiety evokes. Most important, the term is inaccurate, because this hatred of homosexuals appears to be secondary in our society to the fear and hatred of what is perceived as being 'feminine' in other men and in oneself, and not of homosexuality per se" (p. 78). However, I feel that the term homophobia is a good one even when used in its literal sense if it is applied selectively, and only to true homophobes—to those homophobic individuals who are actually phobic of gays and lesbians. In this chapter I will describe the characteristics of these individuals, and try to show how they are true phobics at heart—that is, how they fear, dislike, and then avoid gays and lesbians much in the same way claustrophobics fear, dislike, and avoid being in closed spaces.

True homophobes actually become anxious in the presence of gays and lesbians, much as bridge phobics become anxious in the presence of the need to drive over a bridge. For such homophobes homosexuals represent a trivial prompt—trivial because the prompt makes them anxious not for itself but because of what it signifies: something personal and highly symbolic, such as the femininity of which Isay (1989) speaks. Phobic homophobes avoid homosexuals to reduce their level of discomfort, just as bridge phobics avoid bridges to reduce their level of anxiety. For example, a male homophobe avoided gays to reduce his fear of having his feminine side exposed just as an erythrophobe avoided everybody to reduce her fear of giving away her sexual thoughts by blushing, a public speaker avoided public speaking to reduce her fear of fainting and wetting her pants, and theatre or churchgoers avoid sitting in the middle of the room, and have to sit on the aisle, so they can reduce their fear that their strong feelings will take over and get out of hand, perhaps causing them to become emotional, and weep visibly and uncontrollably.

Homosexuality is a trivial prompt for phobic homophobes because they consciously view homosexuals, homosexuality, and homosexual acts per se as unpleasant; have negative associations to homosexuals, homosexuality, and homosexual acts; have their forbidden erotic or hostile fantasies aroused by homosexuals; and attribute their personal fantasies to homosexuals, enlivening homosexuality as a stimulus, making it unpleasant or threatening in a way that it is not, so that because homophobes feel menaced, they view the stimulus as actually menacing, however neutral it in fact happens to be. Homosexuality also makes them anxious because they endow gays with magical powers and then see them as capable of almost anything—ranging from the ability to undermine society and influence the world's morality in a negative way, to the ability to ultimately take over the world. For example, Pat Robertson (1992) says, "under [homosexuals'] leadership the world will never, I repeat never, experience lasting peace" (p. 329).

Phobic homophobes also behave like other phobics. For example, like other true phobics they display their anxiety in phobic scanning—which is a way to master fear by preparation and foreknowledge. Before entering a restaurant they search the booths for homosexuals hoping not to find them so that they can eat their meal in comfort the same way bridge phobics before setting out on a trip look at maps, hoping to find a route that doesn't require them to drive over high bridges.

Phobic homophobes use the same defenses true phobics use to handle the unpleasant feelings and fantasies they experience in the presence of homosexuals. The primary defense is *avoidance*. They avoid homosexuals as the presumed source of their discomfort and the presumed reason for the danger they believe themselves to be in. The benefits of avoidance include long periods of sustained peace, well-being, and freedom from fear, as well as the pleasurable feelings associated with the anticipated or actual relief of anxiety—pleasurable feelings that are often so intense that sometimes homophobes even come to "love to hate" homosexuals. However, the peace and well-being are illusory, because they come at a price. The price is the complications of avoidance, which require elaborate, exhausting precautions that limit the homophobe's movements, compromise the homophobe's capacity both for enjoyment and love, and reduce the homophobe's potential pool of available love objects. Too, all homophobes have to "ante up" eventually. They cannot avoid gays and lesbians forever. Sooner or later the "devil" comes by to collect his due. The "Homophobe Meets Trivial Prompt" and, because there has been a buildup of undischarged anxiety over time, there occurs an anxiety attack so intense that it makes up for all the pleasurable peace and freedom from fear the homophobe has had until now.

A second defense involves *mastering vulnerability* by surrounding oneself with a homophobic cocoon. Homophobes need their phobia of gays and lesbians as much as agoraphobics need to have their mothers in tow when they venture forth. The homophobia, like the mother, keeps them from feeling unprotected from their enemies (and when they form homophobic societies it also keeps them from feeling isolated).

A third defense involves *mastering fear* by belittling its source. Just as bridge phobics master the bridge by belittling it, saying something like, "you can make it across that bridge; after all it's not exactly the Golden Gate," homophobes belittle gays and lesbians, saying "they are all sick," in order to reassure themselves, "you have nothing to be afraid of, they are too defective to harm you."

A fourth defense involves *making sure that gays and lesbians do not "invade my space."* Phobic homophobes do this by passing laws against gays and lesbians designed to put and keep them in their place. They pass laws to keep them out of the military service, to obscure their presence once they are there ("don't ask, don't tell"), or when that fails, to evict them from the premises once they have become established. For example, one reason they pass laws against gays and lesbians getting married is to thwart the possibility that gays and lesbians will move to the suburbs and live next door to them. Homophobes, then, often advocate anti-gay legislation to curb gays and lesbians, like dog phobics advocate leash laws, or elevator phobics defeat every high-rise building put before the planning board in the town where they live, all so they can minimize contact with, or never have to face, their trivial prompt.

A fifth defense involves *displacement.* There are two kinds of displacement. In the first kind, related to projection, something within that makes the homophobe anxious is displaced onto the external world—that is, onto a specific homosexual, or onto something associated with that homosexual, such as the homosexual lifestyle. Now homophobes become afraid not of themselves but of homosexuals and homosexuality and of what they see homosexuality as standing for, such as femininity. In the second kind we see a shift from the more to the less significant.

Just as a phobic substitutes a fear of heights for a fear of castration, the homophobe substitutes a fear of homosexuals for an even greater threat, such as the fear of castration or dissolution of identity—one reason for the process of what Fenichel (1945) calls, "homosexualization" (p. 434) of a nonhomosexual person or situation.

A sixth defense is *rationalization*. Homophobes like all phobics deny that they are phobic because they need their phobia, because they are ashamed of it, and because society encourages them to hide any taint of what society misinterprets as weakness. They rationalize their phobia as a wish, a preference, an admirable personality trait, or a normal biological condition. They say, "fags are after all revolting and to be avoided at all costs" just as: (1) patients afraid of flying say they take the train not because they fear the plane but because they like the scenery on the ground, or disguise their fear of flying as a general dislike for public transportation then disguise that as a wish not to travel; (2) patients afraid of going out into crowds proclaim a preference for the country over the city; (3) patients afraid of success proclaim a liking for the simple life; or (4) patients afraid of contamination say they are merely taking admirable precautions (the ones that we all need to take) against germs.

A seventh defense is *proselytizing*. Homophobes attempt to make others equally homophobic. For example, they try to get everyone to agree that gays and lesbians shouldn't have their rights. In this they are like other phobics who warn against lurking dangers of other sorts—such as those from dogs, who bite; planes, that crash; and ladders, that, being rickety, drop cans of paint on the heads of those who dare to walk under them. All concerned are indulging in a kind of phobic advocacy composed of equal parts of misery liking company and a wish to normalize their own fear by making others equally afraid.

An eighth defense is *counterphobia*, which often prompts gay bashing. Counterphobic homophobes reverse their course to hide their intended direction. They protest too much about how they hate gays and lesbians to reassure themselves and the world that they are straight, and if they are the slightest bit gay, that they are at least taking all possible measures to counteract the problem. This is hardly different from how a counterphobic afraid of heights takes up parachute jumping to figuratively, as well as literally, "fly in the face of danger."

And finally a ninth defense involves anticipating or actually *creating anxiety* for purposes of mastery, to work out their phobic plan in advance to test out their coping skills should the unexpected occur, and/or to take their pulse to see how they are doing.

Like all phobics, while on the one hand they find the anxiety itself thrilling to experience, on the other hand their anxiety also serves as what they believe to be their deserved punishment for the guilt that drives them—as it drives most phobics—to be phobic. This deliberate creation of the suffering of anxiety helps explain the homophobe's perverse preoccupation with the hated homosexual and the feared homosexuality, the same one that other phobics have with plane crashes or germs. For like all phobics, homophobes are masochists who need to suffer. The homophobic disco singer who calls gays and lesbians sinful and thereby eliminates her entire fan club and in the process kills her career, like all those who avoid gays and lesbians rather than invite them in and along in a joint endeavor for the benefit of every one concerned, has as his or her counterpart the bridge phobic who avoids navigating the bridge to assure that he or she will not get from here to there, the phobic with stage fright who does not give the speech that would make the reputation, and the better-safe-than-sorry agoraphobes who allow a fear of being mugged to keep them from ever going out, or if they do go out, from ever going out alone, without mother, and to someplace interesting and thrilling, such as into the exciting crowds of the big city.

The following cases illustrate some of the points just made:

For one phobic homophobe, gays and lesbians and their homosexual behavior stood in the place of other (typically phobic) fears, such as his castration fears, fears of passivity and compliance, fears of freedom, fears of being flooded instinctually, and fears of his own aggression. In particular, gays having anal intercourse and lesbians using dildoes released his castration anxiety and, in the case of male's anal intercourse, fears of passivity and compliance too. Gays' supposed freedom and loss of self-control released his own fear of instinctual freedom and his anxiety about being flooded from within. And lesbians' so-called swaggering released his own fears relative to masculine aggression.

A veteran displaced his castration anxiety onto gays who were passive in anal intercourse. He had a vendetta going with the government for having "cut off my nuts" by "taking away my freedom by drafting me for the Vietnam war. I didn't resent going to Vietnam so much as I resented having been forced to go there, by Big Brother, that is, by a man bigger than I am, in effect overpowering and raping me." This man criticized homosexuals to contrast himself with them—as a way to reassure himself that his testicles were too big and powerful to be vulnerable to castration, and his penis too firmly attached to be vulnerable to amputation.

One phobic homophobe disliked gays and lesbians for giving in to their homosexual impulses instead of being strong self-deniers who could "control themselves if they really wanted to" and become celibate by mastering their passions. He expected gays and lesbians to change their ways like he expected himself to change, to not step out of line, to not give in to whatever felt good, and to not yield to pleasure that he could only describe as forbidden. He also dealt with his extreme inhibitions by criticizing gays and lesbians' openness about their sexuality, and their outrageousness in expressing it—wearing gay drag, or demanding equal rights/affirmative action as part of a plan that, as he saw it, would give them more freedom than they deserved. Alternatively he condemned the cities in which many of them lived, like New York and San Francisco, thinking them "Sodom and Gomorrahs" to be destroyed because of their excesses. He eventually became too anxious to go to any big city, even when it was necessary for business, as a way to maintain tight control over his feelings to avoid "who knows what [instincts] getting through."

A phobic homophobe instead of condemning homosexuality per se condemned the things that interested gays and lesbians, like ballet (rather than sports), or any intellectual pursuit, which he dubbed an "elitist working with the mind," a feminine thing to do, to be distinguished from "working with the muscles," a masculine thing to do. Still another displaced his guilt about his own oedipal desire to castrate his father, defy the incest taboo, and marry his mother onto a dislike for those who unsanctimoniously defied taboos. As he put it, "gays and lesbians are the first people since Moses to break all Ten Commandments at once." This is why he railed incessantly about gays' and lesbians' refusing to honor the family tradition, and trying to change the "natural order of things," and not for the better, with men wanting to be women, and women wanting to be men, and with gays and lesbians wanting to get married like straights instead of piously leaving things just the way the Lord made them.

The homophobic veteran who said, "Gays and lesbians cannot be in the military because under fire all they would do is their nails," was himself afraid of being a coward who neglected his military responsibility, and took flight at the first sign of danger "like women who, whenever the going gets rough, flee to the ladies room and shut out the world by looking in the mirror, and putting on their makeup."

For another phobic homophobe gays were bad individuals because they wanted special consideration and rights, pushing others aside so that they could be "numero uno" and top dog. In doing this they reminded him of what he did to his own brothers and sisters—pushing them aside so that he could be the one most in the good graces of his mother. As he put it, "getting something always involves clawing your way to the top, and that, in my book, is an example of the worst women have to offer."

While true phobic homophobes avoid gays and lesbians to reduce their own anxiety about something being homosexual stands for, *avoidant* homophobes avoid gays and lesbians as part of their need to avoid everyone. Many claim to be homophobic just so that they can hide how they are avoidant—that is, they admit to being threatened by gays and lesbians so that they do not have to admit that they are threatened by everyone. These avoidant homophobes often strike up a tolerance bargain with gays and lesbians that says, "Gays and lesbians are okay as long as they don't move into my neighborhood, or my home town"—that is, "as long as they keep their distance from me and do not come so close that they act as a constant irritant and reminder of what makes me anxious."

11

Obsessive-Compulsive Homophobes

Obsessive-compulsive homophobes are really sexophobes who criticize themselves and others for having a body that has a physical side. They condemn gay and straight sex alike as sinful, immoral, and revolting. The only exception they make is out of necessity: okaying sex "in the family way," in the missionary position, in the dark, within the confines of marriage, and for the purpose of procreation. All other kinds of sex, gay sex in particular, they condemn. As Morris (1967), expressing himself from the narrow anthropomorphic perspective of the zoologist applying animal models to human behavior might say, for such individuals "the primary function of sexual behaviour is to reproduce the species and this is something that the formation of homosexual pairs patently fails to do" (p. 93).

> An advertisement for Planned Parenthood (1996) puts it this way: "Q. Why are some Politicians in Congress trying to take away birth control? A. Because they believe No Birth Control = No Sex [a] 19th Century Retro-Vision. [They] are promoting the 19th Century idea that sex is somehow 'dirty.' They believe women must be punished if a couple has sex when they aren't 'trying for a baby'"(p. A11).

Obsessive-compulsive homophobes display their sexophobic ideas in the form of rigid and repetitive rituals. The following rituals are among the most commonly found:

1. Condemning/banishing rituals: Obsessive-compulsive homophobes avoid gays and lesbians like phobics avoid gays and lesbians. But in addition, obsessive-compulsive homophobes go beyond merely avoiding gays and lesbians; they also favor condemning, isolating, and

quarantining them. Most phobics will avoid driving over a bridge without condemning bridges. In contrast, an obsessive-compulsive homophobic soldier, especially one who has joined the army to solidify a shaky heterosexual identification, will not only find him- or herself too close for comfort to others of the same sex, and deal with the pressure by avoiding anyone suspected of being homosexual, but will also demand that anyone suspected of being homosexual be condemned and even banished—in the case of the soldier, from the military. This soldier will be too conscience-driven to handle his or her anxiety adequately by simply avoiding the source of that anxiety. He or she will additionally have to condemn and destroy the source of the anxiety, to reassure the conscience that "I am doing everything I can under the circumstances to register the necessary, and appropriate, objections."

At a real-estate closing a seller, at one end of the table, was talking about the theatre with the buyer's lawyer. This displeased the buyer, a "jock" type, because to him anyone who was interested in the theatre was per se a sissy. He handled his displeasure, and his own fear of being a "sissy," by yelling at his lawyer at the other end of the table, "Hey, down there, you are supposed to be talking about sports."

2. Controlling rituals: Controlling obsessive-compulsive homophobes feel both entitled to tell and responsible for telling homosexuals what they should do in their private lives. Controllers brand homosexuals as defiant errant children who should disavow their personal inclinations, hopes, and dreams and go straight, "because that's what I tell you to do." Controllers set forth specific conditions under which they will, and will not, accept gays and lesbians. In particular they will accept gays and lesbians who "submit" to them either by remaining in the closet or by remaining celibate. But they will not accept gays and lesbians who "rebel" against them by coming out of the closet and being sexually active.

Controllers are also moralists who tell others what to do to affirm their own high principles; sadomasochists who get pleasure from discipline and bondage; and narcissists who obtain gratification from the feeling of importance that comes from being in the driver's seat, in charge of others who are in tow, and under their thumb.

One straight man was a past master at what Loraine O'Connell's (1993) article calls, in another context, "Sitting in Judgment" (p. E1). When he caught gay men looking at attractive men he would stare them down in disapproval for cruising. Even though what they were doing was none of his business, he made it entirely so as a way to reassure himself that he was not like them, to satisfy his conscience and thereby to increase his self-es-teem, to manage his environment to handle perceived threats to his mas-culinity, and to feel more masculine by disapproving of "feminine queers." Additionally he derived satisfaction from knowing he carried on the great tradition of his mother and father, who "managed" his life when he was very young. As he put it, "I appreciated how they managed me, for they provided me with the control I wanted and needed, stopping me from gratifying myself in so many bad ways." And he added, by way of reducing his overall guilt about being controlling, that by controlling gays he was actually doing them a favor—the same favor his parents did for him by keeping him from losing control of himself and doing things he might sub-sequently regret.

Another patient himself viewed his excessive need to control others as a leftover from his struggles with his parents over being toilet trained. He perpetuated his rigid toilet training by controlling others as his parents controlled him. He voted for anti-gay-rights bills to teach gays the mean-ing of self-control (as well as to keep them from rising up and destroying society). Underneath it all he wanted to control gays so that he could con-tinue to relate to them. It was, "do what I tell you to do, because otherwise I will have to lose you—because I will have to reject you." In effect he had become like his parents who wanted him asexual to keep him from being a grown-up and leaving home. Along these lines his own mother once sued his dermatologist for taking off a mole on his abdomen near his gen-itals without her permission. He was underage at the time and she said, "I only object because he did the operation without my written consent." But in fact, she was a sexophobic individual who minded her son's having the mole removed because he clearly had had the surgery to improve his sex life. She was a lonely person who feared that if her son were sexually active then he would go off and abandon her. Homophobia for him then was, underneath it all, an attempt to keep homosexuals from beckoning, and thus threatening to take him away from home, and from his mother. Revealingly when he called into right-wing anti-gay talk shows, he did so from home, in his mother's presence, so that she could overhear him and be reassured that he would never leave her, but instead would be with her forever.

Commanding rituals come very close to controlling rituals. For exam-ple, Steven E. Bailey (1996) quotes Dr. Kathleen K. Casey as saying that "'There's really no reason for new cases of HIV in the United States. It's a matter of education and personal choice'" (p. A3). In my opinion she overlooks unconscious forces and overrelies on brute force as a way to change human behavior, something that most psychotherapists know rarely works. The reason for new cases is that sex is a powerful force that has a mind of its own, especially difficult to control when, as is true for many people, there are also unconscious masochistic and depressive personality trends to be contended with.

3. Cleansing rituals: Obsessive-compulsives see gays and lesbians as corrupting them. The commonly held notion that gays and lesbians given rights will corrupt or destroy the fabric of society sometimes origins in a paranoid delusion such as that of the influencing machine (discussed in Chapter 8). But at other times it originates in an obsessive-compulsive fear of contamination. Many homophobes believe that gays and lesbians can "influence" them via a process akin to viral or bacterial contamination, and see gays and lesbians as filthy people— for example, as disgusting buttheads whose dirt will rub off on them. They next handle the possibility of being contaminated by gays and lesbians by creating rituals meant to symbolically decontaminate themselves and their environment. Sometimes such individuals merely hesitate or refuse to touch gays and lesbians, or as a precaution wash their hands thoroughly after shaking hands with a gay or lesbian. At other times they feel that society should take the next step and quarantine gays and lesbians.

> A homophobe was disgusted with gay men because he felt they were all covered with a thin layer of feces. He did, however, "pardon" gays whose homosexuality was ego-dystonic because "at least they were making the effort to clean up their act." He particularly hated active homosexuals, not so much because he viewed them as morally bankrupt, and homosexuality as morally wrong, but because he saw them and their being homosexual as being "dirty and diseased." (He was also not merely a homophobe but a complete bigot. Although he himself was Jewish, he disliked Jews, and even changed his name from one that sounded Jewish, in part because Jews accumulated "filthy lucre." In like manner he disliked blacks because they were "brown like feces"; foreigners because they were "the great unwashed"; and women because they "soiled their panties, with regularity, once a month.")
>
> When dining out, he could hardly go to the bathroom when he suspected there was a gay man in the restaurant because he feared he would contract AIDS by using the same washroom. When he had to use the rest room he developed a severe hand-washing compulsion upon leaving. Convinced he could get AIDS from a contaminated door handle, he had to return to the sink to wash his hands over and over again, only to "recontaminate" them each time he opened the door again. For this individual a fear of contamination by the AIDS virus was really a fear of contamination by feces.
>
> He also didn't defecate as often as he needed to because he felt that defecating was dirty. He ate lightly to avoid making excessive feces, and once even developed bulimia and anorexia nervosa primarily (unconsciously) for that purpose.

In his therapy sessions he couldn't say the word "asked" (one that came up frequently in his conversation) without immediately adding, "Doctor, that sounds like assed." In the supermarket he stood in the middle of the aisle turning the prune jars upside down to watch the prunes fall, ostensibly to see which jar had the thickest syrup, but really, as he came to realize, "as a way to have fun watching turds drop." Each trip to the supermarket he bought as many rolls of toilet paper on sale as he could carry. One time he had 135 packages of multiple rolls stored in, really stuffed into, the closets of his small apartment. The neighbors saw him coming and going with what one, he overheard saying, called a "shit-eating grin" on his face, fresh from his triumph of having gotten another shopping bag full of toilet paper at bargain prices. When it came to disposing of his garbage, in order to not have to go to the incinerator, which he avoided because he was afraid that soot would back up, get on, and dirty his face and clothes, he virtually gift-wrapped his garbage to make it presentable enough so that he could take it down on the elevator without being discovered and safely deposit it in the waste paper baskets on the city streets, in violation of, really because of, the laws against the use of city trash baskets for household garbage.

Once he invited a gay colleague to share his office and then threw him out because his own colleagues were complaining about his association with someone gay. The excuse he used to get rid of this man was that the colleague had ruined his office. What did he ruin? He soiled a 69-cent desk blotter because one day he ate a sandwich and a piece of cole slaw fell on it, as he put it, "staining it irretrievably," and he turned a pair of $28 blinds "to crap" because he simply didn't know how to swing the window closed without catching the blinds in the window frame and bending them. Clearly this was not a financial matter, because a tenth of one month's rent would have covered the damage nicely. It was a personal matter. It involved a gay soiling and contaminating his office, which he saw as an extension of himself.

A psychoanalyst expressed his own contamination fears in the way he analyzed gays, and the reasons for which he analyzed them. He was not analyzing them for being gay; rather he was analyzing the gayness out of them, as if he were purging them of being gay, cleaning them up by giving them the figurative equivalent of a laxative.

Gay bashing or murdering gays is often an unconscious act of self-cleansing.

Two men picked up a soldier hitchhiking in California and had sex with him in the backseat of a car. After complying he pulled out a knife and threatened to kill both of them, in effect, to clean himself off after what he did "because I feel dirty." (They saved their lives by talking him down, really talking to and soothing his guilty conscience, by telling him to "give everyone a break, and just chalk it up to experience.")

4. Denial (reaction formation) rituals: These manage unacceptable impulses by expressing them in opposite form. These rituals cover not only forbidden homosexual but also unacceptable angry impulses. As for the latter, homophobes typically cover their anger with condescending charity, saccharine pity, or with a rigid homophilia. Some individuals become "fag hags" not because they simply like gays but because they are in reaction formation—that is, perversely in love with them, as a way to handle the opposite feelings boiling within—as other individuals become firemen to handle being arsonists or abstinent priests leading boys choirs to handle being pedophiles. When homophilia is not preferential but morbid in this way, individuals do not like gays for their good qualities, such as their brains and looks (factors often cited as being positive features of gays). Nor do they like them because they make good confidants, or flatterers, or, if the homophobes are jealous heterosexuals, because gays don't compete with them for their lovers and spouses. Nor do they like them because they have identified with victimized gays, having been victims themselves in their own lives. Nor do they like them because they are simply opportunists who use gays for what they can get out of them. They like them as a way to resolve a personal conflict about hating them, to absolve themselves of their guilt about their homophobia. They do not really like gays. They have mostly changed their sadism toward gays to understanding, or pity. But they have not gone all the way and turned it into love.

When denial (reaction formation) fails partly or completely and the repressed returns, we see the doing and undoing that is so characteristic of obsessive-compulsive rituals. When homophobes do and undo they look very much like obsessive-compulsives repeating hand-washing rituals. Such homophobes shift from hating to loving gays and back again in a way that is reminiscent of how hand-washers in the process of cleaning up inadvertently touch something dirty, then have to clean up all over again.

An obsessive homophobe constantly worried, "Did I bump you?" and approached gays to ask if he had in fact bumped them. Bump was for him a close relative of bang, and like it a term that referred equally to sexual and hostile desires. Convinced he had bumped his victims, he sidled over to apologize to them, only to get so close that he actually bumped them, so that he had to start the whole process—of self-torture and self-gratification—all over again.

In another ritual with essentially the same meaning, he felt forced to count the dots, stripes, or other decorations on men's ties, but only when the men in question were sitting down, and the tie was in their laps. The count always went from the top of the tie to the tip lying in the crotch, and "then back up the other side of the tie," making both his homosexual and anal wishes clear. Next he questioned whether he got the count right, so that he was forced to repeat it, which allowed him to retrace his forbidden steps, as well as to continue to torture himself for his desire to take these steps.

At still other times he prayed for gays' salvation, doing so hours at a time. He prayed constantly as a way to say something often enough so that it would sink in and cover his anger, and expel his sinful thoughts. In an evangelical fury, he closed his eyes and tightened his facial muscles as if to both give his prayerful thoughts more amplitude and momentum, and to in effect squeeze the evil in his insides out, like toothpaste out of a tube. When he had finished, a beatific look came over him as if he were emptied of sin. Then he became unctiously loving. Soon enough, however, the first signs of a frown spread over his face, signaling that his anger and evil thoughts were returning, popping back in the seams that he could not keep from showing between the prayers.

For this man, there was nothing at all between hate and love. There was no happy medium—no tolerance, permissiveness, acceptance, or even, what many gays would settle for, benign neglect.

Criminalization/exoneration rituals rely heavily on the above-mentioned obsessive-compulsive defense of doing and undoing. These rituals consist of first bashing gays and lesbians as criminals, then feeling guilty and taking it back by forgiving them, then having second thoughts about that and taking it back by bashing gays and lesbians all over again as criminals, and so on. Criminalization makes gay sexual acts into crimes even though there are no victims, then offers salvation and forgiveness, even though there has been no crime.

Rationalization is actually just another kind of denial or reaction formation. Often when homophobes explain their rationalizations they do so in a way that makes them look even more bigoted than before. For example, they say that their gay bashing is provoked, deserved, natural, or biologically based. As one put it, explaining why he demeaned gays and lesbians as inferior mortals, "gay bashing is a natural thing, based on a need for the fittest to survive." Or rationalizers may simply cover up their bigotry by taking it back, saying "This is not gay bashing at all, and I am not a bigot."

5. Ascetic rituals: These, as Meissner (1985) might define them, involve expecting all concerned to renounce "base" pleasure as a way to reduce anxiety (p. 390) for the general good. Ascetics pray that gays and lesbians will be celibate, adding "I am willing to accept them and let them be anything they want to be, so long as they renounce their past homosexual lives, and don't do homosexual things in the present."

6. Jealousy rituals: Jealousy rituals deal with forbidden homosexual wishes by externalizing them onto others. A parallel to the paranoid's

delusional conviction that a spouse is unfaithful is the obsessive's persistent worry that a spouse might be having an affair. Dynamically a consuming fear of the other's infidelity deflects from the homophobe's own wish to be unfaithful, and to be unfaithful in the same way, and with the same person. Obsessive homophobic men become jealous of their wives first because they have a secret wish to be unfaithful to them, and second because they have a secret wish to be unfaithful with the person the wife is presumably cheating with. The so-called straight man jealous about his wife's having a lover consciously thinks he dreads his wife's being unfaithful. But unconsciously he is really troubled by his own homosexual desire for the wife's male lover (the same process, with the sexes reversed, occurs in women). Such can be the reason for double murders, where a man kills both the wife and the possible paramour, both to stop the wife's infidelity from continuing and to keep his own latent homosexuality from surfacing.

7. Intellectual rituals: Meissner (1985) defines intellectualization as "a control of affects and impulses by way of thinking about them instead of experiencing them" (p. 389). We see a systematic excess of thinking, deprived of its affect, used to defend against anxiety caused by unacceptable impulses. As mentioned in Chapter 8, intellectual obsessive homophobes don't hate, they debate. They become contemplative homophobes. They might become preoccupied with the question, "what is sin?" as a way to gain control over the sexual feelings of all concerned by scrutinizing them until they wither and die. Obsessive-compulsives who scrutinize this way do so to prove to themselves that if passion can yield to persuasion, then they can save sinners by preaching to them. Intellectual mechanisms are also used to handle the homophobic anger that is such a significant aspect of homophobia/bigotry. Guilty about their anger they intellectualize it as proper—that is, as provoked. Or they express it covertly in derivative, ideologic form, using philosophical or religious criteria such as "immoral," refinements that avoid their having to state their angry disapproval in more openly aggressive, and so guilt-inducing, ways.

8. Magic rituals: Obsessive homophobes who believe in magic believe that out of mind is out of sight. This technique is illustrated by the mother of a homosexual who, as Jones (1957) reports, wrote Freud a letter asking him about her homosexual son, without even mentioning his homosexuality (p. 195). (Freud had to infer that homosexuality was the problem of which she spoke.) It was as if she had to deny that such a thing as homosexuality even existed. The "don't ask don't tell" homophobic ritual that in essence says, "I accept gays and lesbians so long as they are neither seen not heard" belongs here as well. Magic homophobic rituals also take the form of an individual endlessly praying for abso-

lution for various unspecified guilts, as for example can take place in some formalized interminable psychoanalyses.

9. Perfectionistic rituals: For perfectionists, smoke becomes fire as gays' and lesbians' small flaws become critical defects, and their run-of-the-mill peccadilloes become serious character imperfections. Perfectionistic rituals are also intended to add the quality of thoroughness to other rituals, so that homophobes can completely reassure their consciences that they are doing all they can, with no homosexual transgression overlooked, or allowed to go unpunished. The "let's-try-it-to-see-if-it-works" kind of psychoanalysis undertaken to cure homosexuality is often an exercise in perfectionism. Here every one concerned goes through the motions even though they already know the outcome, or lack of one. They proceed until the very end under the shared delusion that the gay can go straight, just so that they can say that "everything has been tried, and all the bases covered, before we finally had to give up."

12

Personality Disorder Homophobes—I

Personality disorder homophobes abuse gays and lesbians for different reasons, in different ways, and to different degrees, each reflecting their specific underlying personality problems. As examples of the different reasons, homophobes with a paranoid personality disorder bash gays and lesbians to disavow something from within, something they dislike about themselves; homophobes with a depressive personality disorder bash gays and lesbians to enhance their own self-esteem; homophobes with a narcissistic personality disorder bash gays and lesbians because they are different from them; and homophobes with a psychopathic-antisocial personality disorder bash gays and lesbians for personal gain. As examples of the different ways, obsessive homophobes tend to argue gays and lesbians down, while paranoid homophobes tend to beat gays and lesbians up. And as examples of the different degrees, obsessive homophobes, tending to be more contemplative than action prone, tend to be more prejudiced than discriminatory; while passive-aggressive homophobes, tending to be more action-prone (however covertly) than contemplative, tend to be as discriminatory as they are prejudiced.

What distinguishes personality disorder homophobia from other syndromal homophobia is that personality disorder homophobia tends to be more diffuse than encapsulated. However its low-key nature is more than made up for by its persistence and wide applicability. Personality disorder homophobes wake up homophobic, and live, eat, and breathe homophobia until they go to bed at night. They are even homophobic in their sleep, when they have homophobic dreams that reflect on what they thought yesterday and plan for what they are going to do tomorrow. Unlike paranoid homophobes who develop encapsulated delusions about gays and lesbians, paranoid personality disorder ho-mophobes spar with gays and lesbians as a way of life. Both paranoid and paranoid personality disorder homophobes think everyone is queer like they are, and attack anyone even remotely suspect, locking, like bloodhounds, into the mere scent of homosexuality, and following the trail, spotting, seizing, then pinning their victims to the spot, just because as men they like antiques, or as women they hold powerful ad-ministrative positions. And for both the goal is to externalize their own homosexuality. But homophobes with a paranoid personality disorder do not single out an identified victim to bash as do their more discrete paranoid cousins. Instead they bash always and everywhere, and they do so indiscriminately, based on the principle that the wider the net, the larger the catch.

PARANOID PERSONALITY
DISORDER HOMOPHOBES

Meissner (1985) might be speaking of paranoid personality disorder ho-mophobia when he describes patients who "suffer from severe preju-dice, rejection of intimacy through suspiciousness [and jealousy], hy-pervigilance to external danger, and injustice collecting" in this and other ways "attributing [their] own unacknowledged feelings to others," "perceiving and reacting to unacceptable inner impulses . . . as though they were outside the self" (p. 389). For paranoid personality disorder homophobes, gays and lesbians are like a blank screen or an inkblot on a psychological test: stimulating fantasy just by being there. Or, at the most, they are minor stimulants that elicit a major response, one just waiting to happen. For example, Carmen Vazquez (1992) points out that many individuals when asked, "'Why do gay men and lesbians bother you?'" commonly answer the question with, "'Because they act like girls'" or "'because they think they are men,'" and add that "'I don't care what they do in bed, but they shouldn't act like that'" (p. 161). But of course they don't all act like girls, or men. Most people know perfectly well that only some male gays have limp wrists, and only some lesbians swagger. But individuals with paranoid personality disorder homopho-bia need to maintain the myth of altered gender identity in gays and les-bians in the face of much evidence to the contrary, and want to do so so that they can play out the problems they have with their own sexual identity on the smoother turf of the other's supposed problems with his or her sexuality.

A paranoid homophobe, herself greedy and guilty about being greedy, thought she could identify a like-minded greediness in all gays and lesbians, then condemned all gays and lesbians for wanting things for nothing just the way she did. She denounced gay marriage less for the moral reasons she claimed than because she envisioned a world full of hustler-like young gays and lesbians getting something for nothing from their older patrons, without earning what they got—just like she herself wanted to get something from the world, without having to work for it.

A basically straight man, an executive for a large company, found the yoke of masculinity was a heavy one to bear. In his secret fantasies he would, if he could, find relief in coming home, kicking off his shoes, and putting on pumps—not necessarily to be a woman but for the moment to not have to be a man, with all the responsibility that that entailed, and the constant struggle against his feminine side it required. But he only yielded to temptation under the safe umbrella of a public festival, in the play of cross-dressing permissible on Halloween—when, as with all festivals, there is, for a few hours, a socially sanctioned window of opportunity to be yourself in a world that for the moment becomes a permissive place where it is safe to express what has been until now repressed. Halloween night he was among the first to get into drag. But even then he carefully disguised his true desires by not imitating women but by caricaturing them instead. His outfits were not feminine but gross, so that no one would suspect his true yearning. Eventually as the years went by, when he found his own feminine side getting stronger and stronger, he had to disguise his wishes in a more malignant way—by vocally condemning others who yielded up to their feminine side, even when they were only seeking similar relief in play. Knowing that forbidding others to do something was a good way to forbid himself to do the same thing, and that convincing others of a thing was a good way to convince himself of its equal, he spoke constantly in a denigrating fashion of the *real* drag queens, the ones who called themselves by women's names, and who were not playacting, but who were really trying to be Joan Crawford or Bette Davis.

He felt that reality also necessitated his denying his own femininity and his need to be passive like a woman. For being homophobic himself he knew it was right to fear homophobes. At work, for example, he would lose out if he so much as appeared for an instant to be feminine. Someone would zero in on what they, like the rest of society, perceived to be a weakness, and use his behavior to knock him down so that they could advance themselves. As a boss he could not even afford to appear kind and helpful to underlings—gays, lesbians, and straights alike—but especially gays and lesbians. He had to be cruel, selfish, and aggressive to them so that he could look good (i.e., masculine) to his (mostly straight) colleagues and overlings.

Hiding was hard to do as a steady diet. And he needed relief from all the tension associated with denying his feminine side. He needed to throw off his primary masculine identity and relax, even though relaxing itself meant being feminine, and being feminine meant being vulnerable. So he mostly suppressed his desires and kept them private, but did what he wanted to do, one day a year. The other days—for public consumption, for the record, and for his own peace of mind—he condemned those who did what he did, for being serious about it, and for doing it on a regular basis.

Paranoid personality disorder homophobes are particularly adept at defending, really justifying, their homophobia as provoked—that is, as second, not first, strike. They emphasize the ounces of truth buried in the pounds of their distortions, rather like a cardboard cone is buried underneath swirls of cotton candy. They say, for example, that gays and lesbians warrant criticism because they are, as the expression goes, "too much for TV." They blame others instead of themselves, like a patient of mine reported her neighbor blamed her. My patient asked a neighbor's teenage child to please stop playing noisily in the hall, only to have the mother criticize her for scaring the child. Like all paranoids victimizing others, they justify their behavior by blaming the victim. They call them irresponsible, and say that they could have avoided most of their problems if only they had lived their lives differently. Paranoid homophobes call their weapons defensive, not offensive. They say that they are merely responding to real enemies, though they are really creating straw men, and scapegoats, and are not the victims they would like to believe themselves to be, but the perpetrators they deny that they are now or have ever been.

Paranoid personality disorder homophobes bash gays and lesbians not merely to deny their own homosexual urges. They also bash gays and lesbians to handle their anger. They are both projecting it and expressing it to avoid a buildup of unmanageable aggressiveness. For example, aggressive male teenagers gay bash by riding around in cars in Greenwich Village in New York City in the company of other homophobes, hurling things out of the car windows, ranging from epithets to nitric acid, in part as a way to avoid anger buildup. They are discharging their anger on gays and lesbians as a way to handle their rage impulses by simply yielding to them, to get them out of their system and over with.

In the less severe cases of paranoid personality disorder homophobia, homophobes can maintain relationships with gays and lesbians as long as the gays and lesbians meet a specific set of predetermined criteria, criteria which, as they see it, soften the degree to which gays and lesbians aggravate them. For example, they can relate to gays in drag because they simply caricature, and so are not an affront to, "real men." Or they can relate to gays and lesbians with ego-dystonic homosexuality because while they have sinned, and continue to do so, they seem also willing, and eager, to atone for their sins.

SCHIZOID PERSONALITY
DISORDER HOMOPHOBES

While paranoid personality disorder homophobes are uncomfortable in the presence of homosexuals, but not in the presence of heterosexuals, schizoid homophobes, like the avoidant homophobes described in chapter 10, are uncomfortable in the presence of everybody—heterosexuals as well as homosexuals. While paranoids avoid relationships with gays and lesbians to avoid recognizing their own homosexuality, schizoid homophobes avoid relationships with everybody to avoid the anxiety that closeness brings.

PSYCHOPATHIC-ANTISOCIAL
PERSONALITY DISORDER HOMOPHOBES

While paranoid homophobes are guilty people who externalize blame to diminish their own guilt, psychopathic-antisocial homophobes (from now on referred to simply as psychopathic homophobes) are guiltless people who shamelessly externalize blame so that they can get the good things to which they feel entitled. We might say that while paranoid homophobes like to *see themselves* in a favorable light, psychopathic homophobes prefer to *be seen* in a favorable light—so that they can get while the getting is good, and take the money while they can still run. In other words, they externalize guilt not so that they can deny an aspect of themselves, to reduce anxiety, but so that they can diminish the standing of others, to increase their chances of getting something for nothing.

When these homophobes criticize gays and lesbians it is part of their plan to use them. They use them to win an election or to get a coveted job. They devalue their services so that they don't have to pay for them. Much as some people find reasons to complain about the service in a restaurant at the end of an enjoyable meal so that they can reduce the size of the tip, psychopathic homophobes as patients "discover" that their doctor is homosexual so that they do not have to pay a bill they ran up, or as bosses discover that their workers are homosexual so that they can avoid increasing their salaries. Rumor has it that a well-known conductor, who was himself gay, got married to hide the fact, then outed another well-known conductor, a former beloved mentor, but now his rival for the same post, just so that he could get a coveted job. (Neither man got the job. The ones making the hiring decision were probably too bright and too homophobic to let that manipulation fool them.)

Psychopathic homophobes use clever, self-serving ruses to form powerful anti-gay political coalitions. They are good salespeople. Because they are personally appealing they can turn friendship on and off as part of their goal of mesmerizing other homophobes into forming the large groups with clout they need to help them be the winner that takes all. And being manipulative by nature they know how to cleverly excuse their gay bashing with various tricks of logic, to convince themselves, and others, that their mission is admirable. They convince others that they are not homophobic for evil but for good, and not for their own good but for a higher purpose—for the good of mankind, civilization, and God.

While many psychopathic homophobes are covert and sly, others are openly aggressive. They do not simply reason contemplatively that same-sex marriages will destroy the fabric of society. They provoke pitched battles between gay and straight social factions because that serves their purpose—the purpose of tearing the social fabric apart when there is something in it for them, as when a riot is an opportunity for them to achieve a political goal.

BORDERLINE PERSONALITY
DISORDER HOMOPHOBES

Borderlines dismiss gays and lesbians from their lives the same way they dismiss straights from their lives. They get deeply involved in a close relationship then suddenly, and without warning, drop the person, sometimes after years of what at first appeared to be at least a peaceful intimacy. A social worker is still mystified by how a psychiatrist friend of hers, someone she had known for 20 years, dropped her in just this way. This was the only provocation: once the social worker asked the psychiatrist a personal medical question, only to have the psychiatrist tell her off, saying, "Don't you ever call me again. I never mother dykes." Gays and lesbians involved with such people think they have been victimized by a homophobic attack. In fact they have not been treated prejudicially but, unfortunately, equally.

HYSTERICAL (HISTRIONIC)
PERSONALITY DISORDER HOMOPHOBES

Hysterical (histrionic) homophobes develop hysterical hallucinations about gays and lesbians. These are fantasies about homosexuals/homosexual matters concretized into exaggerated visions of what gays and lesbians are and do. Like other hysterics who imagine footsteps in the dark, ghosts, or their name being called in a lonely place, they are overwrought individuals prone to panic easily and extensively. They think the world is going to come to an end because it has gays and lesbians in it. They even have visions of a kind of gay Armageddon. Dynamically they call gays and lesbians the enemy because they hate them, and they hate them because they envy them, because they think they show them up. If they vote against same-sex marriages it is not only because they want to prevent gays and lesbians from getting married for the moral reasons they claim, but also because they think that if gays and lesbians with talent and money were allowed to get married, then the gays and lesbians would have it all, and they would have less in comparison. Hysterical (histrionic) personality disorder homophobia is discussed further in chapter 13.

NARCISSISTIC PERSONALITY DISORDER HOMOPHOBES

Narcissists see themselves as representing the standard everybody else should follow and criticize those who are different. Just as for the general bigot the definition of the good American is "who and what I am," for the narcissistic homophobe "my heterosexuality, family standard, and straight marriage" defines "who and what you should be." Such narcissists often try to convert those whom, as they see it, don't match up. They derive additional pleasure from being dominant and from sitting in judgment, which makes them feel like royalty. Feeling like royalty is especially reassuring to men whose self-esteem is low because they are afraid of their feminine side, and to women who, themselves sexist, believe that a woman is a defective man.

Narcissists criticize gays and lesbians as a way to congratulate themselves. Like the opera buff who boos not to say "You are a disaster beyond belief," but to say "I have the good taste to recognize lack of talent where I see it, and the good sense to want to criticize those who don't have it," narcissistic homophobes condemn gays' and lesbians' blasphemy to brag about the extent of their own faith, and condemn gays' and lesbians' sin to proclaim themselves guilt-free. In general they want to reduce the status of gays and lesbians in society to reaffirm their own high social value and status both in their own and in others' eyes.

Similarly narcissistic are the prolonged self-indulgent temper tantrums they have against gays and lesbians. These tantrums are the puerile kind children have when they feel angry with their parents for having deprived them of something they want. In the case of narcissistic homophobes, they want gays and lesbians to buy into their own lifestyle, and when gays and lesbians do not do it, they act like parents who are hurt because their children have minds, needs, and goals of their own—that is, because the "kids are growing up, defying me, and going to leave."

DEPENDENT PERSONALITY
DISORDER HOMOPHOBES

Isay (1989) notes that gay-bashing adolescents are fighting off "needs and wishes for dependency" on their parents which dependency is perceived as "feminine. . . . [They] assert their masculinity [in an] attempt to deny regressive dependent wishes by expressing their aggression (pp. 77–78).

Dependent homophobes do not merely fear dependency; they also want to be dependent. They think not, like hysterics, in terms of envy but in terms of loss. They are afraid gays and lesbians will fan their own latent homosexuality, then, in yielding to it, they will lose important people in their lives. They fear their spouses will leave them or their children will turn from them. They are also afraid that gays and lesbians will convert and steal away someone they love. Furthermore, many of these dependent homophobes are really sexophobes telling their mothers, "I don't want to be homo-, or any other kind of sexual, because I don't want to grow up and leave you, or worse, have you leave me."

Dependent homophobes tend to form an unholy alliance with gays and lesbians. They need to get close to them, closer than they care to admit, like they need to get close to everyone. Then they fight with them not only because closeness threatens but also because they are threatened with the possibility that they will be rejected, and they want to get there, with the rejection, first.

Developmentally either early rejections or excessive love create the dependent homophobes' excessive need for love. They go through life with one eye open to what their parent substitutes think, so more than most they gay bash to impress a peer group and to shore up a homophobic organization in danger of fragmenting. Here gays and lesbians become useful as the common enemy that keeps the group from dissolving. Perversely, dependent homophobes even want their victims to love them. Some virtually demand that the gays and lesbians they bash accept the bashing, taking it lying down, with equanimity, and even approval for having been bashed, confessing, "I see your point, I deserve what I get, and I thank you for paying attention to me."

OBSESSIVE-COMPULSIVE
PERSONALITY DISORDER HOMOPHOBES

This is a mild, diffuse form of obsessive-compulsive disorder, which is discussed in chapter 11.

SADOMASOCHISTIC PERSONALITY DISORDER HOMOPHOBES

Sadism

Sadistic homophobes are, like hysterics, envious people who prosper and thrive best when their competition is wounded and crippled. But unlike hysterics, who develop personally painful symptoms because of their envy, sadistic homophobes handle their envy by hurting others and making them suffer, while doing little or no suffering of their own. Some do this passive-aggressively, by withholding what gays and lesbians need and standing idly by taking pleasure from watching them "die of neglect." This happened to two gays in a cooperative apartment whose board arranged to make repairs in their apartment without consulting them as to what would be a convenient time or date, then entered the apartment without warning, or concern for what they might find there, and almost let the cat escape out of a window they opened to do their work. Others are more openly aggressive. For example, Bob Herbert (1996), in his article "Radio's Sick Shtick," reports that the talk-show host Bob Grant says it would be "'nice' if police officers had used machine guns to mow down participants in a gay-pride march" (p. A31).

As happens with paranoids, what is at first purely an emotional issue soon becomes a real one. Sadistic homophobes interlock with gays and lesbians in what is at first a one-way hostile relationship. But this progresses to a mutually hostile relationship. Irrational progresses to rational hostility when the homophobe's sadistic attitude toward gays and lesbians becomes at least partly a response to gays' and lesbians' by now angry counterresponse to the sadistic homophobe. Prejudice becomes preference due to provocation when gays and lesbians, having been provoked, straight bait or straight bash to see the enemy wince or to actually do them some harm.

Masochism

Masochistic homophobes do destructive things to gays and lesbians as a way to do destructive things to themselves. They make inept, politically embarrassing, or disastrous slips of the tongue. They become overinvolved in petty, self-destructive vendettas against gays and lesbians, concentrating all their energies on abusing them instead of concentrating the same energies on doing constructive things in their lives. They would rather be lonely than have gay or lesbian friends, and they would rather see their businesses fail than hire gays and lesbians, or serve gay or lesbian customers.

Sadomasochism

Sadomasochistic homophobes swing between the two extremes of de-structive hatred and excessive, self-sacrificing love for gays and lesbians. Sadomasochistic homophobes first thoroughly condemn gays and les-bians, then feeling guilty deny that they are homophobic and prove it to the world in a number of self-destructive ways—say by sacrificing their careers to spend their time doing volunteer work for gay and lesbian or-ganizations. Both the condemnations and the denials are suspect be-cause mostly homosexuality is a nonissue, and, though far less destruc-tive, too much championing of homosexual causes can be part of the same neurotic process as attacking gays and lesbians, only in reverse.

Gays and lesbians interlocked with sadomasochistic homophobes in a mutual love-hate relationship find that each side can neither ignore nor accept the other. In effect all concerned are members of one un-happy family. As such they fight with each other because they are in an unholy (family) alliance. Hating each other more than they know, yet closer to each other than they care to admit, they fight like relatives fight, and mostly for the same reasons: control, position, love, and to maintain their individual identities.

Handling Sadistic Homophobes

Gays and lesbians should avoid getting into sadomasochistic relation-ships with homophobes. In those cases where gays and lesbians bear some of the blame for their victimization, they should stop gratuitously provoking sadists to attack and tempting masochists to beat them over their heads with their bloody bodies.

Pleading with sadists for respect, or mercy, or "playing dead" when at-tacked can help in an emergency, but it does not make a good steady diet, and it can have the reverse effect. Sadists see the pleading/abdica-tion as a sign of weakness, a wound to rub salt in. Being strong and in-vulnerable is a better way to discourage sadists from attacking, or to handle sadistic attacks already under way.

DISSOCIATIVE PERSONALITY
DISORDER HOMOPHOBES

Dissociative homophobes are like two people in one, and in two ways.

1. They are like two people in one in their ambivalent attitude toward gays and lesbians. One part of them sees some gays and lesbians as all good, while the other part sees most gays and lesbians as all bad. As a re-sult, they keep a few good gays and lesbians around as friends and col-

leagues. These they carefully nourish, and distinguish from the bad gays and lesbians they avoid as enemies.

> At one hospital's department of psychiatry, two openly gay psychiatrists were permitted to function "as equals," but only in the selected fields of AIDS-related emotional disorders and drug addiction. They were not suffered gladly in the special province, really in the money-making field, of private practice, which, knowingly at least, admitted only straights. In effect, they were token gays the homophobes could use to make themselves look tolerant and liberal. These gays were permitted to shine as long as, as one homophobe put it, they stayed in "their own ring in the circus." Gays who didn't keep their place and ventured out of the assigned ring became the subject of the negative side of the ambivalence. They were thoroughly mistreated and completely rejected.

Some dissociative homophobes divide gays and lesbians into those who are out and those who are in the closet. While many dislike gays and lesbians who are out of the closet, some actually prefer them. They feel that gays and lesbians in the closet are an unknown quantity, and so an unseen threat. Gays and lesbians who are out of the closet can at least be watched and controlled.

2. They are like two people in one in how they conveniently forget, or actually deny, what they know about themselves so that they can gay bash with abandon. For example, Jonathan Rabinovitz (1995) in his article "Hartford Veterans Agency Nominee Assailed for Remarks" describes how Eugene A. Migliaro, a Hartford Veterans Agency Nominee, some years ago said of a gay lawmaker who "rose to ask a question. . . . 'I hope he doesn't blow me a kiss.'" (p. 24). A few of my patients who saw Migliaro's picture in the paper wondered if he forget to look in the mirror before he assumed the world was out to kiss and otherwise seduce him. Was he physically attractive enough to warrant being sexually approached by strangers? Or, as my patients asked, did, as happens with most bigots, his attachment to the real world lessen to the extent that his attachment to his emotional life increased?

13

Personality Disorder Homophobes—II: Hysterical (Histrionic) Personality Disorder Homophobes

Hysterical (histrionic) homophobes are competitive individuals, rivals in what they view as the ongoing contest of life, in which there can only be one winner. They hate gays and lesbians because they envy them, and they envy them because they think they have it all. They envy them for everything from their hard bodies developed in the gym to their freedom from family responsibility. They deal with their envy by putting them down. They criticize them for what they perceive to be their flaws, although these supposed flaws are either minor, or are virtues misperceived as flaws. For example, one homophobe was in effect demeaning gays and lesbians for their artistic ability when he said that "they made good shower curtain designers but never satisfactory CEOs," and for their ability to dance when he said that "they have a terrific sense of rhythm, but no head for business." The goal of hysterical homophobes is to be, figuratively speaking, the chef, while keeping the homosexual down in the position of the sous chef. And their inspiration is the model room in model homes, where decorators deliberately keep the furniture small, so that they can make the rooms themselves look larger. Such homophobes like being homophobic and resist change, because their homophobia provides them with a refuge from feeling as inferior as they do. For their purposes gays and lesbians make the perfect scapegoats. They are at once the ideal foil and victim—like Achilles, a worthy competitor, but one with a desirably fatal flaw.

Herman Melville (1851/1981) might have been describing a hysterical homophobic patient of mine when he said, "When a person placed in command over his fellow-men finds one of them to be very significantly his superior in general pride of manhood, straightway against that man he conceives an unconquerable dislike and bitterness; and if he have a chance he will pull down and pulverize that subaltern's tower, and make a little heap of dust of it" (p. 232). Victor Hugo (1862/1982) writing in *Les Miserables* might have had the same patient in mind when he said that "genius invites hostility" (p. 995). And Raymond Hernandez (1995) could also have had him in mind when in his article "Youths on Racial Slurs: They're Only Words" he says that cruelty is "hardly always motivated by bigotry alone, and can often mask larger insecurities, frustrations, petty rivalries, hostilities and other emotions that are a part of coming of age" and part of the process of "jockey[ing] to fit in among . . . peers" (p. B2).

My homophobic patient was a flag-waving jingoist who proclaimed "being gay is un-American." He waved the American flag less because he wanted to wave the flag and more because he needed to "erect the flag pole." He waved the flag and raised the flagpole for the same reason he tattooed his arm with a logo that read "Mary," and for the same reason that he regularly wore his favorite T-shirt, the one that proclaimed he was a participant in "Coed-naked basketball." He was not affirming his fidelity to the United States. He was instead reaffirming his masculinity to himself.

This homophobe accepted certain gays and lesbians—the ones he could view as big nobodies because he could see them as in some way inferior to himself. But he hated proud, successful gays and lesbians, especially the ones who came out as if they were not ashamed of being what they were. It followed that he mostly hated gays and lesbians not for what they did wrong, as he claimed, but for what they did right. For example, for many people an intellectual is not a bad thing to be. But for him gays who were intellectuals were elitists, by which he meant inferiors who did not do the real work of the world, like hunting for game or foraging for grain. Gays and lesbians like this he turned on and insulted. And when that did not have the desired effect, he pulled back from them in obvious horror, then shunned them completely.

His counterpart, a homophobic woman, was an antifeminist who hated being a woman and really wanted to be a man. She disliked lesbians because in her eyes they were "like men, and, like men, better equipped than I am to compete in this world, a world where all the important and successful people are men."

DEVELOPMENTAL FACTORS

For many hysterical homophobes gay bashing is the continuation of an old sibling rivalry, so that the homosexual today is a stand-in for a brother or sister that the homophobe envied in the past. Such homophobes compete with gays and lesbians now for the same reasons that they competed with their brothers or sisters long ago—to be #1 among siblings, both to get all the available parental love and to impress parents as to how they, and they alone, make desirable oedipal suitors. Consequently in their homophobic role hysterics are like gladiators in combat. Their homophobia is meant both to kill off the opposition and to impress the spectators.

> A homophobe had a homosexual brother, a successful physician, not someone he felt he could ever match or surpass. For him all male homosexuals were brother substitutes, particularly satisfying as transference competition because "being already one down they were easy to pick on." The recurrent theme of this man's life was: the world is not a place where I lose out to a brother who is more effective than I am. Rather it is a place full of crippled siblings, "sisters" whom, unlike brothers, I can lick with one hand tied behind me.

> I know of one homophobic psychoanalyst whose homophobic analytic theories were in part a way to put down a gay brother whose success he could not readily tolerate. He could not readily tolerate any other successful rivals either. Once after a man he formerly liked built a house bigger than his, he first put such a large new wing on his old house that his friends said he had "not one but two houses." Then he dropped the relationship completely to avenge himself on this man for having beaten him "in the house competition."

DYNAMIC FACTORS

Castration Anxiety

Male hysterical homophobes are often homophobic because they are uncertain of their masculinity. They may actually have a small penis. Or they may think they do though they do not. In either case they view themselves as having what some call "mouse meat"—that is, an organ that is small or shrunken, in fantasy considered to lie somewhere on the continuum between men's and women's genitals. Male gays threaten these homophobes because they see them as winners who have more between their legs than they do. (They also threaten them because they see them as losers, castrated individuals who, because they act like "women" with other men, realize the homophobe's worst fears of being castrated themselves.) Lesbians threaten them for the same reason, once removed. For even though they are still women they act, as one homophobe put it, like they "have a bigger one than I do though in fact what they actually are brings up my worst nightmare—of being someone with nothing at all in between my legs."

Gay men threatened a homophobe by inciting a high level of castration anxiety in him because he thought that "if they have sex with other men it can only be to reassure themselves that castration cannot happen." Then he reasoned, in effect, "if they fear castration, then it must be something to be feared." Gay men having anal sex were particularly threatening to him because they acted "as if it were not there." Lesbians using dildoes were equally threatening because they were trying to replace something, and if they were trying to replace something, "that clearly meant that that something could be lost."

A patient, a graphic artist, suffered from castration anxiety ever since, as a child, he read, on the sly, in one of his father's psychiatric texts, a chapter describing koro, which is, according to Armando R. Favazza (1985), the delusional "sensation that one's penis is shrinking and receding into one's belly . . . [associated with] a fear of death once the penis has sunk into the abdomen" (p. 256). Old enough to understand castration, but not old enough to understand delusion, he took the chapter literally, and swore on the spot, "This will never happen to me." Later in life this complex when reactivated took the form of a need to give up his graphic art because he viewed being an artist as being a sissy, and being a sissy as being a homosexual, which he defined as "someone who used to be a man, but, in the blink of an eye, becomes a woman."

As a partial (emotional) solution he purchased a device which he put in front of his car to hold his fishing rods. These he proudly displayed in all their phallic glory as he plowed through traffic, not merely to get somewhere, but also to demonstrate "his equipment." As one gay man said of him, "Is he driving, and going fishing, or is he showing me his?"

The composer Charles Ives was a notorious homophobe whose homophobia might have appeared in problems he had later in life writing music, which he possibly gave up doing because, as he saw it, it was too effeminate a profession to pursue. According to Stuart Feder (1992), Ives feared (and wrote what he called masculine music to avoid) hiding behind "silk skirts" (p. 337). Ives supposedly asked, referring to the preference for easy listening he saw as a current problem, "Is the Angle (sic)-Saxon going 'Pussy?'" And he proclaimed that his music was "'greater, less emasculated than any of the so-called great masters! [like Wagner and Mozart!]'" (p. 337).

BEHAVIORAL CHARACTERISTICS

Mythmaking

Hysterical homophobes are mythmakers. They are autosuggestible enough to create their own homophobic myths, impressionable enough to believe the myths others create, interpersonally related enough to pass these myths on to and to stampede with others in a kind of gang hysteria, and motivated enough (because they want to see gays and lesbians as the devil so that they can be the angels) to do all of these things simultaneously.

> Lisa Bannon (1995) in her article "How a Rumor Spread About Subliminal Sex in Disney's 'Aladdin'" gives as an example of what I call group hysteria the persistent allegations that Procter and Gamble's moon-and-stars logo symbolizes devil worship. In group hysteria of this sort many people simultaneously see things that are not there. In a typical sequence, first one individual gets "worked up," then eggs others on to become involved, and a general melee ensues. In one of Bannon's cases, an inciter concluded, in a statement that is a paradigm for homophobia, that "it may be Disney . . . but it still smells 'pervert' to me" (p. A8).

> Thomas Gilovich (1991) sheds light on the process of homophobic mythmaking as hysterical hallucination when in another context he quotes the following slip of the tongue by the psychologist Thane Pittman: "I'll see it when I believe it" (p. 49).

Theatrical Overdramatization/ The Tendency to Exaggerate Excessively

One of the favorite beliefs, really sources of emotional panic, of hysterical homophobes is that if you give gays and lesbians a finger they will take a hand, and who knows where it will all end. For example, Cal Thomas (1996) (also apparently unable to distinguish homosexuality from pedophilia) creates the appearance of a crisis about gay marriage as follows: "if 'gay marriage' can be mandated as having equal moral status with marriage between a man and a woman, what's next? On what basis do we . . . prevent adult-child 'marriage'? Preposterous? Not any more" (p. A15).

Name Calling

The names hysterical homophobes call gays and lesbians are not chosen at random. Instead they reflect their envy for gays and lesbians, envy presented in the guise of sour grapes. The envy may appear in the actual name and/or in the act of name-calling. Because envy is the reason for the names, at least some of them, though consciously meant as criticisms, on closer examination sound instead like compliments or even rave reviews. What, for example, is really wrong with being an elitist intellectual?

Hysterical homophobes call gays and lesbians the following names, among others, all of which reveal how much they secretly want to have what they have:

1. *Elitist* (elitist intellectual):

Supreme Court Justice Antonin Scalia in an opinion excerpted from the "Court's Decision on Colorado's Provision for Homosexuals" (*New York Times*, May 21, 1996) hurled the epithet "elitist" to criticize not only gays and lesbians but also those who support them. He said that "this Court has no business imposing upon all Americans the resolution favored by the elite class . . . pronouncing that 'animosity' toward homosexuality, ante, is evil" (p. A21). (I am quoting, not attempting to diagnose, the justice.)

Elitist intellectuals are presumably men who like the theatre and the ballet, as distinct from real men who, if they go to these things at all, do so only because their wives push them to go, and then have the sense to proclaim their dislike throughout, either by vocally protesting, or by silently complaining—by yawning and by falling asleep, so that every one can see, "I am bored." (One gay still complains, whenever given the opportunity, that he was blackballed from a fraternity in the 1950s simply because the admissions committee discovered that he attended the opening night performance of Frank Loesser's musical comedy *Guys and Dolls.*)

In my experience the term "elitist" is favored by homophobes who need to demean bright people because they are themselves dull. Sometimes they feel being bright is the equivalent of being unfaithful to their pedestrian, often lower-middle-class, parents. Such individuals are typically identified with blue-collar workers and put semiprofessional and professional types down for what is the equivalent of "literary pretensions." They conclude that working with their hands is superior to working with their mind because they view manual labor as masculine and intellectual labor as feminine. [As we will see in chapter 18 on how to handle homophobes, it does not help to tell Justice Scalia, or others like him, that gays are good because Leonardo da Vinci was gay. First it does not address Scalia's basic premise, which is that gays and lesbians are "a priori and always evil" (*New York Times*, 5/21/96, p. A21). Second it confirms their fantasies that, as one gay man put it, "all gays doodle, invent gadgets, and paint smiles instead of doing the salt of the earth work that has an immediate and lasting benefit for society." And third it hits home, reminding them of what they are not, which only makes them even more anxious about what they are, and causes them to become even more homophobic than they were before.]

Instead of seeing his own capabilities as being different from, but just as valuable as, those of his gay and lesbian neighbors in the South Side of Boston, a straight man, who had lived in the neighborhood all his life, from the time before it was gentrified, saw his abilities as inferior to theirs. He was good with his hands, and became an able carpenter. They were good with their minds, and became able doctors, lawyers, and business-men. But the suspicion lurked throughout that they had what he did not have, and he was less of a man on that account.

There are, he thought, two kinds of men in this world—superior men who are straight, and inferior men who are gay. The superior men did the real work of the world, and made it go around. They farmed the land, drove the trucks that delivered the milk, and so on. The inferior men did the unnecessary work of the world, and were basically peripheral to and not needed for its progress and survival. These were the elitist intellectuals like his neighbors, people who sat on their butts all day long playing mind games, or the piano.

He concluded defensively that though gays and lesbians had better homes and bodies, more money, and dressed in a more sophisticated way than he did, he was the better person, for he belonged to the class of supe-rior men the world could not do without: simple, honest, direct, uncom-plicated, hard-working people who provided mankind with basic services, however plain, unglamorous, and underpaid. While he went to bed early to get up fresh to do God's work each morning, they arose shortly before midnight for a kind of Walpurgisnacht, to do Satan's bidding. Gays, as he concluded, were expendable, for they belonged to the realm of the effete, a place where bloodless sissies made designer shower curtains and built beautiful but underoccupied homes in trendy resorts. As he put it one day, "these people have 10 bathrooms apiece, though as near as I can deter-mine, they each have only one asshole."

He maintained his me-versus-you-I-am-the-better-person view of life, in spite of its inaccuracies, because it improved his self-esteem. For it al-lowed him to see himself as potent, effective, lovable, and chosen by God, in comparison to gays and lesbians, who, as he saw it, were impotent, inef-fective, and despicable, for they were not chosen by God, but sent by the devil.

2. *Dinks:* The term "dinks" (double income no kids) is really a way to say "You have more than I do," as well as a way to criticize gays and les-bians for being acquisitive (which is the rough equivalent of criticizing Jews for being money-grabbing and of criticizing immigrants for coming

over to go on the dole). Dinks particularly disturb unsuccessful (often blue-collar) homophobes, as well as successful homophobes from blue-collar families who are upwardly socially mobile but feel guilty about being a traitor to their families of origin. (This seems to be a particular problem for newly successful politicians of humble origins whose being successful makes them feel like traitors to the lower-middle-class families they came from.)

> One blue-collar homophobe, whom his gay victims called a "member of the unintelligentsia," mainly complained about gays as piss-elegant people whose only goal in life was to be as much unlike their peasant parents as possible. He frequently cited as an example the gay man who was "excessively enamored of meeting men who wore beautiful clothes at elegant men's bars, and spoke of being in love with a man just because he wore an overcoat with a velvet collar and ate at gourmet restaurants." "Pathetic," he concluded, "if all he wants out of life is to distinguish himself from his low-rent parents." And he condemned another gay man for being able to do no better than hang out at a leather bar down the block to meet handsome strangers costumed in chaps (a kind of leather pants), people he falls in love with just because they are not the home-spun working stiffs he finds next to him on the assembly line. "What a waste," he concluded, "spending your whole life trying to bury your past, and to not go home again."

3. *Superficial:* One homophobe branded gays as wastrels because "they all live their lives in the pages of decorator magazines." He had a small point—that there is more to life than home furnishing. But this was hardly a homosexual problem. For as many straights develop an identity around trivial matters and favor substitute over real gratifications as do gays.

4. *Queens and sissies:* Homophobes who feel castrated by gays' considerable accomplishments feminize gay men to make them, in their eyes, less accomplished. They call them queens to be able to view their own genitals as "king size." They also want gays to be queens to their kings for that way they can dominate gays, much as some men like to and try to dominate women.

5. *Fags:* The term "fags" is one of those f-words whose sound seems to count for as much as its meaning. As for the meaning itself, the term "fagged" (i.e., spent) comes to mind. Fag is a demeaning term meant to conjure up the image of limp-wristed ineffective "nerds" or "creeps." (Webster's disagrees with those who say that the term fag comes from faggot, the bundle of sticks used to burn heretics. Webster's says that the origin of the term is unknown.)

6. *Sick:* Homophobes call gays and lesbians sick to reassure themselves that they are comparatively well, which they define as sane, effec-

tive, and middle-of-the road. (The medical model of homophobia is discussed at length in chapter 3.)

7. *Swish/butch:* Straights deliberately persist in the error that all gays are feminine and all lesbians are masculine to enhance their own masculine or feminine image by comparison. They are also reassuring themselves with fantasies of gays and lesbians as not merely emotionally crippled but also as physically deformed. These fantasies reassure male homophobes who feel their penises are too small, that theirs are at least as big as someone else's, and comfort them with the restitutive idea that, as one put it, "if a woman can have a penis too then having one is not, after all, such a big deal."

8. *Queers:* Hysterical homophobic straights call gays queer to isolate them from the mainstream and so to make them less the competition.

9. *Fruits:* Fruits are a symbol of femininity (one reason why "real men" eat neither fruits nor vegetables).

10. *Child molesters:* Hysterical straights call gays child molesters in part because it is one of the worst things they can think of to call them. They also feel vulnerable in the homosexual presence, as if they are themselves unprotected children, in danger of being abused, or raped.

The following case illustrates how complex are the ideas that are forged into a simple overdetermined name-calling complaint about gays—in this case the complaint that "all gays scream like a bunch of banshees."

A homophobe complained incessantly during his therapy sessions that he could not eat out in New York because he always sat next to "some queer who is screaming so loud that I cannot hear myself think, or concentrate on my meal."

When asked to illustrate one such incident, he described how he sat across the aisle one night from a gay man who was "haranguing" his companion about the details of a *Sound of Music* Tour he took more than a generation ago, in the 1960s. The patient guessed that the man toured a place the Trapp family had lived in, or the set of the movie that was made about their lives.

As the patient related, "the man spoke loudly, and too quickly to leave room for his companion to even make a comment. He regularly dropped the name of Julie Andrews, a star of the movie, as if he were gaining by a fantasied association with her. He was in effect bragging that he knew someone who was rich and famous, while calling himself 'a big unemployed nobody.' And he described, in what was excessive detail, an inconvenience he underwent during the tour, saying, 'They left me at the hotel with all my baggage, and, imagine this, the place had been closed for months.' This man seemed to be taking more delight in what went wrong than in what went right with the trip."

This innocuous incident bothered the patient well beyond what it should have, clearly because it hit a nerve.

When I analyzed what "nerve" the incident hit—that is, what conflicts it aroused—I learned that the following was really what upset my patient:

1. That the gay man wanted to be #1, even if only in a small way. He wanted to tear the other patrons' attention away from what they were doing, and who they were doing it with, and get them to pay attention to him. The evidence for this was his emoting so loudly in the restaurant that everyone could hear, forcing them to pay attention to him. This aroused the patient's own oedipal fears of displacing his father in his mother's affections, and his sibling rivalry and with it all his later fears of competing successfully with rivals, because that meant destroying them. (As the patient said, "I am the sort of person who thrives when surrounded by people I can perceive as failures. For I believe that in any endeavor there is only room for one, and if they are already failures I can get ahead without having to kill them off myself.")

The patient's associations next ran to how as a child he observed the primal scene and reacted to it with mixed feelings. On the one hand he felt left out and wanted to be included. The gay man's wanting to take over, to be #1, to be the center of attention and the object of applause in the restaurant, a look-at-me cry, a plea to be noticed, reminded him of his own wanting desperately to join in the primal scene activities. On the other hand he wanted to be left out too, so that he did not have to contend with his taboo incestuous feelings. The gay man's playing to a restaurant full of strangers reminded him that he himself did not want to get close to his real family, but wanted to make a family out of people he hardly knew, because then there would be no chance of doing anything incestuous.

2. That the gay man seemed to be getting sadistic pleasure from pinning his companion to the wall (and he added, "pinning the rest of us to the wall too"). This revived the patient's successophobia, due to his unconscious conviction that an association existed between accomplishing—"being heard"—and hurting others. He felt guilty, for his sadism was incompatible with his self-image, which was of a nice, kind person.

3. That the gay man was brashly exposing himself, "talking so loudly we could dance to it." My patient was a shy man unable to express himself to others, one reason why he hated people who acted what he called "shamelessly." The gay man's expressing his need to be special also threatened the patient, for the patient was a person who dealt with his own fear of self-expression by fading into the woodwork, never standing out, to assure himself that he would never be rejected, and so would always belong, if only in a limited way.

4. That the gay man could take so much delight in being inconvenienced, humiliated, and abandoned. This reminded the patient of his own troublesome need to be abused, because he was too guilty to enjoy his own life.

5. That the gay man took such obvious pleasure in his brushes with danger, even to the point that he called survival under harsh circumstances "fun." This reminded the patient of his own foolish need to tempt fate to prove he was invulnerable.

6. That the gay man was bragging about his exploits, however modest. Said my patient, "He is going places and I am staying at home." Even though he would not have wanted to go on the tour, he felt he was stuck in the United States with his wife and kids, and missing out on other, equivalent, tours.

7. That the gay man was touring and observing meant that he was not doing, but was appreciating, and confusing being a great appreciator with being a great accomplisher. The gay man's getting satisfaction not from what he did but from associations with others who had done things reminded the patient that his own accomplishments had been modest, and symbolic.

8. That the gay man had Julie Andrews as his hero not, say, James Bond, meant that the gay man did not really want to be a real, and his own, man. This reminded the patient of how his own father did not want him to be his own man, but instead treated him as an extension of the father—and only wanted him to do what the father could never do in his own life.

9. That the gay man was unemployed. This suggested a kind of laziness which suggested passivity, which made the straight man think of his own "feminine" tendency to hold himself back and remain in the shadows.

10. That the gay man was dwelling on the past. This stirred up the patient's own unacceptable nostalgia—that is, his need to dwell obsessively on the good old days because he felt that nothing now or in the future could be as great as what once was, when his parents were alive, and the world was a simpler place, without so many queers and foreigners about, and so much open sex and aggression, everywhere you turned.

14

Personality Disorder Homophobes—III: Passive-Aggressive Personality Disorder Homophobes

The homohatred in passive-aggressive homophobia is not the hostility of the homophobic patient who tried to bomb a woman's college because she believed that the women there programmed the computers to send out rays beamed at and meant to penetrate her vagina. Nor is it the hostility of homophobes who vocally accuse all gays of trying to recruit and seduce all straights in places ranging from the shower to the nursery room. It is, superficially at least, a more polite hostility than that. We do not see physical gay bashing. We do not hear crude jokes about or rude accusations hurled at gays and lesbians. We hear only indirect and refined attacks, indelicate points made delicately. For example, we hear pseudorational concerns such as the worry that gays and lesbians will tear the moral fabric of the nation apart by getting married and adopting children. Or we see gays and lesbians ignored in a courteous and subtle manner, as when a cooperative apartment building changed the locks on its front doors, simply forgetting to contact two gay men who were temporarily out of town, so that they came back from their trip to find themselves locked out—baggage, pets, and all. In short, passive-aggressives install glass ceilings meant to keep gays and lesbians from rising up too far. But because the ceiling is glass, they are able, when gays and lesbians protest, to point up and say, "But you see, there is nothing there."

This "rational," subtle, and indirect hostility is actually the most dangerous and destructive kind, because it is the most difficult kind to identify. Not being able to identify hostility has at least two adverse consequences. First gays and lesbians are left feeling something is wrong, but not knowing what. They then naturally suspect that something is wrong with them—that is, they blame themselves. For example, they think that if they were better people then others would not treat them so shabbily. One felt "if I were a better scholar then I would not have been denied tenure," and another felt "if I were a better doctor then I would get more referrals." These gays and lesbians get the impression that they are paranoid for thinking they are being abused, imagining people are hostile to them when they are not. Then they conclude that they are too sensitive and worry too much about what other people think. And second, when finally gays and lesbians see through it all, they get twice as angry as before, because they feel like fools for accepting the attack without having even bothered to defend themselves, and feel helpless because, having failed to realize what hit them until it is too late, now they cannot protest, repair the damage, or find a way to get revenge.

Being passive-aggressive makes it easier for homophobes to rationalize and deny their homophobia, which they do in part to reduce their guilt about being homophobic, and in part to keep their victims in the relationship, to keep it going so that they can attack them again and again. They rationalize their homophobia in a number of ways: in sociological terms, as when they wonder if gays and lesbians are a threat to society; in religious terms, as when they point to the Bible's justification of homophobia; or professionally, as making "just good business sense to be prejudiced toward and discriminate against gays and lesbians."

> A boss will not fire gays and lesbians. But he will not advance them either. He denies it is because he dislikes homosexuals and because they are not up to doing the job. He says it is because others dislike them and that makes for corporate problems he would rather avoid.

> A psychoanalyst says it is okay to be a plain-vanilla psychiatrist but stereotypes gays and lesbians as too brittle emotionally as a group to be accepted into, really "ordained into," her psychoanalytic institute. She hopes gays and lesbians will not take this personally or as a criticism but see it for what it is, a purely scientific assessment of reality, based on how being homosexual is bound to negatively affect their work with patients.

Or passive-aggressive homophobes say they treat everyone, not just gays and lesbians, badly. Here their hook is, "But I do it to everybody." Gays and lesbians are supposed to tolerate abuse because homophobes abuse straights too. A boss yells at everybody, not just gays and lesbians. The psychoanalytic institute rejects 90 percent of all applicants, straights

as well as gays. Or they rationalize their homophobia as their way of being helpful:

> A scientist swore that she advanced the theory that homosexuality was ge-
> netically determined not to put gays and lesbians down but to do gays and
> lesbians a favor. She insisted that in saying "it is genetic" she meant that "it
> is not something you can help, or be held accountable for." She said she
> was trying to be reassuring and supportive by taking the responsibility for
> being homosexual off the homosexual's shoulders. But, on another level,
> she was really being hurtful, for she was saying, "No one would actually
> *choose* to be a homosexual—it would have to be a birth defect."

Often they simply deny they are bigots. This makes their attack even
more effective, for several reasons. As previously mentioned, by denying
the attack they convince the victim that it is not the attack but the victim's interpretation of the situation that is the problem. Their victims
then blame themselves for being hypersensitive. Also it is as difficult to
counterattack homophobes who say, "You hurt me by accusing me of
being a homophobe" as it is to attack an animal who has rolled over on
its back and exposed its sensitive underbelly.

Their denial often takes the form of a tolerant facade where they
speak of themselves as fair-minded, which they can be, but only when it
does not count for much. Sometimes they do this as part of the above-
mentioned plan to blame the victim for overreacting. At other times they
protest too much deliberately, knowing that that is an effective way to
make the opposite point.

Deniers like to attribute their hostility to others. They attribute their
hostile anti-gay myths to someone else by saying, "I have heard that all
homosexual soldiers are unreliable," or "the Bible tells us that . . ."

> A straight man informs a gay writer that his grandmother always used to
> ask, "Is writing really a way to make a living?" thereby completely invali-
> dating the writer's sincere efforts. Instead of taking responsibility for the
> invalidation, he attributes it to his grandmother's ancient wisdom, al-
> though, as the gay man later said, "this may have been on the level of the
> ancient wisdom that tells us that the earth is flat."

Some homophobes deny their homophobia by being homophobes
only intermittently. In effect they lead double lives. They are like a seed
on the desert that blooms only when after a period of waiting a drop of
water touches it. They do not come alive except under certain rather
specific conditions. As Dr. Jekylls during the day they go about their
business unrecognized, unrecognizable, and manifestly nonhomophobic. But at night, when the talk show host gives them the nudge they

need, they thrive and grow into Mr. Hyde. By morning they have returned to their "resting" state, and resumed their familiar, hidden, identity, the one in which they again proclaim, "I am not a homophobe."

Homophobes also deny they are homophobic by displacing their criticisms from the gays' and lesbians' sexual onto their nonsexual behavior, criticizing them not for what they do in bed but for what they do in their daily lives.

A woman in mock horror complained to a gay man that she had let loose the controls on her diet one day and consumed two, rather than the allowed one, pretzel sticks. The gay man replied, in equally mock horror, "What a terrible thing to have done to yourself." Unexpectedly she spit back, a week later, "You were yelling at me"—that is, "what a crude thing you said, like the crude person you are." She was really thinking, as someone who knew both of them and overheard the conversation later explained, "How dare a gay person like you, with so many problems of your own, criticize a straight person like me who has few, if any, real problems?" But she said, not "gay," but "loud."

A gay man who did not have a car and had to carry groceries home related during a therapy hour how he left the supermarket with a shopping basket in hand and walked home with it, unaware of what he had done until he reached his destination. When he returned it to the supermarket the manager said, "I don't understand how you could have done such a thing—I ought to have had you arrested for stealing." Then he turned around to a fellow manager and gave her a knowing wink, the gay man thought, as if to say, "What more would you expect from a dintsy queen?" But the manager actually said, behind his back, but in a stage whisper easily overheard, not "gay," but "like most of them, too self-absorbed to pay attention to what he is doing."

Another time the same gay man noted that a supermarket checker was piling up all his groceries in one bag, so he asked for two bags so that he could be balanced as he walked home. She got nasty, he thought really meaning to say, "I don't let people like you tell me what to do, and push me around," a way of proclaiming that "if someone is going to be the servant in this relationship, it's not going to be me, but you, because I'm straight, above you people, and proud of it." But she said instead, "I was going to do that, you didn't have to ask"—that is, not "you are to be condemned for being gay" but "you are to be condemned for being pushy." Of course, as he pointed out to her, he was not a mind reader, so how was he supposed to know what she was going to do before she did it?

In another form of denial, homophobes maintain a superficially loving relationship with one member of a couple but get at this person indirectly by attacking the other member of the couple.

Two gay men, one considerably older than the other, have been married for 15 years. The mother of the younger man could not accept her son's being gay. But she never mentioned that to the son. All she told him was, "I love you and want you to be happy, whatever you do and are." However, she made trouble for the son by abusing his lover. She told the older man that she deeply resented his taking her son away from her. (Early in the relationship she had actually barred the older man from the house, and later tried to convince her son to attend a far-off medical school, just to get him out of town and away from this man.)

When the younger man had to have a serious operation, his mother came to the house to help out and baby sit the pets, freeing up the older man to stay with his lover during the surgery and the recovery period. This nice gesture, however, came at a price. The mother got the older man's ear when the younger man was in surgery, and she proceeded to attack him, in the midst of all his worry. She accused the older man of making her son gay, and of liking him only for his youth (implying that his youth was the only thing going for him, though in fact it was a negative factor for the older man, who actually chose to ignore it in favor of the younger man's other qualities). She embarrassed the man about a previous relationship he had with another young man, the son's former friend, citing this as proof that the older man was robbing the cradle on a regular basis, although it was nothing of the sort, for the older man had simply met her son through the younger man's former best friend, and the latter two were not surprisingly of the same age.

She then picked on the older man for his advanced age, using "the pregnant question" to couch her attack in the form of curiosity, asking him, "Just how old are you anyway?"—too often not the kind of question you ask if you are looking for information, but the kind you ask if you already have the information you need and are simply looking to rub it in. (Her next remark made this clear when she asked the older man, "And how come your face fell?") Next she announced that at first she had rejected the older man because of his age and sexual orientation, but that two years ago she bit the bullet and accepted the relationship: a back-handed compliment that in effect said, "I used to think you were defective, but lately I changed my mind."

(Like some other mothers she believed her status as mother automatically conferred on her the right to accept or reject her children's spouses, and that what she thought mattered, and mattered most. And as a straight and a mother she saw herself as doubly anointed, and in a position to be the one to decide whether or not to accept gays. Like locals criticizing tourists for being outsiders, heterosexuals believe they can criticize homosexuals but not the other way around. This practice reflects a social hierarchy where straights, like locals, are the queens, and gays and lesbians, like tourists, are the drones. In her mind whether she would be accepted or not by the gay man was no more a question that needed asking than a man who named his delicatessen "Imalocal" would think of asking the question, "Do the tourists in town accept me?")

In a final form of denial, homophobes qualify their hostility, which they think makes it okay. A neighbor told a gay man, "You are acting like a lunatic." He commanded her to stop calling him names, at which time she denied she was calling him names by reminding him that she said not "you are a lunatic" but "you act like one."

PROVOKING GAYS AND LESBIANS

Passive-aggressive homophobes actively provoke the very behavior in gays and lesbians that they say they merely condemn passively, so that they can justifiably condemn gays and lesbians actively.

> Once I sat near the booth of a man eating dinner in a mixed, gay/straight, restaurant in Greenwich Village in New York City. The man choose the occasion of the St. Patrick's Day Parade (an occasion on which New York gays and lesbians are particularly sensitive to criticism and exclusion given the ongoing prohibition against their marching as an identified group in the parade) to take his date to this restaurant, and then announce, so that any one within earshot could hear, that he agreed with the powers that be that gays and lesbians should not be allowed to march in the parade. This not unexpectedly caused the gays and lesbians in the restaurant to have, as one loudly put it, a "hissy fit of the get you Mary variety." This in turn seems to have influenced the straight man's impression of how gays and lesbians behave in public, and further justify his wanting to deprive gays and lesbians of their civil rights. This was obvious from his next comments, made in a stage whisper, along the lines of "their behavior shows you why we are intolerant and cannot let gays and lesbians push the envelope of equality too far." He was aware only that he was criticizing gays and lesbians for their behavior. In fact he was provoking them to behave badly so that they could merit his criticism of them, one that was already in place.

Here are some specific ways passive-aggressive homophobes choose to provoke gays and lesbians:

1. They give back-handed compliments. A typical example is "some of my best friends are homosexuals," which really means, "I am so liberal that I would even take a homosexual out to lunch." Another is "you make a great neighbor; you are hardly ever home." Some who say they hold homosexuals to higher standards because they really admire them are in fact saying "you have to be twice the person to make it with an impediment like that."

> In one case a gay man's family did not invite the gay man and his lover to any family events. They denied prejudice, citing seating limitations, finan-

cial constraints, and other convenient excuses. Revealingly the truth outed one day in church when the pastor suggested the equivalent of "today everyone express love to those from whom you previously withheld it." At this time the whole family turned to the gay men to shake their hands—to discharge a debt they most certainly owed.

2. They dispense back-handed criticisms. A typical one is complimenting the straight person as a way to criticize the gay one. The woman who told the gay doctor about how her doctors were wonderful because they had big families was doing this. Many straights promote the myth that lesbians are significantly different from gays in positive ways. For example, they supposedly have closer, more long-lasting relationships, and do not cheat on their lovers. Whether or not that is true, and the jury is most certainly still out about that, it is a roundabout way to criticize not only gay men but all men as well, because it perpetuates such myths as the one that all men are less faithful than women because they are more sexual, and this because they have a to-the-ready sex organ that they can hardly control. (It is rare to "accuse" a woman of the equivalent of "not being able to keep it in your pants.")

Another back-handed criticism is shying away from even mentioning homosexuality. The mother who wrote her now famous letter to Freud about her son's homosexuality could not even mention that her son was a homosexual. She put him down indirectly by implying that being homosexual "is an unmentionable."

3. They undermine.

A mother of a man's lover undermined the relationship by reporting back to his lover all the passing negative comments her son made to her about the lover, although they were not positional statements, but said to blow off steam, and made only in the anger of the moment, and to someone believed to be both sympathetic and discreet. (She also puts the lover down to his face, all the while saying how much she loves him, hoping that her protests to the contrary will keep him from hearing her unloving messages, and divining her real intent.)

A mother of a gay man tells all the relatives that *he* does not want to see *them*. She dissimulates this way because *she* does not want *them* to see *him*. She then plays dumb when he complains that his family is rejecting him.

A government internist wanted to obtain an eye consult for a patient with glaucoma before putting the patient on a certain heart medication, which he feared might, as some systemic medicines do, worsen the glaucoma. A homophobic nurse practitioner told him it was not necessary, would waste time, and delay needed treatment. When he still refused, in spite of her "order," to give the medicine without the consult, she complained that he was incompetent, then went behind his back to his straight colleague, who obliged her by filling the prescription. We can only guess that both the nurse and the colleague shared the fantasy that there was a close relationship between the gay man's medical abilities and his sexual practices—that is, they shared the fantasy that being homosexual meant being defective not only sexually but also intellectually as well. (I have found that this idea is often based on at least one cognitive error—that since sex is active, and intelligence is active, therefore sex = intelligence. Hence we have the idea that evil sexual practices make one intellectually defective—one of the cherished beliefs of homophobes, and little different from another, also cherished, belief of sexophobes, the one found in adolescents and in some of their parents, that "masturbation makes you insane.")

4. They ask "innocent" questions. One homophobe asked, "What do two earrings stand for?" or "Are all gays promiscuous?" or, asked of two lovers, one of whom was considerably older than the other, "What is the relationship between you two—is he your father?"

5. They contemplate nonassertively. Aggressivity is refined intellectually—for example, in those psychoanalytic theories that view being homosexual as the result of a developmental lag (such as an oedipal fixation) or a regression, when that is in effect a way to say "you are backward." Often the intellectually contemplative homophobe claims to be reluctantly drawn to the regrettable but inevitable by an unassailable logic which carried to its ultimate and only conclusion can but lead to the homophobic formulation put forth. We frequently hear pseudolegitimate arguments about what constitutes "equal rights" as compared to what constitutes "rights that are more equal than others," whether affirmative action is justified to repay gays and lesbians for past injustices, or creates new injustices (for straights) instead, and whether antidiscrimination laws make gays and lesbians less unfairly disadvantaged or unfairly advantaged. These debates are not meant to discover truth. They are meant to take the homophobic side in a controversy that can never be resolved satisfactorily either because conflicting rights predictably make for different vested interests, or because reasonable differences of opinion are possible in situations where not enough is known for anyone to have all the answers.

6. They are controlling. Controlling passive-aggressives decide what gays and lesbians should want and do, then criticize them not for being homosexual but for any deviation from the arbitrary standard they set for, really impose on, them. One such homophobe criticized her daughter's lover for not working and supporting her, though she was willing to work and actually trying to find employment—but only at something

creative, not just any lowly work that happened to come her way, like pruning trees for a landscape company. Another without considering their needs and wishes, and their right to wear what their taste dictated, gave two lesbians gifts of clothes that were inappropriately frilly, then complained that they never wore any of her presents.

7. They double bind. Double binders put gays and lesbians in an impossible position, the equivalent of being between a rock and a hard place. One criticized gays and lesbians until the polite ones frowned, the best that they could do under the circumstances without actually getting angry. Then she complained both that they were not smiling and that they were too sensitive for their own good.

8. They express ambivalence. Even the straights who appear to accept gays and lesbians often express such reservations as "of course, not all gays and lesbians are perfect, either."

9. They express envy, which is selective. Homophobic straights tell gays and lesbians they envy them for what they have, without giving consideration to what they do not have. For example, straights say they envy gays' and lesbians' freedom from family responsibility but omit how some gays and lesbians feel they are missing out on the benefits of having children. A prototype is one straight with a 9–5 job who envied some gay and lesbian freelancers their independence, though they, unlike her, were making very little money, did not have a regular paycheck coming in, had no benefits, and lacked the structure of a job and the on-the-job "family" that she had as a full-timer.

10. They ignore gays and lesbians. They treat them as if they are invisible. They give them the cold shoulder. Madhusree Mukerjee in her article "Coming Out in the Sciences" (1995) quotes William C. Matthews as calling this "the chilling reception" (p. 24). I call it the secular equivalent of religious excommunication—a kind of declaration of death where another, though still alive, is proclaimed to be deceased, and treated accordingly.

In a clinic there are two social workers. One wrote a paper on hysteria and is gay. The other did not write anything and is straight. The clinic needs a lecture on hysteria. It chooses the social worker who is straight to give the lecture. At one, all-too-typical, office reception for this clinic, the straights were in little clusters, while the gays and lesbians roamed around these, as if lost in space, unable to break in. [Lesbians are not so much ignored as they are condescended to. For example, according to Mukerjee (1995), Matthews quotes a professor who is a lesbian observing that "male colleagues respect my talents more readily than other women's because they do not think of me as a real woman, so it's not so weird that I can do science" (p. 24).]

A doctor will not specialize in proctology because too many of the clientele are gay and he dislikes "working with people of that sort."

A sister of a man's lover subtly humiliates both her brother and his lover by making dates for occasions then canceling them; by not calling unless she has a problem she wishes to discuss, or unload, or needs something done; and by accepting, but not returning, invitations.

A neighbor refuses to nod back at a gay neighbor's hello, thinking, as the old joke goes (but in this case it is no joke), "I wonder what he meant by that?"

11. They withhold. Passive-aggressives' homophobic friends come late to parties only when gays and lesbians are giving them. Then they typically blame the traffic when their personality problems, not the traffic, are the main reason for their being late, for the traffic was a known factor that they deliberately chose to ignore. Or passive-aggressive bosses keep gays and lesbians but not straights on tenterhooks, saying "I have a bone to pick with you," then make an appointment for "later next week" and refuse to have the planned discussion earlier, and will not state in advance what they have in mind.

Passive-aggressive bosses refuse to promote gays and lesbians on the job.

A homosexual teacher and her lover moved from the small town they were living in back to the big city not only because they were unable to handle having their friendly good-mornings met by stony silence and were refused entry into the block alert program because that was "for families," but also because they discovered that on their jobs they were being evaluated, and kept back, in spite of their superior training, experience, and teaching ability because, while they taught children well, they produced none of their own.

They remain unavailable in time of need.

In a semi-gay resort in the 1970s gays were often beaten to a pulp on the beach by local teenagers. Then the police expressed their own feelings about the matter by "never knowing who did it," though they were the only ones who seemed not to have known. (Though the teenagers' parents were just as guilty for not reining in their teenage sons, every one, including some homophobic gays and lesbians, took the parents' side. One said about the father of one of the teenagers, "Poor man, he has so many problems, he can hardly be expected to also solve those of his sons.")

Homophobes often withhold all support from even their best friends when their friends are attacked. Instead they become suddenly unavailable. They do this both to express a disapproval simmering all along, and because they fear being identified with gays and lesbians, and in turn abused because of the association. As a result, gays and lesbians have friends at work, until they need a friend, when they turn to their friends only to have them turn away. Finding strength from within becomes the order of the day, because it is the only order likely to be filled.

A patient asked a gay doctor for a prescription for valium. She wanted it now, and she did not want to wait on line to register for clinic, though registering was clinic policy. The doctor refused to see her unless she registered because he was told by his superior, "If you treat patients without their registering you are in effect in private practice, and the hospital will not cover you for malpractice." The patient replied by complaining about the doctor's uncaring behavior: "He made me wait, and was rude to me too." In the administrative struggle that ensued, every one took the patient's side, not because the doctor was wrong and she was right, but because withholding support from him was a good way to express a hostility to him already in place.

Homophobes typically withhold respect and recognition from gays and lesbians. A gay psychologist was okay to confide in informally, in the elevator, in the clinic. But when he suggested paying for outside counseling in his private office, the response was, "what, pay for something that is all talk?" This gay man also made a good sounding board, but no one ever had the time to listen to him, because they felt that what he had to say to them was necessarily of no importance. In other workplaces straights willingly act the role of expert consultants to gays and lesbians but are unwilling to consult gays and lesbians as the experts. They advise gays and lesbians but never take their advice in turn, even when they are recognized experts in their field. In my experience, black doctors and other black professionals like money managers often experience and complain of this kind of mistreatment. Even when they are tolerated personally, others freeze them out professionally, by refusing to take them seriously.

12. They are excessively critical. Whenever it is possible to view something in a positive or negative light, passive-aggressives abstract selectively and simply withhold the positive in favor of the all-negative view. For example, in contemplating the social problems gay marriages might cause for straights, they overlook the social benefits gay marriage would confer on gays and lesbians, who might in turn no longer fit negative stereotypes and also be in a better position to benefit "straight" society. Homophobic doctors who treat gays and lesbians whose diagnosis is uncertain tend to give gays and lesbians the more serious of two possi-

ble diagnoses. In one case a psychiatrist called a man's lover paranoid simply because he was very worried about the outcome of his lover's surgery, and had a right to be, because the lover was being operated on at a second-rate hospital.

13. They are more giving with straights than with gays and lesbians. Many homophobes are respectful and selfless with straights. They reserve their disrespect, selfishness, and narcissism for gays and lesbians. One consequence is that the gay or lesbian complains about the homophobe's selfishness to straights, but straights, finding the individual perfectly behaved, wonder if the homosexual is "as paranoid as they say most gays and lesbians are."

> At one place of business everyone who lost a parent got flowers—but not one gay man. When his mother died only one person gave him anything— a card. Of course they asked him for funds when they wanted flower money for others who had suffered similar losses.

> A book author is happy to accept a gay editor's editing her book, but will not acknowledge his work in the book itself because she does not want to be associated with gays or lesbians.

> A literary agent held writers she suspected were gay or lesbian to a different standard from the one she used for straights. If she deigned to look at gays' and lesbians' productions at all, she usually merely peeked at them without reading them—and this only if they sent them along accompanied by what she called her convenient waste paper basket (the SASE) she could use to "throw them away," in the likely event they would clutter up her desk, occupy valuable time, drain precious energy, and prove offensive to, and possibly even "contaminate," her.

> One clinic gave straight men things it refused gays and lesbians, holding them to a different standard. In their clinic a straight man was given time off to attend professional meetings that were little more than political jam sessions. But his colleague, a gay man, was not given time off to interview scientists for a paper he was writing for a professional journal, on the spurious grounds that "the rules are that you get time off for meetings, but not for research."

PROVOKING OTHERS TO ACT
OUT FOR THE HOMOPHOBE

Passive-aggressive homophobes get others to act out for them. At work, as in their personal lives, homophobes disavow responsibility for their homophobia and the violent fantasies often associated with it by getting others to act homophobic, and violent, for them. They discriminate against gays and lesbians or hamper their development not directly, by putting gays and lesbians down, but indirectly, by setting them up—with other homophobes.

> A nurse encouraged whatever patients she could approach before anyone else got to them to refuse to see the gay doctor and to pick the straight one. For his part the straight doctor not only did nothing to discourage what was in essence an unethical practice but also used her as a tool to undermine the gay doctor both professionally and personally. For he appreciated the votes of confidence, needed the business, and wanted to shatter the competition.

> Socarides' detractors suggest not only that he condones anti-gay violence but also that he might unconsciously be provoking it. According to Ralph Roughton (1995) Socarides, without necessarily intending to do so, condones antihomosexual violence by "laying part of the blame" for "the murder of a gay man allegedly by the straight man to whom he revealed his secret infatuation during the taping of a television talk show [onto] the gay rights movement [which he sees] as a threat to the natural order. In using such phrases as 'turn the world upside down,' 'playing with the Promethean forces of sexual identity' and 'truly tempting social and personal disaster' regarding this apparently homophobic murder, Dr. Socarides seems to be calling the gay rights movement the aggressor. Thus he comes very close to blaming the victim, which is very close to condoning the violence [and provoking further violence]" (p. 14).

Parents often incite their children to act out for them to avoid guilt or criminal charges falling on the parents. The next-door neighbor's child kicks in a gay's fence for his father, egged on by his father, who can then avoid guilt and prosecution by saying, "I do not have that much control over my kids." Proselytizing homophobes pass on their homophobia to friends and family, particularly to their children, not only because they want everyone to agree with, not challenge, them, but also because they think "my children are my disciples; they can go forth and do my dirty work for me."

MASOCHISTIC TRIUMPHS

Passive-aggressive homophobes suffer masochistically to hurt gays and lesbians. They suffer to "send the bastards a message." In effect they are beating gays and lesbians over their heads with their bloody bodies. Anti-gay small towns that advertise themselves as family-oriented to discourage gays and lesbians from coming there are willing to go broke just to tell the world how much satisfaction they get from doing the right thing, even though they have little more to show for their efforts than the empty stores and other similar trophies the world awards for pyrrhic victories. In effect they do not mind killing Oscar Wilde to tell the world they hate gay men, even though that means they never get to see or hear the beautiful things he could have written, had they let him live.

Masochists often express anger at gays and lesbians by turning the anger inward in the form of disappointment. An example is one homophobe's public attack on gays and lesbians for making her suffer by ruining the family town she thought she was going to live in when she first moved there. We are all familiar with the mother who discovers her son or daughter is homosexual, then proclaims, perhaps in a letter to an advice columnist, that "while I am heartbroken, I will give my child my undying support." At first we feel, "I understand and admire any parent who does not reject the child when he or she discovers the child is homosexual." But next we feel, and we should, "Heartbroken? It is not as if the child has just been branded as a criminal." Or is it?

Masochistic passive-aggressive homophobes like this also express concern in place of anger. They do not accuse gays of being child abusers. Instead they worry that their children might be in danger of abuse from gays. They do not express overt death wishes toward gays and lesbians. Instead they worry about gays' and lesbians' physical health in the face of the tragic epidemic of AIDS.

Pseudomasochists accept or provoke attack as part of a plan to counterattack. Some homophobes take anti-gay stands on purpose, like a stand against gay marriages, because they know that the homosexual community (electorate) will unite, seal over, and attack them, and now they can be the one who is wronged, get the sympathy vote, and build a power base from there, using for a stepping stone gays and lesbians as the common enemy.

PASSIVE-AGGRESSION IN
WOMEN AS COMPARED TO MEN

Mukerjee (1995), referring to a poll conducted by Matthews, suggests that "women are better disposed toward homosexuals than are men" (p. 24). However, in my personal experience women tend not to be less homophobic than men, just more passive-aggressive about it. A possible explanation for this, at least one that pertains to some of the women I have treated (while all generalities are dangerous, nevertheless some do contain shreds of truth), is that women unlike men tend not to abuse gays and lesbians as part of their plan to cleanse themselves of their own forbidden homosexuality. So when they do disapprove of gays and lesbians, it is without the personal involvement and rancor that derives from projection. Because women are less emotionally involved when they put homosexuals down, their criticism of gays and lesbians is less trenchant than the criticism that comes from men. So they can put homosexuals down, if they choose to do so, in a way that is more carefully crafted than otherwise, and often so much so that it cannot be immediately, or even ultimately, traced back to an antihomosexual bias.

HANDLING PASSIVE-AGGRESSIVES

Passive-aggressive homophobes express the most defensive hostility when they are threatened because they sense gays and lesbians are getting too close. For this reason it is always a good idea for gays and lesbians to maintain their distance and not try to get passive-aggressives to warm up to them. Also, like all sadists, passive-aggressive homophobes are inspired by first blood. They either passively wait for it to appear on its own, or they draw the first drop actively. For this reason, passive-aggressive homophobes are best handled not by meek submission, with wounds seeping, but by taking a strong, fully functional, put-up-with-nothing stance.

Gays and lesbians should not "save it up and blow up," but deal, as best they can, with any interpersonal friction directly when it first appears. They should counter passive-aggressive homophobes regularly, pleasantly but firmly, and dispassionately. They should never masochistically put their tails between their legs and run. They can move from a small town to San Francisco if they like the city, and want to be with their own kind, but they should not move as a retreat, going to a faraway place just to get away from homophobes, and to lick their wounds.

When bigots are lonely people who hate others as part of the misery that is their lives, fighting fire with love works, though it is a technique that few can or even want to muster the strength and courage to use.

AGGRESSIVE-AGGRESSIVE HOMOPHOBES

Much gay bashing is not passive but openly aggressive. Examples are given throughout this text. Here is another one:

> Two lesbians were forced to sell their house and move because they were unable to deal with cars driving by calling them dykes from the car windows, having their house windows broken and eggs thrown at their house, police not responding to calls for help, and their new car first scratched with sharp objects then dented by fists punching in the hood.

PART III

Cause

15

Psychological and Biological Factors

In this chapter I study the cause of homophobia from psychodynamic, interpersonal, behavioral, and biological perspectives.

THE PSYCHODYNAMIC PERSPECTIVE

Anxiety and Defense

According to the psychodynamic view, homophobia is a symptom like paranoid delusion or phobia are symptoms. It is a symptom because it is the product of a conflict. The elements of the conflict of which it is composed—the forbidden wishes and guilty fears—remain and are discernible in the resultant homophobic product. For example, a patient who developed the obsessive fear that he would prick his finger on a metal spur on a shopping cart in a Greenwich Village supermarket and inject himself with the AIDS virus was at one and the same time expressing his *wish* to be penetrated by homosexuals, his *fear* of being "pricked," and the anticipated *punishment* for his guilty wishes. His symptom was structurally akin to the erythrophobia of a patient who could not go out in public because of a fear that she would blush and reveal her guilty sexual thoughts, a fear that really referred to and covered her guilty "wish to turn red so that they can all see how hot I am."

As we have seen in chapter 13, even homophobic epithets like "faggot" or "lezzie" are never chosen randomly. Rather they are chosen carefully, specifically to express conflicting wishes and fears of considerable personal importance. For example when, as John Tierney (1995) reports, "the host of a morning show, J. Paul Emerson [calls gays] 'stinking buttheads'" (p. A10), he is quite possibly revealing his own obsessive-

compulsive problem, and, like other obsessive-compulsives, first
dreaming of anal penetration, then reacting in disgust to what he considers to be "his dirty sexual desires."

Also homophobia is a symptom because like other symptoms it is a
defense against anxiety. This can be, according to John Nemiah (1985):
(1) superego or conscience anxiety, (2) castration anxiety, (3) separation
anxiety, or (4) id or impulse anxiety. I add two other anxieties Nemiah
does not mention: (5) real anxiety—that is, fear, and (6) biological
(atavistic or throw-back) anxiety—that is, the kind of fear that was appropriate for primitive man but hangs on though it is no longer appropriate for the presumably "civilized" homophobe of today.

I devote the next section to a detailed discussion of these types of anxiety and how they are related to homophobia. In particular I emphasize
the different anxieties; the different defense mechanisms used to handle
the various anxieties; and how each subtype of homophobia is in turn associated with one or more characteristic defense mechanisms, which in
turn determine the kind of homophobia that presents clinically.

Types of Anxiety

Superego anxiety originates in the homophobe's guilty conscience,
which has three sources. A homophobe's guilty conscience (1) duplicates messages from homophobic/sexophobic parents, (2) duplicates
messages from homophobic/sexophobic society at large, and (3) creates
the cloth of guilt out of the threads of homophobes' raw instincts. As for
homophobic/sexophobic parents, the child punished for infantile masturbation, incestuous desires, or after being caught spying on the primal
scene is likely to condemn others for their homosexuality in particular
as one instance of condemning others for their sexuality in general. As
for homophobic/sexophobic society at large, the conscience merely re-
peats the homophobic party line it hears in school, church, and in the
media. And as for guilt originating in instincts (i.e., in the id), Jones
(1957) explains the process by quoting Friedrich Nietzsche's analogy of
an "animal in the hands of the tamer which beat itself against the bars of
its cage; [and so] create[d] out of its own self [a] torture-chamber . . . it
was this fool . . . who invented the 'bad conscience'" (p. 284). (Nietzsche's formulations help explain why the most sexually repressed spar-
tan "virginal" homophobes are underneath the most sexually driven,
and, if not entirely celibate, are leading double lives that can even qualify them as among the gayest of them all.)

A patient reported that a librarian was looking on when he was checking
out a CD of the Donizetti opera, *Lucia de Lammermore*. A colleague of this

librarian joked, looking now at the cover of the CD of Lucia, and now at her colleague, that "You look just like her." Lucia, as depicted on the album cover, was, according to the patient, young, attractive, and sexy. The librarian did not reply, "Thanks for comparing me to this beautiful person, I am glad to know I look like her," but "You should have your eyes examined." The patient thought her remark translated to, "Anyone who compares me to that slut must be blind," or even "Anyone who thinks I may have sex in me should be struck blind, the best possible punishment for those who yearn to do dirty sexual things, like masturbate."

Homophobes with harsh superegos gay bash to reassure their consciences, "I am not queer, and to prove it I exclude, punish, and exterminate those who are." They also tend to theologize their consciences. They say "my conscience comes from God" when God really comes from their conscience. Those who are primarily sexophobic from the start may also homosexualize their consciences. They subsume all sin under the categorical heading of homosexual sin. At first they use homosexual sin as a metaphor for sin in general. But later what began as a figure of speech ends up becoming an actual (perceived) reality.

Most superego-oriented homophobes claim their so-called homophobia comes not from their superego but from their ego-ideal, which they define as the more positive, inspirational, part of their conscience. They say it is the "what I want to be" rather than "what I, and you, should not be" part of their superego. They make, at least superficially, a persuasive case that they are not homophobes out of a sense of guilt, but subscribers to the idea that heterosexuality is the ideal, and that homosexuality compromises and corrupts this ideal. They deny that their ideals are guilt- or instinct-driven. Instead they swear that their homophobia is not a symptom, but a higher calling.

Castration anxiety, particularly prominent in hysterical homophobes (discussed in chapter 13), refers to a man's fear of being emasculated: literally, figuratively, or both. There is no exact equivalent of castration anxiety in women, which is the reason, some say, that we at least seem to see a preponderance of homophobia in males (a "statistic" I question in chapter 14).

Isay (1989) in effect speaking of castration anxiety says that homophobes' hatred for gay men is often related to fears of "what is perceived as being 'feminine' in other men and in oneself" (p. 78). He also points out that many men are in "conflict about their passive anal sexual desires" (p. 75). In my experience that conflict often creates a feeling of terror. The feeling is partly learned and partly inborn. If the latter it seems as primary as the fear of incest, suggesting that there may be an anal

penetration taboo, perhaps strongest in men, that is the equal of the incest, and other, taboos.

Isay also says that homophobes have a distressing tendency for mis-
taking the "'feminine' aspects of [their] character" (p. 75) as homosexual,
leading to their "fantasies of performing fellatio or being the receptive
partner in anal sex," which they attempt to deal with "through counterphobic attitudes" (p. 77).

Isay adds that "we would expect to and do find homophobia to be
most prevalent in groups in which men are selected to participate because of their 'masculine' qualities and where individuals must deny, re-
press, or suppress their feminine attributes in order to maintain the
public and/or private image of the group and in order to continue to belong" (pp. 78–79). He cites "the military establishment, the CIA and FBI"
among others. "Homophobia is also commonly found in groups in
which a value is placed on the individual's 'feminine' qualities, but
where 'being a man' is prized within the structure of the institution or as
part of the public image of the institution." He cites "the Catholic
Church, and organized psychoanalysis" where a "paradoxical situation
may cause a particularly high degree of anxiety and conflict about . . .
feminine qualities. . . . In the case of the Church, women are excluded
from the priesthood, and in the analytic community gay men are generally excluded from training simply because they are not heterosexual"
(p. 79). Finally he notes that a bias against women is an element in homophobia, because homophobes see their feminine side as "'pollu-
tion,'" much as society associates "such negative traits as envy, jealousy,
pettiness, [and] seductiveness . . . with women" (p. 81).

Separation anxiety is about loss. Homophobes with a high level of
separation anxiety suppress their forbidden homosexual impulses because they fear various losses if these impulses are acted upon, such as
the loss of potency, the loss of (masculine) identity, and, should they be
discovered having gay sex, the loss of their friends and family as well.

Id/impulse anxiety results from feeling flooded by sexual and aggressive instincts that come too fast and furious to be fully integrated.

Real anxiety is the result of reasonable fear. However circular, it is appropriate for homophobes to become homophobic to disavow their
own homosexuality because they know what can happen to homosexuals in a society full of homophobes. As one lesbian put it, "anyone who
gives gays and lesbians even a second look will, like Lot's wife, get turned
into a pillar of salt."

Biological (atavistic) anxiety is shown by homophobes who argue, as
Todd S. Purdum (1996) says, that "gay people committing themselves to a
life-long relationship threaten . . . the American family" (p. B9) then vigor-
ously defend the standard and sanctity of the family and the male-female

design, or become part of homophobic counties like Cobb County (GA) that, according to Kevin Sack (1996) approve a "resolution stating that the homosexual life style is incompatible with the standards to which communities subscribe" (p. A16), doing so in part because they feel the integrity of their tribe or their personal position in it is threatened. (The biological origin of homophobia is discussed in greater detail in chapter 4.)

The Defense Mechanisms

According to Nemiah (1985) "anxiety is a signal to the ego that an unacceptable drive [which may be of a sexual or an aggressive nature] is pressing for conscious representation and discharge" (pp. 885–886), and this signal anxiety "arouses the ego to take defensive action against the pressures from below" (p. 886). The defensive action consists of the use of one or more defense mechanisms. As discussed in chapter 8, these can be first-line, auxiliary/secondary, or supplementary defenses. For example, repression of unacceptable homosexual and aggressive wishes is a first-line defense. Projection, brought into play when repression fails, is an auxiliary or secondary defense. The paranoia that results from the projection is supported by other, supplementary, defenses, such as rationalization, as when homophobes insist that their homophobia is a sign of emotional health, not of mental illness.

First-Line Defenses

First-line defenses are sometimes sufficient in themselves. At other times they anticipate and prepare for the auxiliary defenses. Or, the auxiliary defenses are needed and brought into play because the first-line defenses are simply inadequate.

1. Repression—homophobes first try to forget or suppress their latent homosexual and aggressive anti-gay wishes. (Repression is discussed further in chapter 8.)

2. Narcissism gives homophobes the sense of self-importance they need to feel comfortable and personally entitled enough to proceed with their attacks on gays and lesbians. It helps them suppress their own, often considerable, and considerably obvious, personal defects. Their own anxiety about their personal defects reduced, they can now deny that they are second-class citizens, less than paragons of virtue. Feeling superior to their victims, they can proceed apace to persecute them, and to do so comfortably and without qualms.

Signs of narcissism in a homophobic attorney were how he condescendingly suggested that a gay man buy his, the attorney's, new house because

"I want to sell it so that I can move to a nice place," and selfishly asked gay and lesbian doctors for free medical advice without offering to give free legal advice in return, thinking that if he got without giving he would not have to acknowledge that gays' and lesbians' services, and so gays and lesbians themselves, had a certain value, one that was as great as, or greater than, his own.

3. Stereotyping simplifies fantasies to allow homophobes to use other (secondary or auxiliary) defenses more efficiently. Stereotyping delineates the enemy so that homophobes can better center it in their gunsights. One man's myth that all gays appear on floats on Gay Pride Day simulating anal sex (he saw two of all the gays in the world doing this) served this purpose. (It also helped him project his own anal desires onto gays, and to make the point that he was not gay because he did not do that.) Masculinizing or feminizing every sex act or human behavior is a "good" start for homophobes trying to handle their anxiety about being castrated. If making curtains is sissy work, then men can remain men simply by not sewing, and by condemning others who sew. Proving one's point, or forgetting something that conflicts with it, is much easier when the point is all tied up into a neat little package, for making pure black out of white is much simpler in a world where one does not have to contend with intermediate shades of gray.

Auxiliary/Secondary Defenses

As Nemiah (1985) says, "more often than not, [the first-line defense of] repression is not entirely effective; it is necessary to call into play auxiliary defenses, such as conversion, displacement, or regression." "Depending on the nature of the defenses employed, the individual may develop a variety of psychoneurotic symptoms" where specific symptoms "depend . . . on the defense that predominates" (p. 886).

Projection was discussed at some length in chapter 8. Other auxiliary defenses such as dissociation were discussed in the relevant chapters on the syndromal underpinnings of homophobia. Here I amplify on previous discussions of four auxiliary defenses: dissociation, counterphobia, sublimation, and substitution.

1. Dissociation (splitting, and convenient forgetting) was previously discussed in chapter 12. To condemn gays and lesbians as sinners, homophobes have to conveniently forget that they are "sinners" too. Some are adulterers and practitioners of incest, actual or once removed. The latter was the case for the homophobe who one day slept with his brother's wife and the next day condemned a friend for being gay. He split his conscience into two parts, one of which looked out at his friend,

and saw evil, and the other of which looked in at himself, and saw nothing worth noting. Other homophobes have had homosexual experiences in their own lives, or are even having them now. Some are excusing them—for example, as aberrations of the moment due to the excessive use of alcohol. Others are simply denying them—for example, by renaming them, calling them male bonding. Many homophobes recommend a cold-shower, Boy Scout Manual approach to gay sex after conveniently forgetting that all sex, gay as well as straight, is difficult to resist, as Freud (1927) puts it in *The Future of an Illusion*, because "arguments are of no avail against . . . passions" (p. 8).

Homophobes accuse gays and lesbians of being "perverts" after forgetting that straights do exactly the same things that gays and lesbians do—that is, that sodomy is not an exclusively homosexual practice. Homophobes who criticize gays for bringing AIDS on themselves have to forget that some straights act in equally self-destructive ways, by overeating, smoking, and drinking themselves to death. Even some lesbians have a double standard when on the one hand they decry homophobia and on the other hand they keep gay men out of their bars, as when the bartender at a lesbians' restaurant politely rejected two gay men by listing the gay men's restaurants in the neighborhood and highly recommending they try one—tonight—qualifying herself as no less the bigot than the manager of the exclusionary country club who will not admit blacks or Jews.

2. Counterphobia: Just as couples who reaffirm their marriage vows on a regular basis both to themselves and others often do so because they are not getting along well, homophobes who reaffirm their masculinity on a regular basis often do so because they question it in the first place.

3. Sublimation: While some homophobes are openly aggressive, others, preferring to be more covertly sadistic, and liking to congratulate themselves for their forbearance, refine their raw aggression and instead of bashing gays attempt to control and change them.

4. Substitution: Aggressiveness can substitute defensively for repressed forbidden sexual feelings, one reason why Isay (1989) can speak of homophobia as due to "the aggression that . . . anxiety evokes" (p. 78). (Due to the return of the repressed, the aggressive epithets homophobes hurl at gays and lesbians often reveal an underlying attraction to them. Calling gays "lollipops" certainly qualifies.)

When a gay man asked a neighbor to curb his dog, he responded not by telling the man, "I will" or "I will not" but, "Faggot, go back to New York where you came from, with all the rest of the queers." As it turned out, his aggressiveness was at least partly a way to squelch the many anxious guilty thoughts he himself was having about going to New York City, a place he envisioned as being full of sin. (It was also a way to get vicarious pleasure by putting the gay man up to doing what he himself secretly wanted but was unable to do.)

Supplementary Defenses

Supplementary defenses support and justify a homophobia already in place. They include:

1. Rationalization: Rationalization provides the convincing fallacy homophobes need to make their homophobic attitudes, beliefs, or behavior acceptable to themselves and society, and so incontestable all around.

2. Depression: In chapter 9 I discussed depressive homophobia where individuals became homophobic as a way to elevate their (depressive) low self-esteem. Here I discuss how homophobes can use depression as a way to maintain their homophobia. However painful this depression is, it serves as a supplementary defense when it allows homophobes to deal with their guilt about being homophobic by tithing, making it okay to be homophobic as long as they feel bad about it and/or do self-destructive things to themselves to atone. Such homophobes can be as hard on themselves as they are on the gays and lesbians they persecute. They torture themselves with pictures of sexual evil, and gays and lesbians burning in hell. Or they actually hurt themselves. Their tongue slips and they say something that ruins them politically. Or they commit bias crimes whose real intent is to get caught. How else can we explain why a group of straight teenagers would be so reckless as to yell anti-gay epithets out of the car window at a passing gay man, knowing, at least subliminally, that the police are cruising in a marked patrol car, right behind them?

3. Denial: Homophobes use denial to fool themselves into thinking that they are not homophobic. According to Johnathan Rabinovitz (1995), after Eugene A. Migliaro, the Hartford Veterans Agency Nominee, calls gays "lollipops" he denies he is homophobic, saying, "'I don't have a prejudiced bone in my body. It's just the way an old marine talks'" (p. 21).

Missing Defenses

Homophobes rarely use mature defenses like altruism, what Meissner (1985) defines as "the vicarious but constructive and instinctually gratifying service to others." And few of them have a sense of humor, as defined by Meissner as a state that "allows one to bear . . . what is too terrible to be borne," (p. 390), such as the awareness that no one is perfect.

Incomplete Repression and the Return of the Repressed

Mostly repression is incomplete and the repressed returns so that the warded-off impulses achieve some degree of expression in the symptoms. Meissner (1985) says that "the 'forgetting' of repression is unique in that it is often accompanied by highly symbolic behavior, which suggests that the repressed is not really forgotten" (p. 389).

> One individual joined the army to deal with his own forbidden homosexuality, then became homophobic, thinking, to quote him, "if you cannot join 'em, beat 'em." Experiencing a return of the feelings he tried so hard to suppress, he behaved in a way that suggested that his repressed sexual wishes were still active, revealing his true colors in the very act of being homophobic. For example, his setting out to cleanse the army of homosexuals only seemed to increase his contact with them, and so the possibility that a relationship might form.

The cowardice that is the reason for defensive homophobic gay bashing comes through when teenagers "bravely" drive around the streets of gay resorts, or gay "ghettos" in cities, yelling "faggot" from the safety of their cars, attacking pedestrians in a manner that roughly approximates shooting fish in a barrel.

Sometimes the defenses fail completely, the repressed returns with a vengeance, and the problem spreads and new countermeasures are required. The case of the homophobic man in chapter 8 who could not walk near gay bars is illustrative. The man went further and further out of his way to avoid the bars, only to find that his circuitous route took him to other bars, which he had also to try to avoid. Eventually he became virtually a prisoner in his own home. In many cases like this, what starts as homophobia spreads to become sexophobia, then sinophobia, then a paralyzing obsessive-compulsive scrupulosity that affects all areas of potential enjoyment, until homophobes burn in the same hell on earth in which they want gays and lesbians to burn, both now and in the afterlife.

Homophobes whose homophobia is an attempt to control anger can become violent when their defenses against anger fail and the anger returns. The unlucky homosexual who picks up a stranger in a bar, or hitchhiking, and takes him (rarely her) home to have sex, only to be tortured and strangled afterward, is often the victim of such an individual.

Developmental and Dynamic Considerations

Fixation

For fixated homophobes, homophobia begins at home, and gays and lesbians are the catalyst for the homophobe's childhood reminiscences.

Homophobes often see gays and lesbians as their fathers and mothers. They might call gay men "queens" because they remind them of their own imperious mothers, or "sissies" because they remind them of a father who was not a real man. Or they might call lesbians "lezzies" or "bull dykes" because they remind them of an aggressive mother.

Identification and Counteridentification

When a homophobic parent creates a homophobic child in his or her own image, the homophobic children abuse gays and lesbians the same way their parents abused them when they were young. They do this partly because they have the same genes that their parents had, and so the same genetically determined attitudes and behaviors, and partly because they have identified with their parents, having learned all too well what their parents taught them. Male children seem at particular risk for becoming homophobic when they have a homophobic father who additionally is dominant, controlling, scrupulously religious, and resolutely nuclear-family-oriented. Both male and female children seem at particular risk of becoming homophobic (and sexophobic) when the mother condemns early manifestations of sexuality, checking for budding sexual activity, then punishing the child harshly for "touching it down there," creating masturbatory guilt.

Fathers and mothers who "desex" their children to keep them at home indefinitely tend to teach their children to be both homophobes and sexophobes. Controlling parents also tend to produce controlling children who too readily involve themselves in the personal lives of others, and in matters that are of no concern to them. They stick their noses into places that are none of their business, and speak without having been first spoken to, offering their opinions without actually having been asked for them. They like to get into power struggles with gays and lesbians, to dominate and control them like their parents dominated and controlled their children. They expect gays and lesbians to be submissive and do what they are told, unquestioning, just as their parents expected the same thing of the children.

Cruel parents produce homophobic children who are cruel to gays and lesbians. Children of parents who are less homophobic in specific than they are cruel in general are likely not only to become generally cruel but also to develop not simply into homophobes but into total bigots. These generally cruel total bigots try to change others, not with positive but with negative reinforcement, not with reward but with punishment, not by encouraging them but by discouraging them, and not by supporting them but by humiliating them—into submission: with threats, not promises, and with sticks, not carrots. And they target not only gays and lesbians but also Jews, blacks, women, and foreigners. They hate everyone like their parents hated them; put every one down like their parents put them down; humiliate every one like their parents humiliated them; and abuse everyone emotionally and physically just as they were abused themselves—often simply because they were there, and in the line of fire. When the parents were rejecting, homophobia becomes primarily an excluding mechanism—from the army, from religious groups, from jobs, or from doing psychoanalysis, as homophobes exclude gays and lesbians now as they felt excluded by their parents in the past. They mock gays and lesbians when their own infantile sexuality was mocked, as when they were thrust aside for being a lowly child, a big nobody, too small to be taken seriously sexually, and too insignificant and unimportant to count in any way.

It is common for children to act like their parents out of a fear of defying them because they want to maintain a loving relationship with them. This aspect of identification is often part of the resolution of oedipal conflicts: a way to tell the parent of the same sex, "I identify with you" as a way to say, "I love you too much to compete with you as a rival."

Sometimes homophobia originates not in identification with a cruel but in counteridentification with a kind, nonhomophobic parent. These homophobes shun or abuse gays and lesbians not because they had mean parents and have turned out to be like them, but because they had kind parents, and want to be as much unlike them as possible.

Shifting identifications and counteridentifications can make homophobes into a study in opposites. They are charitable and loving one day and aggressive and exploitative the next. They become now homophiliac, accepting homosexual friends and getting close to them just to spite their parents, and now homophobic, dropping and punishing their friends for being homosexual as a way to return to the parental fold. Such homophobes can specialize in criticizing gay men *or* lesbians but not both. For example, one homophobe first identified with a cruel critical mother who hated passive men, then came down hard on gay men for being too passive, calling them "sissies" or "swishes." Then he counteridentified with his cruel critical mother and came down hard on gay men again, but this time for being too pushy or assertive.

Sometimes the doing and undoing process occurs because the homophobe has identified with a Janus-like parent—for example, a father who is a castrating homophobe and a castrated passive latent homosexual combined.

The father of one such homophobe was a passive, shrinking, retiring, don't-make-trouble sort of man until he zeroed in on homosexuals, when he became absolutely inspired to abuse them, in part to pronounce himself resolutely heterosexual and so prove his masculinity to himself and others. During the week he was a Milquetoast. But on Saturday night he went out with the guys to a go-go bar and drank the evening away, all the while making jokes about "homos" to test himself and prove how much he really hated them. Of course he also hoped to fail the test, so that he could have a little gay horseplay along the way—before he came to his senses and denied his errant ways. Later in life he alternately gay bashed and was gay himself. He was the kind of bisexual whom gays call "rough trade" to refer to men who passively accept fellatio—men of whom gays say that "today's rough trade is tomorrow's competition."

Sibling Rivalry

Homophobes fight with gays and lesbians like brothers and sisters fight with each other. Some homophobes exclude gays and lesbians like a first child who wants to stay an only child excludes the second child to come along. The homophobe who tells gays and lesbians to get out of my town is spiritually akin to the firstborn who tells the secondborn, "I was here first, so now get out of my house." Many hate gays and lesbians as a way to distinguish themselves from a homosexual sibling; with the gays and lesbians they abuse those who remind them of that sibling. These homophobes sometimes reveal how they came from a family where there were gays and lesbians in the way they groom themselves. They look, as one gay man put it, "like closet cases." For example, one homophobe's Mr. Clean appearance (shaven head, mustache, tight T-shirt) though intended to make him look virile, in fact made him look just like some of the gays he said he thoroughly detested.

Early Deprivation/Trauma

Gay bashing today can have its roots in deprivation or actual bashing (witnessed or received) yesterday. For a homophobe whose mother beat him with a strap for playing doctor with the other little boys in their apartment complex, bashing gays was a way to handle the fear of passivity and helplessness associated with being traumatized. Seductive same-sex parents can disgust a child who grows up to be disgusted with "seductive" gays and lesbians, as happened to a son whose father constantly kissed him on the forehead to "take his temperature" and whose mother bathed him well past puberty, in spite of his firm protests.

One homophobe had a particularly unhappy home life. He had a controlling critical homophobic gay-bashing father and a distant alcoholic mother. As a child he dealt with his unhappiness by making animals feel what he felt. He burned caterpillars to see them squirm, and smashed eggs from the nests birds built around his house so that he could in effect "evict the babies from their home." This homophobe saw four lesbians eating dinner together in a gay restaurant. He thought, "The different women with a little stretch of the imagination could be mother, father, brother, and sister." He then became upset because they looked so happy together, and he went on a rampage condemning gay marriage. He thought, "That's disgusting, a perversion of the natural order of things, a travesty. Gays and lesbians who get married are like circus chimps dressed up as babies; or like aliens from another planet—the wrong people doing all the right things." He condemned them to deal with his own unhappiness. He wanted to make others squirm, and to foul their nests, if only in his thoughts, to deprive them of the happy home life he himself felt deprived of when he was a child.

Homophobic Myths as Symptoms

Myths are like symptoms because:

1. They reflect the operation of defense mechanisms. Many myths, especially those built around the defense mechanisms of projection and denial, reveal more about the mythmaker than the subject of the myths. The belief that gays are promiscuous often reveals a secret wish to be sexually free, while the belief that all gays are sex-crazed men who recruit in the shower room often denies an active wish by creating the image of oneself as the passive victim.

2. They reduce anxiety—the primary gain of the symptom. The myth that all gays and lesbians are sinners reduces the homophobe's anxiety about being a sinner by defining sin narrowly—that is, homosexually. The myth that gays and lesbians cannot be soldiers is a hopeful way for the homophobe in the military to reduce his or her contact with gays and lesbians to keep them from getting close enough to become threatening.

3. They promise a real, wish-fulfilling advantage—the secondary gain of the symptom. If gays and lesbians are defective, then straights get all the promotions, and can more efficiently live out their enslavement desires—and now not merely in fantasy.

4. They increase self-esteem. Homophobic myths give homophobes smug self-satisfaction by making them feel more perfect than, holier, or closer to God than thou.

5. They are the product of the unconscious, in two ways. First, many mythmakers are unaware they are mythmaking. Instead they think that even their most dereistic and irrational myths are true, though they are as false as delusions, and as irrational as phobias, and, like them, misperceptions held tenaciously and reiterated compulsively. This uncon-

scious aspect of myths helps explain why conscious argument does not dissuade homophobes from their myths any more than it dissuades schizophrenics who are hallucinating from hearing their voices, and why the stupidest myths can exist in the most intelligent people.

Second they originate in unconscious fantasies. The myth that all gays are theatrical people who want to be movie stars and live on an old movie set, barely in contact with the real world, in lofts in Greenwich Village, surrounded by cats, watching old movies, and longing nostalgically for a wonderful past to avoid a depressing present and an even more distressing future, originates in part in unconscious escapist fantasy. The myth that all gays and lesbians show an appalling lack of self-control, are all impulsive and pleasure-oriented, and are regularly unable to postpone pleasure even when doing so would be life-saving, originates in part in unconscious fantasies of liberation. The myth that all homosexuals are promiscuous, and gay relationships never last, or if they do are never monogamous, originates in part in unconscious erotic fantasy.

It follows that translating myths into the unconscious products from which they arise gives us broad insight into the homophobe's specific needs and intentions. For example, we can translate such epithets (which are really minimyths) as elitists, pansies, sick-os, dinks, flits, sissies, queers, fags, femmes, swishes, dykes, and butches into the specific fantasy of intent from which they arise. To illustrate, the epithet "sick" sometimes suggests that the homophobe has fantasies about having oral sex with gays, and is now taking the consequences: retching and vomiting up the secretions. To take a line from Leviticus 18:25, he or she has identified with "the land [that] vomited out her inhabitants."

6. They are syndrome-specific. For example, the idea that homosexuals could control themselves if they would ("you brought AIDS on yourself") has an obsessive-compulsive ring to it, for like obsessives, who favor self-control as a way to solve all their problems, they leave little room, when it comes to sex, either for the hormonal effect or for human fallibility, both of which make sexual desire into an irresistible force that predictably meets a movable object. Furthermore, obsessive homophobes who think gays and lesbians could control their being homosexual by simply doing the equivalent of taking a cold shower are very much like obsessive neurotics who rely on magical avoidance rituals like not stepping on a crack in the sidewalk to control a fearful wish to "break their mother's back," or who repetitively wash their hands to control their "dirty" sexual desires (and to atone for presumedly "dirty" past sexual acts).

7. They begin in childhood. For example, in the developmental history of what some gays call control queens—or what some straights call control freaks—individuals who subscribe to the myth that gays and les-

bians could simply decide to stop being homosexual if they only would listen—we find that the parents dealt out discipline by simply demanding that the child "cut it out" (for example, "just say no to touching yourself down there") without attempting to help the child understand the reason for the command, and without supporting the child as he or she tried to change.

8. They are hostile. For example, the myth that gays and lesbians are child abusers persists because it expresses the homophobe's abject hatred for gays and lesbians. Child abuse and incest are two of the worst things people can think of to accuse gays and lesbians, or anyone else, of. (In fact, most gays and lesbians, like most straights, prefer adults to children. They may like adults who look like children, but rarely children themselves. They may even dislike children completely because in their helplessness they remind them of how they themselves were once weak and passive.)

THE INTERPERSONAL PERSPECTIVE

Hernandez's (1995) previously cited discussion of racial slurs is applicable to the interpersonal aspects of homophobia. He says in effect that those who use racial slurs are making an interpersonal statement. They "view race and religion as the handiest and most hurtful differences to seize upon as they jockey to fit in among their peers." They are "lashing out at . . . authority figure[s]," or "intimidated by . . . a certain hardened, 'street attitude' of some . . . students" (p. B2). Rachel Kranz (1992), in her book *Straight Talk About Prejudice* says that the reasons for prejudice consist of "cultural differences" (p. 10), "economic competition" (p. 12), and "insecurity from feeling that there is very little that can be counted on or controlled" (p. 15). Morris (1967) might be explaining one reason why homophobes fear gays when he notes that "couples [who produce no offspring] will put heavy demands on their pair-bonds, which may break under the strain. These individuals will then constitute a greater threat to other pairs that are attempting to rear families" (p. 100).

THE BEHAVIORAL PERSPECTIVE

Kirk and Madsen in *After the Ball* answer such common questions as "Why are people bigoted?," "Why do people not like homosexuals?," and "Why is it humiliating to be told that someone of the same gender has a crush on you?" in strict behavioral terms. They say that homohatred develops in the individual as a learned reaction with "anger and/or fear in response to an arbitrarily defined outgroup: fags [learned] in accord with certain fundamental laws of behavioral conditioning—specifically, two: *Rule 1: Associative Conditioning.* When a person experiences, either by direct sensory perception, or in the form of a thought or emotion, two things either simultaneously or in immediate succession . . . an Associative Link is formed between the two so that, in the future, experiencing one of the things will tend to evoke the other thing . . . [and] *Rule 2: Direct Emotional Modeling.* . . . an immediate [automatic] kindling of the same, presumably appropriate, emotion(s) . . . an excellent example with which [all] are quite familiar [being] the cattle stampede" (pp. 120–124).

THE BIOLOGICAL PERSPECTIVE

If Morris were to write about homophobia he would almost certainly view it from the perspective of the behavior of the animal within humankind. For example, he might agree that homophobes who compete with gays and lesbians are like animals who compete with each other for food, lodgings, sex, or simply for position. One patient speaking of strife between straights and gays in his place of work illustrated his point by repeating the following anecdote about some animal behavior he once observed:

> There were two sea gulls sitting on a street light. Let's call them #1 and #2. A third sea gull, #3, flew over, and pushed #1 off its perch; whereupon #1 flew over and pushed #2 off its perch and #2 flew away; whereupon #3 flew over and pushed #1 off its new perch, and #1 flew away. There was #3, I thought, master of the street light, like some homophobes I know, at the top, but all alone, and with very little to show for their efforts.

Physical disorder early in life can be another factor in the formation of later homophobic attitudes. For example, in one of my patients an undescended testicle was high on the list for creating a latter-day fear of femininity associated with an extreme sensitivity to castration/humiliation. This flared later in life when gay men's supposed femininity reminded him of the potential vulnerability of his testicles. Also the patient's mother delayed his treatment for an undescended testicle because she "only wanted me to have one" because "she liked me the way I was, as only half a man." Because he felt like half a man he had to try to make himself feel whole again. To do this he condemned other "half-men," particularly Jews, blacks, and gays and lesbians, as defective so that he could have "bigger balls, comparatively." (The biological aspects of homophobia are also discussed in chapter 14).

16

Cognitive Errors

In this chapter I describe some of the cognitive errors that contribute to homophobia as well as to other forms of bigotry. The most familiar of these are the ones that Aaron T. Beck (1985) identifies as contributing to depression (pp. 1432–1438). But there are others as well, not per se associated with depression. These have been relatively neglected in the literature, so I have had to identify, label, and define them myself. This has been no easy task because it is difficult to distinguish among the different errors, since they tend to overlap conceptually and occur together. As an example, homophobes often combine selective abstraction with part=whole cognitive errors (both of which I define below) to create two homophobic logical fallacies in vogue these days: the belief that all homosexuals are sick, and the belief that gay marriages will undermine the fabric of society.

INCONSISTENCY

For homophobes, what is good for the goose is not necessarily good for the gander. Homophobes do not like even playing fields. They tend to forget that the homophobic brush paints two ways. For example, those who say that being homosexual is unnatural should also say, to be absolutely consistent, that if God had wanted us to smoke He would have put chimneys in our heads. Analysts who will not let gays and lesbians be analysts because they did not resolve their oedipal problems should also exclude/defrock the not inconsiderable number of analysts who are adulterers, have a psychosomatic ailment, or even, like one analyst I used to know, cannot say the word "hostile" without stuttering, because he gets stuck on the H, and can proceed only with extreme difficulty, and sometimes not at all, as his analyst might say, "because of a preoedipal anal fixation even more primitive than the oedipal fixation that causes homosexuality."

RATIONALIZATION

While scientists search for truth, using the scientific method, which starts with a premise that is elaborated into a conclusion, homophobes (and other bigots), using sophistry, start with a fixed belief then search for a way to justify it. They need this justification to make their prejudice seem to be something other than the flat assertion it is—to make it look like the fact-driven inevitable conclusion it is not. An inability to like gays and lesbians, and the need to dislike and abuse them, is already in place. Then one or more reasons are found to justify the dislike with "facts." Finally the process as a whole is justified, really covered and obscured, to reduce guilt, and make the homophobe look like he or she has a considerable degree of social awareness, or even, as one claimed, "big breasts producing the milk of human kindness."

DISSOCIATION

Homophobes are hypocrites who condemn gays and lesbians for doing the same thing that they do, after conveniently forgetting that they themselves also do it. Gays and lesbians are not the only ones who stay up all night and go to singles bars; promiscuity is not confined to homosexuals; and sodomy is hardly an exclusively homosexual behavior (straights like to sanitize it and call it "foreplay.")

TAKING THINGS TOO SERIOUSLY

The incongruous gender behavior some homophobes find so unpalatable and frightening is in fact mostly little more than genderbending, a humorous put-on, a theatrical event, a joke, to be taken not seriously but with a grain of salt. Gay men do call themselves and others Mary, and say things like "get her" to and about other men, but they do not, as some people believe, mean to change their anatomy. They are mostly having fun, and perhaps getting a little relief from what can be a depressing reality, at least for some gays and lesbians. In fact there is no predictable relationship between effeminancy in men/masculinity in women and sexual preference. Any such relationship is an inconstant one, and often determined after the fact, so that "I see you as gay because I see you as feminine" is really "I see you as feminine because I see you as gay." (As mentioned throughout, homophobes, and to some extent the rest of us, get a skewed view of who is gay or who is a lesbian because, failing to recognize any but the most obvious gays and lesbians, they equate homosexual with being obviously homosexual and stereotype accordingly in a way that excludes the vast majority of homosexuals. Many mythmaking homophobic therapists see only pathology in gays and lesbians because they only come in contact with gays and lesbians with problems. They would be right in their stereotypical negative observations about gays and lesbians, except for one thing: they are basing their findings about gays and lesbians not on a knowledge of gays and lesbians in general but upon gays and lesbians who come to see therapists in specific.)

PART=WHOLE

Part=whole dyslogic judges the whole according to the part. Many homosexuals' workplace problems originate with part=whole cognitive errors made by homophobes who judge gays and lesbians in their entirety by the sexual yardstick, although this is only one measure of any person. For example, many homophobes judge homosexual doctors' capabilities at the bedside by the yardstick of their behavior in bed. They view homosexuality as a "disability," then, taking the next step, conclude that a disability in one area is a disability in all areas, and that a homosexual's sex life necessarily spills over into a homosexual's professional life to spoil it.

In fact, even if being homosexual were a disability, which it is not, most disabilities are compartmentalized—that is, they do not affect the ability to function occupationally. And this is particularly true of "sexual disabilities." Even true sexual disabilities, like pedophilia, can leave the rest of the ego intact, so that we are often surprised when an individual who appears perfectly normal turns out to have a paraphiliac disorder, or when an individual who is paraphiliac turns out to behave otherwise in a perfectly normal way. Most homosexuals are indistinguishable from heterosexuals in the workplace for another reason: sex comes from a different part of the brain from work/other activities of everyday living. While I cannot say that there are no cases where one's homosexuality does not mesh imperceptibly or even perceptibly into personal or professional (occupational) disorder, in most cases homosexuality produces no effect on the individual's ability to do his or her work. Homosexual doctors may not decorate their offices with the "requisite" family pictures, but they do not often lose their diagnostic and therapeutic skills on account of being homosexual. Homosexual lawyers can prosecute or defend with a brilliance equal to that of straight lawyers—if only society would let them. Homosexual artists are neither great nor inferior artists because they are homosexual. But even some psychotherapists, who should know better, think that being homosexual personally spills over into being homosexual professionally, and not merely to become a blemish on, but to completely mar, the whole person.

Many part=whole thinkers do not merely passively conclude that because gays and lesbians are less than perfect then they are no good at all. They also search actively for something about gays and lesbians that they can call imperfect, so that they *can* view them as defective. These homophobes not only believe that one bad apple can spoil the whole bunch—that is, that being homosexual spoils the entire person—they also play their favorite game, which I call "bobbing for bad apples."

Discrimination in the workplace based on part=whole cognitive errors has serious negative effects on gays and lesbians. They go through life striving to do well professionally, but they do not, because so often they do not stand a chance. They do not stand a chance because they try to improve their work, thinking they are being judged fairly according to the work they do, when in fact they are being judged unfairly according to the sex they have. Ultimately their self-esteem falls when they come to believe the ad hominem evaluation of others. They get angry and they cannot express their anger, partly because they think their anger is unjustified, and partly because they know that expressing it will not do any good, or will actually do considerable harm. Then they get depressed or, if they tend to somatize, they get high blood pressure, or suffer from asthma.

There are a number of what are essentially part=whole errors, with different names depending on the specific mechanisms used, as follows:

Overgeneralization: Conclusions about all gays and lesbians are drawn based on a few examples. When conclusions applicable to some are applied to all, the false belief that characteristics of one individual apply to the whole group to which that individual belongs is born. Overgeneralization is a particularly invidious form of part=whole illogic when it is used to smear gays and lesbians by making being gay a buzzword for something evil. Prejudiced people pick the few gays and lesbians that prove a negative point they wish to make, then tar all gays and lesbians with the same brush, forgetting that there are gays and lesbians of all types in all walks of life. Examples of overgeneralization include statements to the effect that being homosexual is a conscious choice when applied equally to prison homosexuals and homosexual hermaphrodites, and the belief that gays molest children, or are recruiters, because some gays are pedophiles, or try to enlist others in the gay cause. Mona Charen (1996b) in her article "Homosexual Ruling Worse Than Bad Law" makes this error when she in effect says that because a few gays and lesbians are brushed with the tar of the sexual underworld, and are "raunchy and vulgar" (p. A21), that is the way all gays and lesbians have to be.

Guilt by association : Just as the T-shirt that reads "New York, London, Paris, Jersey City" puts Jersey City in an excessively positive light, homophobes put gays and lesbians in an excessively negative light by knowing them by the company they keep. Charen (1996a) makes gays and lesbians guilty by association when she asks, "if we grant recognition to homosexual marriages, by what principle can we deny it to polygamists or those who engage in bestiality, incest, or necrophilia?" (p. A21). So does Robertson (1992) when he says that lasting peace will come only when "drunkards, drug dealers, communists, atheists, New Age worshipers of Satan, secular humanists, oppressive dictators, greedy moneychangers, revolutionary assassins, adulterers, and homosexuals are [no longer] on top" (p. 329).

Selective abstraction: According to Beck (1985), this is the process of drawing conclusions about a situation or event based on "a [single] detail taken out of context ignoring other, more salient features of the situation, and conceptualizing the whole experience on the basis of this element" (p. 1437). Selective abstraction is the soul of anti-gay discrimination for it focuses on the negative and overlooks the positive things about gays and lesbians. Some bigots selectively quote the Bible. They pick those parts that make their point, while overlooking the other parts that weaken their position. As Spencer (1995) asks, "Why should those biblical sections which appear to deplore same-sex loving be believed in so fanatically, when other sections that praise it, for example the love of Jonathan and David, are ignored?" (p. 400).

Homophobes often use selective abstraction to justify opposing gay marriages. They cite the antitraditional features of gay marriages while overlooking, as Charen (1996a) quotes Sullivan as saying, how gay marriages might give gay men "'incentives for responsible behavior, monogamy, fidelity, and the like'" (p. A21).

> Charen (1996a) in equating many gays and lesbians with "male marchers sport[ing] masks and pierced nipples . . . 'Dykes on Bikes' . . . transvestites, spankers, foot fetishists, and sadomasochists among many others" (p. A21) presents about as accurate a picture of gays and lesbians in general as the one that a gay man, satirizing her, presented when he equated all straights with proprietors of tattoo parlors. To make her point she eliminates from consideration gays and lesbians who are none of these things, which is most gays and lesbians. By reasoning the way she does she maneuvers herself to the real point of her argument, which is that "the chasm between the sexual underworld [= gays and lesbians] and the heterosexual majority is wide and the notion that gay marriage can bridge it folly" (p. A 21).

> A boss intends to embarrass and punish gays and lesbians because he feels that is what they deserve, then to excuse his aggression toward gay and lesbian workers as provoked, as second, not first, strike, to make it

look as if he is acting the part not of the homophobe but of the avenging angel. He concludes that *no* homosexual can perform equally to and certainly not in a way that is superior to straights, and so should not be promoted in his company, and perhaps not allowed to work there at all. He arrives at his conclusion by preselecting his examples, omitting all that disprove the point he is trying to make.

Psychoanalysts like Socarides who cite what they call the equivalent of "typical gay pathology" overlook mitigating factors that make the behavior in question less pathological than it might at first appear to be. It is true that some homosexual relationships are sadomasochistic because they are characterized by the wish to humiliate, or stifle, a partner. But even in those cases when the wish is there it is often under control and softened by other, less exploitative, more loving, factors. Mostly what some consider to be stereotypical gay behavior is intermittent and situation-specific. One patient said to me, "I walk my cocker spaniel every day past a lesbian bar in New York City. When the weather is warm, there are probably what some view as stereotypical bull dykes sitting outside, but even the ones that can be imagined to fit that description break the stereotypical aggressive mold by fawning all over the dog, and cuddling her, proving how easily that the stereotypical bull dyke role is undercut. I am forced to conclude it must be not innate but created (and able to be relinquished) out of, and for the need of, the moment."

Psychoanalysts use selective abstraction when they cite certain developmental and dynamic reasons to explain homosexuality, though these may be neither necessary nor sufficient, and as frequently found in straights as in gays and lesbians, and so possibly incidental, not causal. For example, a man can love his father, even too much, without having anything so sinister as a reverse oedipus complex, and without becoming a homosexual.

Homophobes use selective abstraction to create the idea that all gays and lesbians are out to seduce them (some are), then to create the myth that all gay men are promiscuous (some are), then to conclude that it is dangerous to take a shower in the locker room (it can be, but it rarely is).

Physicians discriminate against homosexual psychiatrists after overlooking how being homosexual can have certain advantages for psychiatrists treating both gay and straight patients. Many patients feel, and not without justification, that their doctors cannot understand them because they do not themselves have anything like their problems. Some would even prefer it if their doctors were to be more like them even to the point of having suffered as they have suffered. (This belief is one of the cornerstones of the community psychiatry movement—namely, that untrained professionals from the same background as their patients are better equipped to treat the patient than trained professionals who come from walks of life and have life experiences significantly different from those of their patients.) They also overlook how being openly homosexual can be adaptive. It can reduce anxiety, helping gays and lesbians to function. And it can be motivational, prompting gays and lesbians to help others avoid experiencing the same pain some of them have experienced in their own lives.

Magnification: This swells the point that selective abstraction creates until the point fills the whole canvas and becomes the entire picture. For example, strangers feel complete disgust and revulsion toward gays and lesbians as the result of seeing only the base aspects of their sex acts, up close and unsoftened by the erotic bath that changes "animalistic behavior" into ethereal experience.

Paralogical predicative thinking: According to Jules R. Bemporad and Henry Pinsker (1974), in paralogical thinking "the slightest similarity between items or events becomes a connecting link that makes them identical." The purpose is "to give . . . some semblance of meaning [to reality] to protect [the patient] from the anguish that a realistic appraisal of his environment would engender." For example, many homophobes reason falsely that if A can be meaningfully equated with B in any respect and A can be meaningfully equated with C in any respect, then A=C. Bemporad and Pinsker quote Silvano Arieti's example: the "patient who believed she was the Virgin Mary because she also was a virgin" (p. 532).

A gay man who moved from Massachusetts to the Maryland shore (and hated it because of all the homophobes there) reasoned in just this way, making his original decision to move based on the following formula: gays and lesbians live beside the sea in gay resorts like Provincetown; the Maryland shore is beside the sea; therefore there are gays and lesbians (and other interesting folk) at the Maryland shore.

In like manner homophobes reason that: sex involves seduction, homosexuals are sexual people, therefore homosexuals seduce other people. And: homosexuality is unique, sick people are unique, therefore homosexuals are sick. Ad hominem thinking, also discussed below, is at times just one form of paralogical thinking because homophobes judge nonsexual performance on the basis of sexual orientation, forming their conclusions based on shared characteristics of what are at bottom disparate behaviors. Ad hominem thinkers judge gays and lesbians' work performance on the basis of their performance in bed when they reason: work is a performance, sex is a performance, therefore sex=work. Many homophobes confuse male sexual with male personal passivity, conclude that male homosexuals are personally as well as sexually passive, then assert that gays can never be effective professionally (outside of certain "gay" professions) because they are not forceful enough. The same kind of reasoning, in reverse, is applied to lesbians. They are kept from being in authority because they are perceived to be too forceful—that is, because they are not passive (motherly) enough.

Similar=the same thing: These errors are also a form of predicative thinking, for they promote unwarranted extensions to the general from the specific. Many politicians confuse similar (really dissimilar) things with the same thing when, asked to vote pro-gay, they say that this would mean voting for transvestites and practitioners of bestiality. Such individuals are indulging in the predicative thought, "some transvestites are gay, you are gay, therefore you are a transvestite," which is little different from Arieti's patient's delusion: I am a virgin, the Virgin Mary is a virgin, therefore I am the Virgin Mary. In like manner bisexuality is like, but not the same thing as, homosexuality, so that some but hardly all gays and lesbians are frustrated straights. Analysts who "cure" homosexuality are often merely curing bisexuality, especially the kind that, being the result of oedipal heterophobia—that is, a fear of the opposite sex because of incest fantasies—is due to conflicts about straight sex that can, like any other conflicts, be potentially resolved via psychotherapy.

Equating the symbol with what it symbolizes: Quoting Wesley C. Salmon (1997) this is like saying, "(i) the chair has four legs. (ii) [the symbol] 'Chair' has five letters. [Then] (iii) This chair has five letters [which] is nonsense" (p. 685). In like manner, homosexuals are first symbols of evil, and then evil incarnate, then the devil, or Satan, himself.

Some=all: A familiar example of this error is the belief that all gay men act like women, and all lesbians act like men. Some=all thinkers forget that not all homosexuals are alike. They forget that there are many homosexualities, not just one, because homosexuality is a common final destination for many pathways, so that any generalizations, to be at all meaningful, and not simply stereotypes, have at the very least to distinguish among the different homosexualities. Prison (or reactive) homosexuality, for example, is only distantly related to endogenous homosexuality, and homosexual pedophiles are different from gay and lesbian adults in a voluntary, consensual, committed relationship with an adult partner.

TANGENTIAL THINKING

Tangential thinkers use minor, incremental logical distortions to make large major illogical leaps. Their logical missteps are each so small and the falsifications each so gradual that these shifts are imperceptible, making the process as a whole convincing.

One (schizophrenic) patient was asked, "What are you eating?" and, though he was eating a bowl of cereal, he answered, "A bowl of confines" because he wanted to talk not about what he was eating but about getting out of the hospital. He bridged "what are you eating" to "my confinement" with a series of part concepts. A bowl is many things, one of which is an item that has sides and holds its contents in so that they cannot get out. This patient chose to speak only of this aspect of the bowl—that is, this part concept of bowl—because that was the aspect that allowed him to veer toward the discussion he wanted to have—of how he felt imprisoned by hospital walls, just as his cereal flakes were imprisoned by the sides of the bowl.

The lemming-like proof that gay marriage is unacceptable because it breaks the social mold, which breaks with tradition, which creates a generation of nontraditionalists, who will create a new, nontraditional society, that will overthrow the old, is a familiar example of how homophobic tangential thinking crawls rather than leaps from premise to false conclusion heading, like a crawling infant, not to where it is supposed but to where it wants to go.

ONE THING LEADS TO ANOTHER, OR THAT IS HOW IT STARTS

Homophobes like to create the illusion that gays and lesbians are poised to get rapidly out of control so that if they give gays and lesbians a finger they will take a hand, and if they give them a hand they will take an arm, so that gay rights will lead to gay marriages, gay marriages will lead to a violation of the sanctity of the family, and a violation of the sanctity of the family will lead to the downfall of society, if not to all of the human race, until the end of the world is upon us. Cognitive errors are not the only cause of this kind of reasoning. It is also caused by emotional thinking due to hysterical excessiveness and/or schizophrenic *weltuntergang:* the delusional belief that the world is about to come to an end, based on very little, if any, evidence. As for the cognitive contribution, this is the kind of reasoning elementary schoolteachers (by reputation) use to deny a child's wish to go to the bathroom in the middle of a class. As they put it, according to legend, "If I let you go I will have to let every one go, and my class will be disrupted, emptied out before the final bell." They say this without determining if indeed every one has to go, which is unlikely, since in any large class at any one time most children can hold their water until the final bell, just as in any one homosexual population at any one time, few gays and lesbians are actually interested in trying to disorganize society.

AD HOMINEM REASONING

In ad hominem reasoning, homophobic criticism of the producer becomes homophobic criticism of the product, so that the work is judged
by the worker.

> Citing the damage done by the homophobic play reviewer George Jean
> Nathan, Lyle Leverich (1995), writing in "Tom," says "Nathan was also
> wise enough in his ways, especially in the ways of the theatre, to have
> pegged Tennessee [Williams] as a homosexual, and he was outspoken in
> his loathing of sexual deviation. He was first among a few critics to let
> their homophobic feelings prejudice them against not only the play-
> wright but his plays, as well. Nathan would ultimately give *The Glass
> Menagerie*—as a play . . . a sneering review and finally, despite the great
> success of *A Streetcar Named Desire*, dismiss the playwright as 'a Southern
> genital-man'" (p. 554).

In effect, homophobes like Nathan judge gays' and lesbians' higher
ego functions by their lower instinctual behavior. In psychoanalytic
terms, they equate ego with id.

CIRCULAR REASONING

A homophobic government employee who reasoned in a circular fashion said, "It is reasonable to not hire gays and lesbians because you cannot trust gays and lesbians to work for the government because they are
subject to blackmail," then reasoned that "gays and lesbians are subject
to blackmail because homophobes will not hire them into, and will fire
them from, government service." It is circular reasoning to define an entity homophobically then apply the definition prejudicially. For example, Lisa Schiffren (1996) pleads, "Don't redefine an important institution." Gays and lesbians, as far as she is concerned, cannot marry, but
that is because of the way she defines marriage, as an "institution [that
is] a lifelong compact between a man and woman committed to sexual
exclusivity and creation and nurture of offspring . . . imbued with an aspect of holiness" (p. A21). In like manner others say homosexuality is an
illness because it is not normal, and it is not normal because it is an illness. They call to mind how in some circles intelligence is defined by
one's IQ, and one's IQ in turn defines one's intelligence.

INEXACT LABELING

Inexact labeling, according to Robert J. Ursano and Edward K. Silberman
(1988), refers to the "tendency to label events in proportion to one's

emotional response to them rather than according to the facts of the situation" (p. 870).

HOMOSEXUALIZATION

Homophobes often attribute their dislike for gays and lesbians to their being homosexual, however much they dislike them for other reasons. Homosexuals do the same thing to themselves. A psychiatrist thought he had trouble filling his private practice because he was gay. In fact he had trouble filling it because he hated, and refused, to work nights and weekends.

A PRIORI (FLAT ASSERTIONS)

Flat assertions form the basis of airtight anti-gay propaganda that looks believable though it starts with what we might call "original error." Just as schizophrenics make (or used to make) their case for being Napoleon by announcing "I am he" and refusing to entertain rational arguments to the contrary, gay bashers deem gay bashing right because homosexuality is wrong, and that is where the matter begins and ends. For example, Socarides (1996) says, speaking out on gay marriages, that the "redrawing of the male-female design doesn't make life more fruitful, only more barren" (p. A28) yet cites no specifics (for whom? and how?) or evidence, and offers no persuasive argument to justify his point.

PERSONALIZATION

Homophobes who personalize believe that everything the homosexual does is relevant to them, the homophobe—one reason (besides being a control freak) that they make gays' and lesbians' behavior their business, concern, and source of anxiety. Personalization leads to ideas of reference, where individuals think that gays and lesbians are cruising them when they are not. One gay man complained that some homophobes stared back at him in the gym, thinking he was cruising them, though he was merely looking to see if they were finished with the machine they were using so he could use it next.

ABSOLUTISTIC AND DICHOTOMOUS THINKING

In absolutistic and dichotomous thinking an individual or groups of individuals are divided into all good and all bad, angel and devil, and judged accordingly. Gays and lesbians are all bad and straights are all good, although real life is not so simple.

RELATED PHENOMENA

Denial: Many bigots say the most bigoted things then proclaim, "I am not a bigot." They pass anti-gay laws, then we hear, "This is not about homophobia, or gay bashing," though that is exactly what it is about.

The plain unvarnished untruth: Not all mistakes of logic are due to cognitive errors. Some are pure dissimulation for effect, and some are misstatements made out of ignorance or deliberately. I think Socarides (1996) is simply wrong when he says "homosexuality dares to exempt humankind from the sexual bipolarity that runs up the evolutionary ladder of earthly beings" (p. A28) because homosexuality in animals is a well-known phenomenon. For example, Morris said (1967) "There is nothing biologically unusual about a homosexual act of pseudo-copulation. Many species indulge in this, under a variety of circumstances" (p. 93).

DYNAMIC ORIGIN OF COGNITIVE ERRORS

Cognitive errors do not arise de novo but are created to satisfy specific emotional needs. For example, one homophobe who proclaimed that the only valid marriage is between one man and one woman in a union blessed with children was not so much defining marriage as he was condemning those who defied family tradition by striking out on their own, doing things in their own way—that is, refusing to listen to him. A homophobe who flatly asserted that gay marriage violates the holy sanctity of matrimony did so to deal with her own conflicts about rebelling against her parent's values by instead abjectly submitting to her parent's idea of what constitutes a good marriage. Cognitive errors make the discharge of anger possible. They also serve a defensive purpose. For example, the dissociative errors that enable adulterers to unabashedly criticize gays and lesbians facilitate the narcissism homophobes need to cover their own low self-esteem. Cognitive errors also help homophobes gain specific advantages, as when illogic is used to provide the homophobe with a competitive edge.

> A man who could not walk down Christopher Street in Greenwich Village because he felt *all* gays on the street were criminals trying to steal his wallet from a fanny pack he wore over his crotch was less fearful of his wallet being picked than he was eager to have his genitals fondled. The same male could not shake any gays' hands because he became delusionally convinced that *all* gays had scabies, which he would contract: a symptom that was both an expression of his desire to touch gays and his fear of and punishment for getting too close to them.

PART IV

Treatment

17

Treatment of Homophobes

Homophobes need treatment for two reasons: they cause serious problems for gays and lesbians, and they also cause serious problems for themselves. For example, when they abuse or avoid gays and lesbians they deprive themselves of many of the pleasures of life. As spectators they do not attend certain performances, look at certain works of art, or read certain works of literature by, for, or about gays and lesbians. As bosses they refuse to hire, or they harass or fire, some of their most talented workers because they are homosexual, not only impoverishing their own lives, but also ruining their own companies. As patients they avoid the gay doctor who could make the right diagnosis in favor of the straight doctor who has made the right family. And as neighbors they shun the gays or lesbians who move in next door, though what they gain fighting sin and maintaining their smug morality they lose in the potential friends and helpers they could have otherwise had and enjoyed. And finally, being bigoted and "morally" right diverts them from what they should be doing both personally and professionally because it takes time, effort, and energy away from being effective.

Kenneth Hausman (1993) in his article "Military Ban" quotes a letter Melvin Sabshin, then the president of the American Psychiatric Association, wrote to President Clinton, noting that "the military's policy [on homosexuals] is based solely on 'ignorance and bigotry' and 'is a stain on the fabric of America's cherished ethic: All citizens should be judged by their conduct.'" Sabshin adds, referring to the self-destructive nature of this homophobic attitude, "that the annual cost to American taxpayers to discharge gays and lesbians and to train their replacements now exceeds $27 million" (p. 11).

According to Lois M. Rogers (1996a) there is hope that Episcopal Bishops who ordain gays and lesbians will not have heresy charges brought against them and that the church will make "a decision . . . that stresses scripture, reason and tradition, and which recognizes the 'valuable contributions made by lesbians and gays to an inclusive church'" (p. A3).

And though mostly they do not know it, homophobes, by being homophobic, are actually damaging their reputations, and not merely with gays and lesbians. They are also damaging their reputations with themselves, and with the very straights, family and friends, they are trying to impress and win over. As for themselves, how can a moral religious individual preach compassion and love for all, and then make exceptions based on sexual orientation, without on some level feeling guiltily hypocritical? And how can presumably logical people wear T-shirts that say, "How can a moral wrong be a civil right?" without wondering if they are making the mistake of comparing apples and oranges? And as for their straight family and friends, all the world loves a lover, so that, at least in my experience, even some drinking buddies who approve of the homophobes' militant anti-gay stands at the bar the night before think twice the next morning and, finding the homophobes off-putting and sadistic, ignore them as friends, do not vote for them as politicians, and make sure that their sisters marry someone else.

Nevertheless homophobes avoid getting help for their problems for at least three reasons. First, through a process of self-denial, they do not believe that they are homophobes. For example, Kay Lazar (1996) in her article "Ban on Unisex Wedlock Debated" reports that Assemblywoman Marion Crecco introduces a bill to ban unisex wedlock saying, "allowing same sex marriages . . . 'goes against the grain of society and undermines the foundation of the family upon which civilization was built'" (p. A1) only to add "'This has nothing to do with morals, nothing to do with values'" (p. A6). Second, if they do believe they are homophobes they do not realize that they are causing problems for themselves. And third, if they do believe they are homophobes they deny that they are causing problems for others—beyond, that is, what they feel others deserve.

As a result, while there are many homophobes who are in psychotherapy, most of them are there for a reason other than their homophobia. Few if any homophobes enter treatment with the chief complaint, "I am homophobic," and with the expressed goal of curing their homophobia. Should their homophobia come up at all during the session they often do not want to discuss it, and if they do discuss it they resist any suggestion that they change. As a result, therapists who chose to handle homophobia have to do so indirectly if they are to make any inroads.

A therapist was treating a homophobic obsessive-compulsive patient who washed her hands because of sexual guilt and who abhorred gays and lesbians because of a sense of moral superiority that was a side product of that sexual guilt. The therapist chose to deal with the patient's homophobia indirectly, by treating the sexual guilt that caused it, without even mentioning the homophobia itself. In this case the outcome was favorable, for the patient became less homophobic when her obsessive-compulsive problem was successfully treated, thereby lessening her need to express her guilt by criticizing others.

In a very few cases homophobes are insightful enough so that their homophobia can be handled like any other symptom. In these situations cognitive therapy is particularly useful, for it helps homophobes to evaluate gays and lesbians rationally, and to judge them fairly. It helps them to distinguish gay passion from gay profession—that is, gays' and lesbians' sexual orientation from gays' and lesbians' ability to do a job. It helps them to distinguish homosexuality from character pathology in gays and lesbians so that they do not condemn gays and lesbians for being homosexual when they really mean to call attention to a personality problem or disorder more or less independent of the homosexuality. And it helps them learn that there are significant differences between homosexuals and polygamists, wife beaters, and murderers, for mostly sex, gay and straight, when it is loving, is not an exploitative, hostile, or criminal act. Some religious homophobes can even learn to distinguish between true and anthropomorphic God, and determine if they are homophobic because God wanted them to be, or if God is homophobic because they wanted Him to be—that is, if they are displacing their personal homophobia onto God, giving Him ideas that originated with them, and saying that they originated with Him.

Interpersonal therapy can help insightful homophobes distinguish what they do not like in others from what they do not like in themselves. They can learn how they project their own flaws onto and condemn others for something inside themselves, something that needs to be, if not condemned, then at least changed. They can learn how their involvement in others' homosexual practices is really an overinvolvement when these practices are between consenting adults, and no one is getting hurt, either physically or emotionally. They can learn to recognize that gay life holds no immediate importance for them, and is neither a good nor a bad thing as far as they are concerned, but is instead a nonissue. They can understand that it is neurotic to make private homosexual behavior of public concern. They can stop proselytizing against same-sex marriages and instead discover why they are so involved with the topic, why they seem so threatened by the possibility, often to the point of hysteria, and why they waste so much time and energy on upholding laws when they do not work for a law enforcement agency. They can stop emulating the individual who received a flyer for a sexually oriented book in the mail and could not simply throw it away and forget all about it, but had to get involved, endlessly protesting to the authorities about the lax laws of today, until we had to question his true motives.

In especially favorable cases, where patients are insightful and motivated to change, therapists can even interest homophobes in dealing with the social problems their homophobia creates, as when homophobes collectively sacrifice social gain for individual personal triumphs that are more like pyrrhic victories.

> The family orientation of one town was partly to blame for the empty stores that were a silent testimony not to any poor economic conditions that prevailed at the time but to the conflicts its inhabitants had about allowing gays and lesbians to live and work there. The town advertised itself as a family town (it even had a "family tattoo parlor") to get the message across that it did not like gays and lesbians, or anyone else too different—blacks, Jews, and Latinos included. Once when two gay men tried to open a microbrewery, which would have rehabilitated an abandoned eyesore building near the center of town, the project was defeated, using as an excuse that it was a few blocks from an elementary school, where it could corrupt children. This decision was not made on practical grounds, since no children would be served or otherwise involved in any way. The town fathers were simply resolving their own feelings about drink and sex by "protecting the children" from the demon rum and the devil homosexual, much in the same way people rate movies not based on what they want their children to see, but on what they themselves dislike, really fear, having to watch.

This town is a parable for the self-defeating aspects of homophobia. In banishing gays and lesbians who pay taxes but do not use the schools (making their tax money mostly profit), fix up their houses, and open up attractive businesses that encourage tourism and attract even more business, it acts the part of the enterprise that could have been profitable, except that it deliberately set out to discourage some of its best customers.

18

How Gays and Lesbians Can Deal with Homophobes

IDENTIFYING HIDDEN HOMOPHOBIA

Gays and lesbians cannot eliminate all the homophobia in the world. But they can at least learn to better handle the homophobia the world has to offer them.

First, gays and lesbians need to recognize hidden homophobia. Too often gays and lesbians deliberately or unconsciously overlook homophobia so that they can deny they have real enemies. That temporarily helps them feel less depressed. But to use a medical analogy, it is as if they are denying they are coughing up blood, just hoping it will go away. It spares their day, but it ruins their life. Gays and lesbians can handle homophobia best if they learn when and where it exists. If they know what they are dealing with they will know when they have been discriminated against, and are not just imagining it. So they will not feel paranoid when they are in fact being persecuted. Here are some discriminatory put-downs that some gays and lesbians did not immediately recognize as signaling the presence of hidden homophobia:

A gay man was asking reasonable questions about a straight man's sister. After a few questions the straight man snapped, "You are asking me more questions about my sister than I care to answer." Notable for its absence was, "I am answering fewer questions about my sister than you care to ask."

An individual finds gays unacceptable as equals—that is, as friends or neighbors. However, she dwells on their virtues when they are in her employ, doing her a service like catering her affairs or installing her window shades.

A doctor's colleagues found one excuse after another to avoid sharing an office with him. He wondered if his being an International Medical Graduate or his practicing alternative forms of medicine was the problem. It was not. He was being excluded simply because he was gay.

A gay man asks a homophobic supermarket checker, a patient of mine, if he may have a plastic rather than a paper bag. She thinks, "That faggot is making just too many demands for a sissy," and replies, pointing at a garlic clove that he forgot to take out of his basket, "and may *I* (reestablishing dominance) have that garlic clove?" She thinks, "sissies don't demand; sissies don't take. Sissies ask; and sissies give." "Sissies," for this individual, are acceptable. But they are acceptable only so long as they are supplicants, figuratively speaking down on their knees.

The same homophobic checker tells a gay man checking out flowers in her supermarket that the flowers he bought are $5.95, which surprises him, for they were in the $2.95 flower bin. He decides not to purchase the flowers and asks the checker if it is okay if he returns them to the bin. She does not answer his question, but instead asks him another one: "If they are too expensive why did you take them in the first place? The price is clearly marked right on the bouquet." Then for good measure she raps the gay man's knuckles for having put the flowers on top of her scale, which she pointedly reminds him has to be kept clear so that she can weigh his other purchases for him.

The nurse who told the gay doctor that he was being too cautious asking for an eye consult before giving a possibly contraindicated medicine to a patient with blinding glaucoma in both eyes adds for good measure that everyone agrees that he must not know much if he has to ask. Another time she demands that the doctor take a patient off diazepam because "it is the wrong medicine for elderly people"—though it can in fact be used if one is conservative in dosage, avoiding medication buildup. The doctor complains to her superior, who admits that she could have expressed herself differently, but denies that she was stepping out of line. (She is right to think she can get away with abusing this doctor because the doctor is afraid to complain. He knows that being gay makes him vulnerable, because to make his point he would have to express the belief that she had it in for him personally, then say why. Of course by not complaining now the doctor only leaves himself open to more of the same in the future.)

A gay man wanting to buy a shirt he is holding in his hand approaches a salesperson at a branch of a well-known men's haberdashery established in a homophobic neighborhood. He is about to say, "may I have this?" But he stops, and he does not buy the shirt, because as he nears, she backs off almost reflexively.

A lesbian at the bank goes directly to the area of the safe-deposit boxes, as other tellers told her to do when she needs to get into her box. The teller manning the area that particular day puts her down, complaining, "You are trying to jump ahead of the line, before the other people who are waiting in the anteroom." The teller says this even though she knows the other people are waiting for something else.

A social worker got a patient to write 11 letters of complaint about a lesbian doctor to the hospital administrators, after first giving the patient the names of the administrators to write to. The social worker encouraged the patient to act out for him because he was angry at the doctor for refusing to write a prescription for him to have filled to carry to the patient on a home visit. The social worker knew these were the rules. He knew the doctor could not write a prescription without first seeing the patient. But he deliberately put this doctor in this impossible position and made the most of his patient's anger so that he could launch an attack on the doctor personally, primarily because she was a lesbian.

A gay man said to a friend, "I would invite you over for dinner this summer except that I know you go to the seashore summer weekends." His friend says, "That's okay. Invite me. Of course I just might put you off."

UNDERSTANDING THE HOMOPHOBE

As a colleague of mine who wishes to remain anonymous said, "Until you understand what is going on with homophobes you cannot prevent homophobia the next time." Gays and lesbians can win more easily with homophobes if they understand how homophobes achieve their negative effects. For they can use this understanding to move against homophobes in a way precisely geared to counter the ways that homophobes have just moved against them.

For example, gays and lesbians need to recognize that homophobes are intimidating them by taking over with more confidence than is warranted, simply proclaiming that they are wise enough to know what is right, and important enough to expect compliance. They need to recognize that homophobes are casting the first stone hard and fast enough to stun gays and lesbians, hoping they will overlook how the homophobes are themselves sinners who forgot to first look within before hurling accusations at others.

Bob Herbert (1996) in his article, "Radio's Sick Shtick" calls radio's Mr. Bob Grant a "garbage-spewing individual" then adds that "There is no free-speech issue here. The First Amendment is not an employment guarantee for self-hating bigots who feel the need to vent during drive time. (Yes, self-hating. Try to imagine the loathing Bob Grant feels whenever he takes off that rug and stares into a mirror. At some level he knows how vile and spiritually empty he is.) But Mr. Grant is more than ugly . . ." (p. A31).

Homosexuals cannot let homophobes mesmerize them and they cannot be too busy defending themselves to have the time or inclination to stop and analyze homophobes in enough depth to be able to see their flaws clearly.

Gays and lesbians must recognize that homophobes are double binding them, putting them in a no-win position. Homophobes attack gays and lesbians for being homosexual, though the only alternative is abstinence, something homophobes would not expect of themselves. Or they force them to come out of the closet to defend themselves, for they either have to admit they are homosexual for self-protection or listen to anti-gay remarks with silence and aplomb, all the while hating themselves for not fighting back. With most people self-defense is adequate. For gays and lesbians self-defense requires "self-incrimination." Of course the gay or lesbian can say, "Some of my best friends are homosexual," and defend them instead. But that is so obvious that even the suffering of silence is often a better alternative.

Gays and lesbians must not buy into the illogical thinking which homophobes use to intimidate them, simply because they do not have the training or experience they need to recognize homophobic cognitive errors and understand homophobic illogic. Some homophobes merely state, and repeat, flat assertions, mistaken notions like "all gays are sick." For example, Lazar (1996) quotes the New Jersey Assemblywoman Marion Crecco: "citing her observations during [a] drive-through safari [Crecco proclaims] that animals do not engage in homosexual behavior." Lazar adds: "On that point, Crecco is mistaken. 'Throughout the animal kingdom, including mammals, sex between same gender individuals is frequent,' said Dr. Larry S. Katz, an animal behaviorist at Rutgers University" (p. A6). Other homophobes are more subtly sophistic. They reason rings around all but the cleverest gays and lesbians. They can do this because they are shrewd, preoccupied with, and motivated by their homophobia, so much so that they have little better to do with their lives than to practice being homophobes until they can give it their best shot. (Homophobic cognitive errors are discussed in detail in chapter 16.)

Gays and lesbians can avoid being intimidated by thinking of serious homophobes as troubled individuals with emotional problems diagnosable even without formal psychological training. The following are the most common types of emotionally disturbed homophobes: paranoid homophobes, who dislike gays and lesbians because they are delusional about them—for example, thinking, "Given an inch, gays and lesbians will take a mile, then take over the world"; schizoid homophobes, who are too shy to relate to anyone—gays and straights alike; borderline homophobes, who get too close to gays or straights and then reject, and quickly drop, them; narcissistic homophobes, whose (1) self-love takes the form of a superior attitude that convinces them that they have the ability and right to abuse gays and lesbians, (2) whose self-love convinces them that their homophobia is an exact science, resting on a fixed platform in space such as the family standard, and (3) whose self-love gives them so much self-confidence that they proceed apace to abuse gays and lesbians regardless of what others think about the homophobes, and independent of what they ultimately come to think about themselves. Finally, it helps for gays and lesbians to view homophobia as a transference disorder that says more about the prejudiced individual than about his or her victim. For as Levinson (1982) implies, if homophobes say the same thing about blacks and Jews as they say about gays and lesbians, and about all gays and lesbians even though they are a heterogeneous group, then what they say has to come from within, not from without, i.e., that what they say "depends . . . upon their own psychology" (p. 57). Gays and lesbians have to understand that homophobes who appear to be criticizing them are in fact driven by a secret personal agenda, and responding to gays and lesbians as if they were a blank screen onto which they project their personal fantasies. (The principles of understanding and diagnosing homophobes are discussed throughout this text.)

DECIDING ON PASSIVITY VERSUS ACTIVITY

Recognizing homophobia in all its manifestations and understanding where homophobes are coming from is particularly useful for gays and lesbians trying to decide whether to be active or passive with homophobes and whether to fight homophobes or ignore or avoid them.

Gays and lesbians are in danger both from being too passive and from being too active with homophobes. As for being too passive, on the positive side homophobes may leave passive gays and lesbians alone, and in peace, for people tend not to notice the flowers they have trampled on. It is also true that passivity is a helpful, though not perfect, way to deal with gays' and lesbians' legitimate fears, such as the fear that standing up for oneself will particularly displease homophobes who depend on their victims' cooperation. It is also a helpful way to deal with gays' and lesbians' emotional fears, such as guilt about being assertive because assertion is confused with aggression, and the belief that being assertive will necessarily make things worse by driving others away, or provoking them to retaliate in kind. But on the negative side, gays and lesbians who allow themselves to be passive stay beaten down until they become too weak to care much about life. Besides, when gays and lesbians silently acquiesce in being a target, and suffer in silence, instead of speaking up after having been spoken about, they let homophobes get away with murder. That usually inspires the more sadistic homophobes to become even more homophobic. Because gays who act emasculated and lesbians who act defective provoke sadists who are homophobic because of their own emasculation fears and fears of being defective, sadists who are actively homophobic to avoid being passively homosexual, sadistic homophobes become even more sadistic when they see what they interpret as a weakness, and smell what they think is blood.

As for activism, on the positive side it is a good way to increase self-esteem and convince certain (stable) homophobes that their negative views are unjustified. But on the negative side, activism can be a waste of time, for protesting against homophobia can be to as little avail as protesting against schizophrenia. And activism can also present a personal danger to gays and lesbians. Many homophobes are quick on the trigger, and armed, especially the paranoid ones who keep guns in case of an "attack from the rear." Gays and lesbians sometimes get killed when they "assault" such people, because the assault touches on the homophobe's worst fears, while simultaneously inflaming their deepest desires.

SELECTING THE RIGHT COUNTERSTRIKE

Passive-aggressive counterstrikes are often the best response to anti-gay aggression. Here gays and lesbians attack with their wits, not with their fists.

> One gay man found an effective counterattack was to sue for harassment. This worked particularly well with a homophobic neighbor, who took every opportunity to stare this gay man down and make nasty comments about him under his breath. At first the gay man complained to him to his face. This only led to more harassment, so he complained to the police, who for their own, partially homophobic, reasons said they could not help him unless there was an actual physical attack. A nuisance lawsuit stopped the abuse because it showed the homophobe, "I may be a homosexual, but I am not a doormat." (It simultaneously relieved the gay man's depression, although it did not improve either his financial position or his character.)

The altruistic counterstrike is often effective, though some gays and lesbians find it undoable. Here gays and lesbians make homophobes guilty by loving them in direct proportion to how hateful the homophobes have just been to them.

> One gay man did not know how to respond to straights who stared at him. Were they staring at him with hate in their eyes or were they cruising him?

He wanted to avoid getting into a fight, say by telling them to keep their stares to themselves, or by staring back, and he knew that meeting vicious dogs' eyes provoked them to attack. And he recognized that making flip remarks like "have you never seen a queer before?" was out of the question because should he misfire and needle the wrong person his targets could become assaultive. Still he wanted to feel better about himself. For him, smiling and saying good morning was the best solution. If others were cruising him they would appreciate his smiling back. If they were staring at him and staring him down then they might be too ashamed of themselves to abuse him further—or they might even come to like him for his solicitude. And the more paranoid ones would easily tire of him because he did not act the part of the adversary paranoids need on which to base their delusional system.

The depressive counterstrike is often effective, though as often equally unacceptable. Here gays and lesbians induce guilt by beating homophobes over their heads with the gays' and lesbians' bloody bodies. A more acceptable counterstrike is the hypomanic one: living well as the best revenge. Here gays and lesbians ignore the put-downs and the glass ceilings, and thrive and prosper regardless, or out of spite. Being defiantly generative is a useful variant:

> Kenneth Hausman (1994) reports Robert Kertzner, a psychiatrist, as saying: "Generativity remains a 'hallmark of middle age' for gay men and lesbians as it is for heterosexuals. For the former groups, however, resolving how to leave their mark on the world, when most have no children of their own and many have 'strong feelings of loss concerning their childlessness,' becomes more challenging. . . . To a substantially lesser [sic!] extent than for heterosexuals entering middle age, elements of normative midlife development are still evolving for homosexuals. Its potential . . . will eventually be determined by 'medical advances against HIV and the continuing evolution of social tolerance and legal rights such as domestic partnerships, parenting rights, homosexual marriage, and antidiscrimination measures.'" "'Although sexual orientation may be largely constitutional, midlife development may, indeed, be something gays and lesbians choose'"(p. 10).

In the aggressive counterstrike, offense is thought to be the best defense, regardless of the dangers involved. Here gays and lesbians face homophobes down and counterattack, turning the tables, to give them a taste of their own medicine. Loraine O'Connell (1993) in her article, "Sitting in Judgment," using as her source Chris Rosenthal, a mental health counselor, describes ways to handle judgmental people. She calls this aggressive form of counterstrike "confrontation" and suggests that "aggressive counterstrike" might be helpful because "judgmental people are at their worst with those who allow them to get away with it" (p. E1).

Two gays who were living in a small town were unable to set foot in the local restaurants because the diners stared them down throughout their
meal. At first they merely looked the other way, complained to each other,
and went home feeling deflated and paranoid. Eventually they discovered
that it helped them, at least emotionally, to mutter something aloud, such
as, "It's rude to stare." Sometimes that stopped the behavior. They did get
through to homophobes who had not completely lost their humanity.
Those felt guilty, turned red, then turned away. Or if they did not get
through to and stop anybody, then at least the gays felt better about themselves, and could, as they put it, "swallow their food because they didn't
swallow their sword."

In the passive counterstrike, what O'Connell calls "agreement," the
homosexual handles judgmental homophobes by deciding that "some
things just aren't worth getting upset about" (p. E1). This is rarely applicable to serious bigotry, but there are certain occasions when it is the better part of valor to retain one's sense of humor, and let things pass.

In the narcissistic counterstrike, what O'Connell calls the "fogging
technique," the individual counters that what you criticize me for is
"'one of the things I like best about myself'" (p. E1). Using this technique
gays and lesbians can counter homophobia by citing the advantages of
being homosexual. They can accentuate the positive aspects of being
homosexual and negate everything bad said about homosexuality with
something good to be said for it. They can note how often expressing
one's homosexuality relieves symptoms built out of repressed sexuality.
They can also mention that being homosexual can serve a defensive
function. For reaffirming gay identity is uplifting. Gay pride helps to
maintain self-esteem in a way that makes up for how gay shame lowers
it. I know some gay activists who feel that, for certain homosexuals, even
promiscuity itself, when transitional, and adequate protection against
disease is taken, can be a legitimate source of elevated self-esteem, pro-
viding the individual with a constant input of interpersonal supplies
that would not otherwise be available. Some argue that we tend to unfairly shrink from saying that promiscuous lives can be rich and satisfy-
ing in their own way. And they point out that some people make such
lives work for them. For them, notches on the gun serve as a source of
pride. Besides, as they say, monogamous relationships/marriages are
not right for everybody. Closeness threatens some people, straight or
gay, just too much. Gays and lesbians can also stress the practical advantages of being homosexual. For example, when being homosexual
bridges the gap between classes it puts gays and lesbians in contact with
some very special individuals not ordinarily available otherwise. Sometimes there is also a positive relationship between gayness, intelligence,
and creativity. Perhaps this is because gays and lesbians sublimate their

reproductive potential into creativity—one possible reason why so many homosexuals seem to be so creative.

Many gays think that the best counterstrike for them to use is a compromise: a nonthreatening but firm approach. Here homosexuals act with silent strength and without cloying passivity, discouraging abuse without crossing the line that separates self-protection from aggravating another's paranoia. For example, gays might set limits without speaking of sensitive things that rub salt in the wounds of a homophobe's forbidden instincts, like telling homophobes that "you are as queer as you think I am, because it takes one to know one." This approach is effective yet it avoids the Scylla of passive submission and the Charybdis of dangerous confrontation. It avoids shouting matches between those on the offensive and those on the defensive. And it removes the reward of the pleasure of the kill from those sadists who, absolutely inspired by the screams of pain of the masochistic response, attack even more when they see the reds of the eyes of gays and lesbians who have been weeping.

The following is a list of caveats pertaining to counterstrike, some of which I have already mentioned.

1. Counterstrike should never be first strike—that is, not protection against, but provocation of, homophobes.

2. The aim of counterstrike is more actual accomplishment than it is emotional satisfaction.

3. Counterstrike is dangerous when homophobes are unstable. The safest thing gays and lesbians can do in such circumstances is to make their point, but in a roundabout way, and get a measure of revenge, but only what they can get by proceeding cautiously. Aggressive counterstrike, in particular, must be done in a controlled fashion, and only when adjudged safe.

4. The timing must be right. Gays and lesbians should try to avoid having to think on their feet, which often means thinking emotionally. They should counterattack only after they have thought out their approach carefully, and given consideration to the best time and place for the counterattack.

BEING PRACTICAL AND MAKING COMPROMISES

There are several practical compromises in life gays and lesbians might find worth considering.

Gay Marriages

Joan Beck (1996) in her article "Domestic Partnerships Better Than Gay Marriages" advocates domestic partnerships as a form of marriage for gays and lesbians, saying "Anything less than marriage on equal terms with heterosexuals won't satisfy many gays who consider this an issue of civil rights, as well as love and benefits and who want the symbolic stamp of mainstream approval and respect. But expanding the concept of domestic partnerships and pushing their acceptance by employers, government and society would help. And it would not dilute the sanctity of marriage, as the world has generally understood it for millennia" (p. A23).

Promotion at Work

Handling occupational troubles often requires a creative compromise between what is ideal and what is practical:

> Hausman (1994) reports that psychiatrist Kertzner notes that there is a "subset of gay men working in institutional or business settings who resist assuming greater identities as 'company men' as they ascend work hierarchies. This is done in an effort to avoid being in a position where management colleagues [sic] will learn of their homosexuality and use this discovery to derail future career advancement. . . . [and because] revealing their sexual orientation at work has meant the end of valuable mentor relationships, a rejection that 'may rekindle feelings of early loss, with resultant decreased self-esteem and depression.'" (p. 10).

> Hal Lancaster (1996), in his article on "Managing Your Career": "That Job That's Open Might Be a Step Up But a Bad Step for You," gives advice that is as applicable to gays and lesbians in the workplace as it is to straights when he notes, quoting Tod White, a business consultant, that individuals offered a promotion should at least consider staying in their present job because they might be "'better off where they are'" (p. B1).

THINGS TO AVOID
Trying to Win Homophobes Over

While gays and lesbians can accentuate the positive about being homosexual (as described above), they should think twice before trying to argue homophobes out of being homophobic, or attempting to convince homophobes to like them by appealing to their humanity or guilt. This mostly threatens homophobes and makes them more hostile, for it confronts and challenges their defenses, is seen as part of the passivity (or aggressivity) they detest, and gets too close for the homophobe's comfort and for the gays' and lesbians' safety. In particular, gays and lesbians, like anyone else, should not masochistically try to convert people who cannot and will not love them—that is, not choosing desirable objects to adore but undesirable objects to bring around. Gays and lesbians who come out of the closet because they only want the straight person who hates them to tell them that they are lovable, and as good as the next person—that is, gays and lesbians who feel that the only way to increase their low self-esteem is to change the minds of the very people who lowered it in the first place—will usually not get what they want, and will eventually become panicky about not having gotten it. In a panic for love they will go to extremes and try to get it from anyone. For example, they will stay up all night cruising for sex, and be unable to work the next day. That makes work, which can be a major source of gratification, into something that instead interferes with their social lives, adding a professional to a personal problem.

It is particularly masochistic to abdicate to homophobes professionally then rationalize it as being a good thing to have done. For example, gays and lesbians should first try to resolve as many problems as possible before quitting their jobs because of "all the homophobia at work," concluding that what they did was right because "it was the job or my stomach lining."

While gays and lesbians can rarely convince or cower homophobes into no longer hating them, they can sometimes help pass laws that keep homophobes from acting on their hatred. Education and psychoanalysis are the best ways to change a homophobe's mind. But legislation is fastest way to change a homophobe's behavior.

Starting Off Life on the Wrong Foot

One psychiatrist I know suggests gays and lesbians should do as well as they can professionally early in life, when others can still see them as straight but not married just yet—that is, before their homosexuality becomes obvious. Now when they are discovered, or come out, they will at least be far enough along in their careers to keep their homosexuality from mattering quite so much.

He adds that gays and lesbians should avoid choosing the wrong profession right from the start. They should ask themselves, "Is it worth it to pick a field where it is difficult for me to do well?" So often gays and lesbians chose difficult professions without forethought, and struggle to succeed in them, but they cannot, for even when they are highly trained professionals what they do in their office is not nearly as important for their career as what they do in bed. As a paradigm for all gays and lesbians, he cites how some people in the know think homosexual doctors should consider avoiding going into pediatrics and psychiatry because they are two fields where being homosexual can present real problems. As for pediatrics, some homophobes argue that gays and lesbians should not be pediatricians because they are treating children, who should be protected from all intimate contact with gays and lesbians. And as for psychiatry, he reminds gays and lesbians that many straights in a position of power argue that gays and lesbians should not be psychiatrists, because psychiatry uses the very interpersonal relationships that gays and lesbians supposedly have so much trouble forming and maintaining.

> Remarking on how many gays and lesbians do not stand as much of a chance in psychiatry as do straights, Robert Paul Cabaj (1995) in his article, "Psychiatry Needs to Lead Way in Eradicating Gay Bias in Medicine" reaffirms that psychiatry is a profession where gays are particularly unwelcome by straights, noting that many homosexual "psychiatrists reported some of the highest rates of discrimination, in terms of career and job-related problems, [including] denial of referrals" (p. 13).

He also reminds gays and lesbians that many patients avoid homosexual psychiatrists. Most patients do not care if their anesthesiologists are homosexual, but patients with an emotional disorder want to know about their doctor's personal life, and they manage to find out about it sooner or later. Often they see gays and lesbians with their friends or lovers in the supermarket, or on the beach, and become inquisitive or even openly hostile. In a clinic setting these patients may even complain to the administration about something or other, and back up their complaints by deliberately presenting a distorted picture of the doctor's behavior both in and out of the office. Most psychiatrists think they can handle this. But it is not easy, and even if it were it would be better if they did not have to spend so much time and energy dealing with such problems in the first place.

Psychiatrists can form support groups, and try activism, or, as one did, stomach a long commute to and from work to avoid living where he worked, so that he did not run into patients all the time who would then find out about his personal life. But as the psychiatrist I am quoting points out, this would have been unnecessary if they had gone into another field in the first place. He even told one gay man, "go into dermatology, for there the patients won't care if you are gay—only if you cure their skin problem." Then he added, wryly, what he thought could be a prototype for an outline of a life plan for all gays and lesbians, whatever their profession: "Maybe you should go into parasitology. There, at least if you are homosexual, the worms you run across won't care. Or matter."

Bibliography

"Activists Are Targeted in Bishop's Excommunication Order." 1996. *Asbury Park Press*, May 16.

Adorno, Theodor W. 1982. "Prejudice in Interview Material." In Theodor W. Adorno, Else Frenkel-Brunswik, Daniel J. Levinson, and R. Nevitt Sanford, *The Authoritarian Personality* (Abridged Edition). New York: W. W. Norton & Company.

Adorno, Theodor. W., Else Frenkel-Brunswik, Daniel J. Levinson, and R. Nevitt Sanford. 1982. *The Authoritarian Personality* (Abridged Edition). New York: W. W. Norton & Company.

Altman, Dennis. 1987. *AIDS in the Mind of America*. New York: Anchor Books.

American Psychiatric Association. 1994. *Diagnostic and Statistical Manual of Mental Disorders (DSM-IV)*. 4th ed. Washington, DC: American Psychiatric Association.

The American Psychiatric Press Textbook of Psychiatry. 1988. Ed. John A. Talbot, Robert E. Hales, and Stuart C. Yudofsky. Washington, DC: American Psychiatric Press, Inc.

Ames, Linda. 1995. Letter to the Editor, "An Obvious Bias?" *Clinical Psychiatry News*, February.

Anonymous flyer: "Homosexuality: Is It an Alternate Life Style?"

Bailey, Steven E. 1996. "Some Aren't Listening." *Asbury Park Press*, February 20.

Bannon, Lisa. 1995. "How a Rumor Spread About Subliminal Sex in Disney's 'Aladdin.'" *The Wall Street Journal*, October 24.

Beck, Aaron T. 1985. "Cognitive Therapy." In *Comprehensive Textbook of Psychiatry/IV*, ed. Harold I. Kaplan and Benjamin J. Sadock. Baltimore, MD: Williams and Wilkins.

Beck, Joan. 1996. "Domestic Partnerships Better Than Gay Marriages." *Asbury Park Press*, March 21.

Becker, Judith V. and Richard J. Kavoussi. 1988. "Sexual Disorders, Homosexuality." In *The American Psychiatric Press Textbook of Psychiatry*. Ed. John A. Talbot, Robert E. Hales, and Stuart C. Yudofsky. Washington, DC: American Psychiatric Press, Inc.

Bemporad, Jules R. and Henry Pinsker. 1974. "Schizophrenia: The Manifest Symptomatology." In *American Handbook of Psychiatry*, 2nd ed., ed. Silvano Arieti and Eugene B. Brody. New York: Basic Books.

Cabaj, Robert Paul. 1995. "Psychiatry Needs to Lead Way in Eradicating Gay Bias in Medicine." *Psychiatric News*, January 20.

Carter, Bill. 1995. "After Killing, Hard Questions for Talk Shows." *New York Times*, March 14.

Carter, James H. 1996. "Racism and Mental Health Professionals." *Psychiatric News*, October 4.

Charen, Mona. 1996a. "Giving Approval to Gay Marriage Begs: What Next?" *Asbury Park Press*, June 11.

Charen, Mona. 1996b. "Homosexual Ruling Worse Than Bad Law." *Asbury Park Press*, May 28.

Clymer, Adam. 1996. "Bitter Debate, Then a Vote for Rejecting Same-Sex Marriages." *New York Times*, May 31.

Couser, Thomas. 1996. "Marked Car." *Brown University Alumni Magazine*, March.

Darnton, John. 1996. "Scottish Inquiry's Focus: Why Strict Gun Law Failed." *New York Times*, March 18.

"Doctors Urged to Stop Trying to Change Homosexuals." 1994. *Asbury Park Press*, December 22.

Drescher, Jack. 1995. Letter to the Editor, "Dr. Socarides' Views." *Psychiatric News*, June 16.

Dunlap, David W. 1995. "An Analyst, a Father, Battles Homosexuality." *New York Times*, December 24.

Dunlap, David W. 1996. "Reform Rabbis Vote to Back Gay Marriage." *New York Times*, March 29.

Egan, Timothy. 1995. "Men at War: Inside the World of the Paranoid." *New York Times*, April 30.

"Excerpts from Court's Decision on Colorado's Provision for Homosexuals." 1996. *New York Times*, May 21.

Favazza, Armando R. 1985. "Anthropology and Psychiatry." In *Comprehensive Textbook of Psychiatry/IV*, ed. Harold I Kaplan and Benjamin J. Sadock. Baltimore, MD: Williams and Wilkins.

Feder, Stuart. 1992. *Charles Ives: My Father's Song*. New Haven: Yale University Press.

Fenichel, Otto. 1945. *The Psychoanalytic Theory of Neurosis*. New York: W. W. Norton.

Fox, Thomas C. 1995. "Can the Pope Be Wrong?" *New York Times*, November 25.

Frenkel-Brunswik, Else. 1982. "The Interviews as an Approach to the Prejudiced Personality." In Theodor W. Adorno, Else Frenkel-Brunswik, Daniel J. Levinson, and R. Nevitt Stanford, *The Authoritarian Personality* (Abridged Edition). New York: W. W. Norton and Company.

Freud, Sigmund. 1927. *The Future of an Illusion*. Reprint, no date given. New York: Doubleday & Company, Inc.

Freud, Sigmund. 1957. "Dostoevsky and Parricide." In *Collected Papers*, Vol. 5. Trans. by Alix and James Strachey. London: Hogarth Press.

Gibbon, Edward. 1776–1788. *The Decline and Fall of the Roman Empire*. Reprint. London: Viking Press, 1980.

Gilovich, Thomas. 1991. *How We Know What Isn't So: The Fallibility of Human Reason in Everyday Life*. New York: The Free Press.

Gosling, John A. 1995. Letter to the Editor, "There Is Nothing to 'Fix' in Homosexuals." *New York Times*, December 27.

Graham, Renee. 1995. Book review, "A Grieving Mother Faces Up to Her Homophobia." *The Boston Globe*, October 9.

Gray, Jerry. 1996. "House Passes Bar to U.S. Sanction of Gay Marriage." *New York Times*, July 13.

Guthke, Karl S. 1996. "The 'Deaf Musician.'" *Harvard Magazine*, September–October.

Hausman, Kenneth. 1993. "Military Ban." *Psychiatric News*, January 15.

Hausman, Kenneth. 1994. "Homosexuals Said to Face Unique Midlife Issues." *Psychiatric News*, July 15

"Helms Takes Stand Against AIDS Bill." 1995. USA Today. June 1.

Herbert, Bob. 1996. "Radio's Sick Shtick." *New York Times*, May 3.

Hernandez, Raymond. 1995. "Youths on Racial Slurs: They're Only Words." *New York Times*, June 26.

Hicks, Daniel W. 1995. Letter to the Editor, "Dr. Socarides' Views." *Psychiatric News*, June 16.

Hugo, Victor. 1862. *Les Miserables.* Reprint. London: Penguin Classics, 1982.

Hyde, Margaret O. 1994. *Know About Gays and Lesbians.* Brookfield, CT: Millbrook Press.

Hynes, Samuel. 1994. "A Disconnected Life." Book review, "E. M. Forster: A Biography" by Nicola Beauman. *New York Times*, April 3.

Isay, Richard A. 1989. *Being Homosexual: Gay Men and Their Development.* New York: Farrar Straus Giroux.

Jones, Ernest. 1953, 1955, 1957. *The Life and Works of Sigmund Freud,* 3 volumes. New York: Basic Books.

Kakutani, Michiko. 1996. Book review of *T. S. Eliot, Anti-Semitism and Literary Form* by Anthony Julius, entitled "Was Eliot Anti-Semitic? An Author Says He Was." *New York Times*, June 4.

Kirk, Marshall and Hunter Madsen. 1989. *After the Ball: How America Will Conquer Its Fear and Hatred of Gays in the '90s.* New York: Doubleday.

Kranz, Rachel. 1992. *Straight Talk About Prejudice.* New York: Facts on File.

Lancaster, Hal. 1996. "The Job That's Open Might Be a Step Up But a Bad Step for You." *The Wall Street Journal*, September 10.

Lazar, Kay. 1996. "Ban on Unisex Wedlock Debated." *Asbury Park Press*, June 18.

Leverich, Lyle. 1995. *Tom.* New York: Crown.

Levinson, Daniel J. 1982. "The Study of Anti-Semitic Ideology." In Theodor W. Adorno, Else Frenkel-Brunswik, Daniel J. Levinson, and R. Nevitt Sanford. *The Authoritarian Personality* (Abridged Edition). New York: W. W. Norton & Company.

Levinson, Daniel J. and Nevitt Sanford. 1982. "Preface." In Theodor W. Adorno, Else Frenkel-Brunswik, Daniel J. Levinson, and R. Nevitt Sanford, *The Authoritarian Personality* (Abridged Edition). New York: W. W. Norton & Company.

Macmillan Dictionary of Quotations. 1989. New York: Macmillan Publishing Company.

Marmor, Judd. 1994. Letter to the Editor, "Homosexuality." *Psychiatric News*, March 4.

Martin, Douglas. 1996. "Summertime, and the Living Is Single." *New York Times*, August 4.

McCormick, Brian. 1994. "Anti-gay Discrimination Impedes Careers, Health Care." *American Medical News*, July 11.

McGowan, William. 1995. "A New Paradigm for Race Relations?" Bookshelf: *The End of Racism* by Dinesh D'Souza. *The Wall Street Journal*, September 21.

McGurn, William. 1996. "The Iconoclast Who Found God." *The Wall Street Journal*, April 17.

Meissner, William W. 1985. "Theories of Personality and Psychopathology: Classical Psychoanalysis." In *Comprehensive Textbook of Psychiatry/IV*, ed. Harold I. Kaplan and Benjamin J. Sadock. Baltimore, MD: Williams and Wilkins.

Melville, Herman. 1851. *Moby Dick*. Reprint. New York: Bantam Books. 1981.

Meyer, Jon K. "Ego-Dystonic Homosexuality." 1988. In *Comprehensive Textbook of Psychiatry/IV*, ed. Harold I Kaplan and Benjamin J. Sadock. Baltimore, MD: Williams and Wilkins.

Morris, Desmond. 1967. *The Naked Ape*. New York: McGraw-Hill Book Company.

Mukerjee, Madhusree. 1995. "Coming Out in the Sciences." *Scientific American*, April.

Narrett, Eugene. 1995. Letter to the Editor, "Airbrushing Louis Farrakhan." *The Wall Street Journal*, October 30.

Navarro, Mireya. 1993. "Ethics of Giving AIDS Advice Troubles Catholic Hospitals." *New York Times*, January 3.

Nemiah, John. 1985. "Neurotic Disorders." "Anxiety States (Anxiety Neuroses)." In *Comprehensive Textbook of Psychiatry/IV*, ed. Harold I Kaplan and Benjamin J. Sadock. Baltimore, MD: Williams and Wilkins.

Niebuhr, Gustav. 1996a. "Methodists Keep Rule Against Homosexuality." *New York Times*, April 25.

Niebuhr, Gustav. 1996b. "Baptists Censure Disney On Gay-spouse Benefits." *New York Times*, June 13.

O'Connell, Loraine. 1993. "Sitting in Judgment." *Asbury Park Press*, August 12.

O'Connor, John J. 1995. Television review, "Gay Show Broadens Beyond Parochial Views." *New York Times*, February 28.

"Origins of Homosexuality Debated at Annual Meeting." 1995. *Psychiatric News*, July 7.

Ovesey, Lionel. 1969. *Sexuality and Pseudohomosexuality*. New York: Science House.

Planned Parenthood. 1996. Advertisement. *New York Times*, August 12.

Purdum. Todd S. 1996. "White House Is Avoiding Gay Marriage as an Issue." *New York Times*, May 16.

Purnick, Joyce. 1996. "Recalling a Gay Rights Non-Crisis." *New York Times*, March 21.

Rabinovitz, Jonathan. 1995. "Hartford Veterans Agency Nominee Assailed for Remarks." *New York Times*, February 11.

Rich, Frank. 1995. "Banned from Broadcast." *New York Times*, November 25.

Rich, Frank. 1996. "A Gay-Rights Victory Muffled." *New York Times*, May 22.

Robertson, Pat. 1992. *The New World Order.* Boston: G.K. Hall & Co.

Rogers, Lois M. 1996a. "Heresy Finding Imminent." *Asbury Park Press*, May 15.

Rogers, Lois M. 1996b. "No Grounds for Heresy Charge." *Asbury Park Press*, May 16.

Roughton, Ralph. 1995. Letter to the Editor, "Blaming Gay Victim in Talk TV Murder?" *New York Times*, March 26.

Sack, Kevin. 1996. "Vote Dares Committee to Reroute the Torch." *New York Times*, May 15.

Salmon, Wesley C. 1997. Logic. *Encyclopedia Americana*, International Edition, Vol. 17.

Sanford, R. Nevitt, Theodor W. Adorno, Else Frenkel-Brunswik, and Daniel J. Levinson. 1982. "Measurement of Antidemocratic Trends." In Theodor W. Adorno, Else Frenkel-Brunswik, Daniel J. Levinson, and R. Nevitt Sanford, *The Authoritarian Personality* (Abridged Edition). New York: W. W. Norton & Company.

"San Francisco Station Ousts a Blunt Host." 1995. *New York Times*, February 17.

Satinover, Jeffrey Burke. 1995. "Pot Calling the Kettle Intolerant." *Clinical Psychiatric News*, February

Schiffren, Lisa. 1996. "Gay Marriage, an Oxymoron." *New York Times*, March 23.

Schwarz, K. Robert. 1994. "Composers' Closets Open for All to See." *New York Times*, June 19.

Socarides, Charles W. 1996. Letter to the Editor, *New York Times*, March 15.

Socarides, Charles W., Harold D. Voth, C. Downing Tait, and Benjamin Kaufman. 1995. "AMA and Homosexuality." *Psychiatric News*, May 5.

Spencer, Colin. 1995. *Homosexuality in History.* New York: Harcourt Brace and Company.

Stein, Terry. 1994. Letter to the Editor, "Homosexuality." *Psychiatric News*, March 4.

Stein, Terry S. 1996. "Homosexuality and Homophobia in Men." *Psychiatric Annals*, 26,1: 37–40.

Steinfels, Peter. 1995. "An Editor Speaks on the Paradoxes of the Roman Catholic Church's Teaching on Homosexuality." *New York Times*, February 18.

Stoudemire, Alan. 1988. "Somatoform Disorders, Factitious Disorders, and Malingering." In *The American Psychiatric Press Textbook of Psychiatry*, ed. John A. Talbot, Robert E. Hales, and Stuart C. Yudofsky. Washington, DC: American Psychiatric Press, Inc., pp. 533–556.

Tierney, John. 1995. "A San Francisco Talk Show Takes Right-Wing Radio to a New Dimension." *New York Times*, February 14.

Thomas, Cal. 1996. "Senate Stands Firm in Refusal to Back Same-Sex Marriage." *Asbury Park Press*, September 13.

Ursano, Robert J. and Edward K. Silberman. 1988. "Individual Psychotherapies: Other Individual Psychotherapies: Cognitive Therapy." In *The American Psychiatric Press Textbook of Psychiatry*, ed. John A. Talbot, Robert E. Hales, and Stuart C. Yudofsky. Washington, DC: American Psychiatric Press, Inc.

Vazquez, Carmen. 1992. "Appearances." In *Homophobia—How We All Pay the Price*, ed., Warren J. Blumenfeld. Boston: Beacon Press.

White, Edward L. 1994. Letter to the Editor, "Homosexuality." *Psychiatric News*, April 15.

"White House Apologizes for Rubber Gloves." 1995a. *New York Times*, June 15.

"White House Inhospitality." 1995b. *New York Times*, June 16.

"Who's Being Disgusting on AIDS?" 1995c. Editorial, *New York Times*, July 9.

"Zimbabwe Leader Condemns Homosexuality." 1995d. *New York Times*, August 2.

Index

Abdicating to homophobes, avoiding, 205

Absolutistic (dichotomous) thinking, cognitive error of, 187

Activism as way to handle homophobes, 71–72

Ad hominem, cognitive error of, 183–184, 186

Adorno, Theodor W., ix, 6, 79, 82

Affirmative action, homophobes against, 150

Aggressive-aggressive homophobes, 157

Aggressiveness in homophobes, 11, 48–49

Aggressor, identification with, defense in paranoid homophobia, 86

AIDS, 42, 167

Alcoholism and drug use in paranoid homophobia, 88–89

Altman, Dennis, 22, 23, 24

Altruism, missing defense of, 168

Ambivalent attitude of morbidly religious homophobes, 44

American Medical Association: old position on homosexuality, 24; present position on homosexuality, 25

American Psychiatric Association, 35–36

American Psychiatric Press Textbook of Psychiatry, x

Ames, Linda, 24

Anger: the role of in homophobia, 82–84; unacceptable, 114

Anonymous flier on religion and homophobia, 42

Antiaggression, Christian, 11

Antihomosexual hysteria, 5–6

Anti-intraception, attitude of, in paranoia, 81–82

Anti-Semitism, 5, 6, 7

Anxiety: belittling source of, defense in phobic homophobia, 103; biological (atavistic), 162, 164–165; as cause for homophobia, 161–165; as cause of true paranoid homophobia, 78–80; castration, 162, 163–164; dynamics of castration anxiety in hysterical homophobes, 133–134; id (impulse), 162, 164; real (fear), 162, 164; separation, 162, 164; superego (conscience), 162–163

Anxious, homophobes making gays, 67–68

A priori, cognitive error of, 187

Arguing with depressive homophobes, futility of, 95

Arieti, Sylvano, example of paralogical thinking, 183

Avoidance, defense of, in phobic homophobia, 102–103

Avoidant (phobic) homophobes, 106–107

Avoid, things to, in handling homophobes, 204–206

Bailey, Steven E., on HIV, 111

Bannon, Lisa, 135
Barr, Bob, Representative, 79
Beck, Aaron T., 177, 181
Beck, Joan, 203–204
Becker, Judith V., 21
Behavioral perspectives on homophobia, 175–176
Bemporad, Jules R., 183
Bias, against women, 164
Bible, the, 14, 45–46; in Freud's *The Future of an Illusion*, 45; in Margaret O. Hyde, 45–46; Sodomites in, 42
Bigotry, general, 6; in small towns, 69–70; as source of self-pride, 94
Biological: homophobia, 176; model of homosexuality, 47–49; sexophobia, 16
Bisexuality, 34, 96–97; and conflict, 79
Blood sport against gays and lesbians, 98
Blue-collar homophobes, 138
Borderline: homophobes, 124, 198; personality disorder, misdiagnosis of by homophobic psychiatrists, 29–30
Butch, myth of lesbians as being, 94

Cabaj, Robert Paul, 22, 26
Carter, James H., xii
Casey, Kathleen K., 111
Censoring in paranoid homophobia, 88
Charen, Mona, 180, 181
Child molesters, name hysterical homophobes call gays and lesbians, 139
Church, Catholic, homophobia in, 164
Circular reasoning, cognitive error of, 186
Closet homophobes, 75–76
Closet queens, two kinds of, 80
Clymer, Adam, 87
Cocoon-making, defense of, in phobic homophobia, 103

Cognitive errors: as cause of homophobia: 177–188; circular reasoning, in law enforcement model, 46; dynamic origin of, 188; equating sex with intelligence, 150; of homophobic psychotherapists, 29–31
Cognitive errors, list of: Absolutistic (dichotomous), 187; Ad hominem reasoning, 186; A Priori, 187; Circular Reasoning, 186; Dissociation, 178; Homosexualization, 187; Inconsistency, 177; Inexact labeling, 186–187; One thing leads to another (that is how it starts), 185; Part=whole, 179–184: Guilt by association, 180–181, Magnification, 183, Overgeneralization, 180, Paralogical (predicative) thinking, 183–184, Selective abstraction, 181–183, Similar=same, 184, Some=all, 184, Symbol=what is symbolized, 184; Personalization, 187; Rationalization, 178; Taking things too seriously, 178–179; Tangential thinking, 184–185
Cognitive therapy of homophobes, 193
Columnists as manipulative paranoids, 91
Combination disorder (true and manipulative paranoia), 92
Compassion, lack of, in morbidly religious homophobes, 41
Compromises in handling homophobes at work, 204; gay marriage and, 203–204
Confined versus general homophobia, 10–11
Conflict: as basis of homophobia, 8–9, 161–162; origin of anxiety in, 79

Conscience, punitive, as product of parental homophobia, 55–57

Conscious versus unconscious homophobia, 11

Contamination, delusions of, 85; fear of in obsessive-compulsives, 112–113

Control, defense of, in paranoid homophobia, 88

Controlling attitudes of morbidly religious homophobes, 43

Control queens (freaks), 174–175

Corinthians, biblical book of, and "sin" of homosexuality, 42

Counteridentification with nonhomophobic parent, 171

Counterphobia: auxiliary defense of, 167; defense of in phobic homophobia, 104; macho, 164

Counterstrike: against anti-gay aggression, 200–203; aggressive, 201–202; by agreement, 202; altruistic, 200–201; compromise, 203; depressive, 201; hypomanic, 201; narcissistic, 202–203; passive, 202; passive-aggressive, 200; warnings about, 203

Couser, Thomas, 67

Covert versus overt homophobia, 11

Cowardice, in homophobia, 169

Cowell, Henry, 46

Creating anxiety for purposes of mastery, in homophobia, 104

Crecco, Marion, 192, 198

Criminal (Law Enforcement) model of homosexuality, 46

Cruel parent, identification with, 170–171

Darnton, John, 85

Dealing with homophobes, 195–206

DeBell, Grace, Pollyanna paranoia of, 77–78, 96–97

Decompensating, projection of the feeling that one is, 85

Defense mechanisms: first-line versus auxiliary versus supplementary, 165; and homophobia, 162, 165–169; missing, 168

Defense mechanisms, types of: Auxiliary (secondary), 166–168: Counterphobia, 167, Dissociation, 166–167, Sublimation, 167, Substitution, 167–168; First-line 165–166: Narcissism, 165–166, Repression, 165, Stereotyping, 166; Supplementary, 168: Denial, 168, Depression, 168, Rationalization, 168

Delusional disorder, paranoid type, as cause of homophobia, 75–76

Delusions, encapsulated, in paranoid homophobia, 119–120

Delusions, litigious, 75–76, 86

Delusions, paranoid, in alcoholism, 89

Denial: of abuse, 69–70; of bigotry, 188; of hostility, 145; passive-aggressive, of homophobia, 145–148; rituals of (reaction formation, doing and undoing), 114–115; supplementary defense of, 168; and tolerant facade, 145

Dependency, misdiagnosis of, 34–35

Dependent personality disorder homophobes, 126

Depression: in gays from effects of homophobia, 32, 68–69; in homophobes, 8, 9, 168

Depressive homophobia, 93–100

Deprivation, early, 172–173

Dereism in homophobia, 3–4, 44

Developmental causes of homophobia: 169–173; of hysterical homophobia, 133

Diagnostic and Statistical Manual-IV (DSM-IV), x

Dinks: epithet of, 94, 137–138

Discrimination: by doctors against gay patients, 27; by patients against

gay doctors, 35; and prejudice, 11; by psychotherapists against gay patients, 28–35; as result of medical model of homosexuality, 26–35; in workplace based on part=whole error, 180
Disgust about sex, 13
Dishing of homosexuals by other homosexuals, 54–55
Displacement: defense of, in homophobia, 103–104
Dissociation: auxiliary defense of, 166–167; cognitive error of, 178
Dissociative personality disorder homophobes, 128–129
Doing and undoing rituals, 114–115
Don't ask, don't tell, 116
Drescher, Jack, 22
D'Souza, Dinesh, 64–65
Dunlap, David W., 39–40
Dynamic factors in hysterical homophobes, 133

Egan, Timothy, 79–80
Ego-ideal, origin of homophobia in, 163
Eliot, T. S., bigotry in, denying of, 98
Elitist (intellectual): epithet of, 93–94; 136–137
Emerson, J. Paul, 17–18, 161–162
Endogenous versus exogenous disorder, 31–35
Envy, as motivation for hysterical homophobes, 131–132; aspects of in all homophobes, 10
Epithets: 135–141, 161–162; minimyths, 174
Erotic wishes as basis of homophobia, 8
Erotomanic delusions, and paranoid homophobia, 85
Erythrophobia and homophobia, 161
Essential (as distinct from nonessential) homophobia, 11

Exogenous versus endogenous disorder, 31–35
Extrasystoles, as model of homosexual "illness," 36–37

Fag-hags, 114
Fags, name hysterical homophobes call gays and lesbians, 138
Family standard in straights, 97–98
Favazza, Armando R., 134
Fear of rejection from gays and lesbians, development of, 96–97
Feder, Stuart, 134
Feminine, gays as, 94, 101
Fenichel, Otto: conflict about sex, 13; ego's unfriendliness to the instincts, 16; guilt over masturbation, 15; homosexuality and narcissism, 20; homosexualization of guilt and punishment, 86; homosexualization of threat in phobia, 104; on the mechanism of developing litigious delusions, 86; on the mechanism of developing paranoid delusions, 85; on the nature of projection, 66
Fixation in development of homophobia, 169–170
Fluoxetine, danger of giving to paranoids, 78
Fogging technique (form of narcissistic counterstrike), 202
Fox, Thomas C., 86
Frank, Barney, 87
Frenkel-Brunswik, Else, ix, 6, 79; subtypes of bigots, 10–11
Freud, Sigmund: 167; on creativity, 36; on homophobia and politics, 46–47; homosexuality not an illness, 18; and letter to mother of homosexual son, 116; view of religion, 44–45
Fruits, name hysterical homophobes call gays and lesbians, 139

Future of an Illusion, The, and Freud's
    view of religion, 44–45

Gay rights movement, 155
Gender identity, myth of altered, 120
General (as distinct from confined)
    homophobia, 10–11
Genesis, biblical book of, and the sins
    of Sodom and Gomorrah, 42
Gibbon, Edward, 95–96
Gilovich, Thomas, 135
God, fantasy of being, 44
Gosling, John A., 22, 25
Graham, Renee, 40
Grandiose paranoia, 83
Grandiosity/narcissism in
    homophobia, 4
Grant, Bob, 127, 197
Gray, Jerry, 79
Group hysteria, 135
Guilt by association, cognitive error
    of, 180–181
Guilt, origin in the instincts, 162–163
Guilty conscience and anxiety,
    162–163
Guilty wish as basis of homophobia,
    8–9
Guthke, Karl S., 15

Handling homophobes, 71–72
Hausman, Kenneth, 191, 201, 204
Hedonists, criticism of gays as being
    pleasure-oriented, 95
Helms, Jesse, 23
Herbert, Bob, 127, 197
Hernandez, Raymond, 98, 132, 175
Hicks, Daniel W., 25
Histrionic attitude of homophobes
    (excessiveness), 5–6
Hitler, Adolf, 83
Holding grudges in paranoid
    homophobia, 88
Homophobia in homosexuals:
    developmental aspects, 55–57;
    due to avoidant personality
    disorder, 59–60; due to cognitive

errors, 61–62; due to
    dependency, 59; due to
    depression, 57, 58–59; due to
    dissociative disorder, 61; due to
    histrionic personality disorder,
    61; due to hypomania, 59;
    innate (as distinct from
    acquired), 57; manifestation of
    as back-stabbing, 55;
    manifestation of as cheating, 54;
    manifestation of as name-
    calling, 55; due to narcissism,
    60–61; outing and, 55; due to
    paranoia, 57–58; due to
    posttraumatic stress disorder,
    61; due to psychopathy, 59; due
    to sadomasochism, 58–59; due
    to sexophobia, 57
Homosexuality, separating from
    extant pathology, 31
Homosexualization: cognitive error of,
    187; of conscience, 163; of guilt
    and punishment, 86; of
    nonsexual guilt, 16
Hostile parents as cause of
    homophobia in homosexuals,
    55–57
Hostility, indirect, 143–144
Hugo, Victor, 132
Humor, sense of, missing, 168
Hyde, Margaret O., 39, 40–41, 45–46
Hynes, Samuel, book review of
    biography of E. M. Forster, 51
Hypersensitivity to rejection in
    morbidly religious
    homophobes, 43
Hypocrisy in paranoid homophobes,
    81; in morbidly religious
    homophobes, 44
Hypomanic homophobia: as by-
    product of elevated self-esteem,
    97–98; as by-product of
    narcissism, 97–98; consensual
    validation, 99; counterphobic
    certainty, 99; counterphobic
    denial, 99; dissociative denial,

99; publicizing and proselytizing, 99; rationalizing, 99–100

Hysterical (histrionic) homophobes, 29–30, 66, 124–125, 131–141

Ideas of reference, 187
Identification in development of homophobia, 170–172
Identifying with gays and lesbians: and feelings of loneliness, 96; and postpartum depression, 97
Identifying hidden homophobia, 195–197
Impersonalization, defense of, in paranoid homophobia, 87–88
Imprinting as possible cause of homosexuality, 37
Incestuous desires, punishment for, origin of guilt in, 162
Inconsistency, cognitive error of, 177
Indirect approach to treating homophobia, 192–193
Inexact labeling, cognitive error of, 186–187
Infidelity, fear of, 116
Influence, question of (effects gays have on others), 11
Influencing machine, delusion of, 76, 112
Insight in homophobes, 193–194
Intellectualization, defense of, in paranoid homophobia, 87
Interpersonal aspects of homophobia, 175
Interpersonal therapy in homophobes, 193–194
Intimidating gays and lesbians, 197
Isay, Richard, 163–164; definition of homophobia, 101; femininity in homosexuals, 101; gay-bashing adolescents, 126
Ives, Charles, 134

Jealousy, delusions of, 85
Jones, Ernest, 18, 116, 162

Judgmental homophobes (obsessive-compulsive), 110–112
Julius, Anthony on T. S. Eliot, 98

Kakutani, Michiko, book review of, 98
Katz, Larry S., 198
Kaufman, Benjamin, 18
Kavoussi, Richard J., 21
Kertzner, Robert M., 201, 204
Kings I, biblical book of, abominations in, 42
Kirk, Marshall, ix, xiv, 48, 175–176
Koch, Edward I., 79
Koro, 134
Kranz, Rachel, 175

Lancaster, Hal, 204
Latent homosexuality, 81, 89
Law-making, anti-gay, 26, 103
Lazar, Kay, 192, 198
Leverich, Lyle, 186
Levinson, Daniel J., ix, xii, 5, 6, 79; homophobia as self-statement, 7; internal origin of homophobia, 199; sadistic homophobes, 9
Leviticus, biblical book of, 41, 42, 68
Litigious paranoids, 75–76, 86
Lot and the sins of Sodom and Gomorrah, 42

Madsen, Hunter, ix, xiv, 48, 175–176
Magnification, cognitive error of, 183
Manipulative paranoia, 77, 89–92
Marmor, Judd, 26
Martin, Douglas, 31
Masochism in homophobes, 104–105, 127; triumph of, 155–156
Masturbation: guilt, and sexophobia, 15; infantile, punishment for, origin of guilt in, 162; prohibition of, and sexophobia, 15
Matthews, William C., 151, 156

McCormick, Brian, 27
McGowan, William, 64–65
McGurn, William, 8
Meissner, William, 51, 64;
    definitions of: altruism, 168;
    ascetic rituals, 115; being
    paranoid, 120; "forgetting" of
    repression, 169;
    intellectualization, 116; sense of
    humor, 168
Melville, Herman, 36, 132
Meyer, Jon K., 7
Migliaro, Eugene A., 129, 168
Misdiagnoses made by homophobic
    psychotherapists, 29–35
Mixner, David B., 47
Models of homophobia: biological,
    47–49; law-enforcement
    (criminal), 46; medical, 4, 17–37;
    political, 46–47; religion, 39–46;
    sociocultural, 47
Moralists, obsessive-compulsive,
    110–111
Morbid religious homophobia,
    39–46
Morris, Desmond, 16, 21, 43, 44, 176;
    homosexual pairs not
    reproducing species, 109;
    homosexuality in animals, 188
Mukerjee, Madhusree, 11, 151, 156
Multiple personality disorder,
    misdiagnosis of, 34
Mythmaking, behavior of hysteric
    homophobes, 135
Myths: and defense mechanisms, 173;
    hostile nature of, 175;
    increasing self-esteem by
    using, 173; origin of in
    childhood, 174–175; origin
    of in unconscious (erotic,
    escapist, liberation) fantasies,
    174; reducing anxiety by the
    use of (primary gain), 173;
    secondary gain and, 173;
    syndrome-specific nature of,
    174

Names that hysterical homophobes
    call gays: banshees, 139; butch,
    139; child molesters, 139; dinks,
    137–138; elitist (intellectual),
    136–137; fags, 138; fruits, 139;
    queens, 138; queers, 139;
    screamers, 139; sick, 138–139;
    sissies, 138; superficial, 138;
    swish, 139
Narcissism, 30–31, 125, 198–199;
    defense mechanism of, 165–166;
    misdiagnosis of in gays, 32, 34;
    in morbidly religious
    homophobes, 44
Narcissistic personality disorder
    homophobes, 125
Narrett, Eugene, 17, 98
National Association for Research and
    Therapy of Homosexuality
    (NARTH), 22
Negative effects of homophobia,
    67–72
Nemiah, John, 162, 166
Nerds, epithet of, 94, 138
Niebuhr, Gustav, 40, 41
Nietzsche, Friedrich, 162
Nonactivism as way to handle
    homophobes, 71–72
Nonessential (as distinct from
    essential) homophobia, 11

Obsessive-compulsive homophobes:
    9, 75, 109–117, 126;
    misdiagnosis of disorder in gays,
    32–33
O'Connell, Loraine, 110, 201
Oedipal fears in a gay man, 140
Oedipal guilt causing sexophobia, 15
One thing leads to another, cognitive
    error of, 185
Orthodox homophobes, 10–12
Othello jealousy of homophobes, 75
Overgeneralization, cognitive error of,
    180
Overt (as distinct from covert)
    homophobia, 11

Paralogical predicative thinking, cognitive error of, 183–184

Paranoia: 7, 8, 9, 75–92, 198; in homosexuals, 31; vera, 8; versus affective disorder, 78; versus provocation, 127

Paranoid, making gays and lesbians feel, 144

Paranoid personality disorder, 120–122

Parent, homophobic, identification with, 170–172

Part=whole, cognitive error of, 179–184

Passive-aggressive homophobes: 143–157; handling, 157. *See also* Counterstrike; Denial; Rationalization; Sadomasochism

Passive-aggressivity, in sadistic homophobes, 127

Passive, fear of being, 9

Passivity versus activity, 199–200

Perfectionistic attitude of morbidly religious homophobes, 44

Personality-disordered homophobes, 119–157

Personalization, cognitive error of, 187

Phobic/avoidant homophobia, 5–6, 9, 101–107

Pierce, Chester, xii

Pinsker, Henry, 183

Political model of homosexuality, 46–47

Politicians: as homophobes, 138; as manipulative paranoids, 91

Pollyanna paranoia, of Grace DeBell, 77–78, 96–97

Positive aspects of being homosexual, 202–203

Postpartum depression, 97

Preference, legitimate, explanation for homophobia, 92

Preoccupation with homosexuality, as a quality of homophobia, 9

Prevention of effects of homophobia, 205–206

Pride, homophobes reducing gay, 68

Primal scene: latter-day effects of, 140; spying on, punishment for, origin of guilt in, 162; viewing of, as origin of sexophobia, 15

Professional opportunities, limited, 26–27

Projection: of aggression, in paranoid homophobia, 82–84; second-line defense of, in paranoid homophobia, 81–86; of sex, in paranoid homophobia, 82

Projectivity, 81–82

Promiscuity, 30–31; as manifestation of inhibition-celibacy, 52

Promiscuous, myth of gays as being, 94

Proselytizing, 14; in paranoid homophobia, 87; defense of in homophobia, 104

Provoking gays and lesbians, 67–69, 148–154; with back-handed compliments, 148–149; with back-handed criticisms, 149; by being excessively critical, 153–154; by contemplating nonassertively, 150; by controlling, 150–151; by double-binding, 151; by expressing ambivalence, 151; by expressing envy, 151; by ignoring, 151–152; by asking the innocent question, 150; by treating them unequally, 154; by undermining, 149–150; by withholding, 152–153

Provoking others to act out for the homophobe, 154–155

Prudes, anal, 13; hypocritical, 13–14

Pseudodemocratic facade, 11

Pseudomasochists, 156

Psychoanalysis, organized, homophobia in, 164

Psychodynamic causes of homophobia, 161–175

Psychopathic-antisocial personality disorder homophobes, 123–124

Psychopathy, misdiagnosis of, 32
Psychotherapists, homophobic, 28–35
Purdum, Todd S., 47, 164
Purnick, Joyce, 79

Quarantine, fantasy of for gays and
    lesbians, 8, 24, 110, 112
Queens, name hysterical
    homophobes call gays and
    lesbians, 138, 170
Queers, name hysterical homophobes
    call gays and lesbians, 139

Rabbis and homophobia, 39–40
Rabinovitz, Jonathan, 129, 168
Racism, 6
Rational homophobia: 63–66; as an
    aspect of human nature, 63;
    because provoked, 64–66; due to
    cultural factors, 63; due to
    healthy (mature) asceticism, 64;
    that is preferential, 64
Rationalization: cognitive error of,
    178; defense mechanism of, 104,
    165, 168; in passive-aggressive
    homophobes, 144–145
Reaction formation (undoing),
    defense mechanism of, in
    paranoid homophobia, 87
Reference, ideas of, 86; in alcoholism,
    89
Reformed homophobes, 10–11
Religious homophobes, morbidness
    of, 40
Repressed, return of the, 80–81; and
    ritualistic doing and undoing,
    114–115
Repression, defense mechanism of,
    165; first-line defense of, in
    paranoid homophobia, 80–81
Responsibility for making changes,
    bigots' designation of, 11
Rich, Frank, 17, 46, 83, 85
Ring of the Nibelungen, The, 15
Rituals (in obsessive-compulsives):
    ascetic, 115; cleansing, 112–113;

condemning/banishing,
    109–110; controlling, 110–112;
    doing and undoing
    (criminalization and
    exoneration), 114–115;
    intellectual, 116; jealous,
    115–116; magical, 116–117;
    perfectionistic, 117
Robertson, Pat, 82, 85, 181
Rogers, Lois M., 41, 191–192
Romans, 10:13, biblical book of, how
    homosexuals can be saved, 42
Roughton, Ralph, 155

Sabshin, Melvin, 191
Sack, Kevin, 165
Sadistic pleasure, of a gay man, 140
Sadomasochism, misdiagnosis of in a
    gay man, 33
Sadomasochistic homophobes: 9, 95,
    127–128; handling, 128
Salmon, Wesley C., 184
Sanford, R. Nevitt, ix, xii, 6, 79, 81–82;
    homosexuals as "criminals," 83;
    paranoid personality trait, 86
Santayana, George, 20
Satanists and homosexuals, 83
Satinover, Jeffrey Burke, 25
Scalia, Antonin, Justice, 46, 136
Scanning, phobic, 102
Schizoid: homophobes, 123, 198;
    misdiagnosis of personality
    disorder in a gay man, 34. See
    also Avoidant homophobes
Schizophrenic weltuntergang, 8
Schopenhauer, Arthur, 15
Schwarz, K. Robert, 46
Selective abstraction, cognitive error
    of, 181–183
Self-esteem: improving, 71–72; low,
    32, 72, 202; lowered due to
    discrimination, 180
Self-homophobia: camping and, 53;
    hustling and, 53; suicide and,
    54; distancing and, 52;
    inhibition/celibacy and, 51–52;

interest in pornography/onanism and, 53; self-destructiveness and, 52–53; overuse of substitute gratifications and, 53–54. *See also* Homophobia in homosexuals

Self-referential qualities of homophobia, 7

Sexophobia, 9–10, 13–16, 30; as cause of homophobia in homosexuals, 56; and dependent homophobes, 126; obsessive-compulsive, 109; in parents, 162; in society, 162

Sexophobic parents, identification with, 170

Sexual excitement, origin of sexophobia in, 16

Shame, homophobes inducing in gays, 68

Sibling rivalry, 172; in a gay man, 140

Sick, name hysterical homophobes call gays and lesbians, 138–139

Silberman, Edward K., 186–187

Similar=same thing, cognitive error of, 184

Simplistic attitude of homophobes, 5

Sin, viewing homosexuality as a, 42

Sissies, epithet of, 170; name hysterical homophobes call gays and lesbians, 138

Socarides, Charles W., 18, 20, 22, 24, 188; pathologizing of homosexuality, 25, 182; provoking gay violence unconsciously, 155; on reparative therapy, 24; support of Colorado's Amendment Two, 26

Sociocultural model of homosexuality, 47

Some=all, cognitive error of, 184

Sorting capacity of the ego, defect of, as cause of anxiety, 79

Spencer, Colin, ix, 47, 76, 181; homosexuals as barbarians, 49

Stable relationships in homosexuals, 3–4

Stein, Terry, 25–26, 75

Steinfels, Peter, 18, 39, 40, 43

Stereotypes about straights, 4

Stereotyping, defense mechanism of, 166

Stoudemire, Alan, xii–xiii

Straight-bashing in homophobes, 75

Straights, pathology in, overlooking of, 30–31

Strengths, overlooking of in gays by homophobic psychotherapists, 30

Sublimation: auxiliary defense of, 167; defense in paranoid homophobia, 86–87; negative, 87; positive, 86–87

Submissiveness, in morbidly religious homophobes, 43

Substitution, auxiliary defense of, 167–168

Subtypes of homophobia, 10–12

Successophobia in a gay man, 140

Suggestibility in morbidly religious homophobes, 43

Sullivan, Andrew, 18, 39, 40, 43, 181

Superficial, name hysterical homophobes call gays and lesbians, 94, 138

Swells, epithet of, 94

Swish/butch, name hysterical homophobes call gays and lesbians, 139

Symptomatic nature of homophobia, 8–9

Tait, C. Downing, 18

Taking things too seriously, cognitive error of, 178–179

Talk radio, medium for paranoid homophobes, 88–89

Talk-show hosts, as manipulative paranoids, 91

Tangential thinking, cognitive error of, 184–185

Theatrical overdramatization,
    behavior of hysterical
    homophobes, 135
Theologization of conscience, 163
Thomas, Cal, 135
Tierney, John, 161–162
Transvestites, myth of gays as, 94
Trauma, early, 172–173
Treatment of homophobes, 191–194
Trivial prompt, stimulus in phobic
    homophobia, 101–102
True paranoid homophobia, versus
    manipulative and Pollyanna,
    77–78
True projective paranoia, 78–89

Unconscious versus conscious
    homophobia, 11
Understanding, as way of dealing with
    homophobes, 197–199
Unfaithfulness, conviction of in
    jealous homophobes, 115–116
Unoriginality/derivativeness of
    homophobia, 4–5

Unreasonable demands made by
    morbidly religious
    homophobes, 43
Unresolved oedipus, as causal theory
    of homosexuality, 36
Untruthfulness of homophobes, 188
Ursano, Robert J., 186–187
USA Today, on Jesse Helms, 23

Vasquez, Carmen, 120
Violence, in homophobes, 78
Voth, Harold D., 18

Wellness, homosexuality as, 35
Weltuntergang, 8; cause of anxiety in
    paranoid homophobics, 79
White, Edward L., 31–32
White House inhospitality, 23–24
Wilde, Oscar, 156
Women: as compared to men,
    homophobia in, 11, 156–157
Worthlessness, personal feelings of,
    in depressive homophobes,
    93–97

About the Author

MARTIN KANTOR is Clinical Assistant Professor of Psychiatry at the University of Medicine and Dentistry of New Jersey. He is the author of five other Praeger titles, including *Occupational Disorders: A Treatment Guide for Therapists* (1997) and *Understanding Writer's Block: A Therapist's Guide to Diagnosis and Treatment* (1995).

ISBN 0-275-95530-3

HARDCOVER BAR CODE